A History of
Walton-le-Dale
and Bamber Bridge

David Hunt

Research sponsored
by Baxi Partnership

Carnegie Publishing, 1997

A HISTORY OF
WALTON-LE-DALE AND
BAMBER BRIDGE

For Anne

The publishers are deeply grateful to
the Baxi Partnership for contributing
towards the costs of research of this volume

First published in 1997
by Carnegie Publishing Ltd,
Carnegie House, Chatsworth Road,
Lancaster LA1 4SL.

ISBN 1-85936-043-2

Typeset and originated by Carnegie Publishing
Printed and bound by The Alden Press, Oxford

Contents

Introduction

A sad and harassing quantity of sentiment, hypothetical antiquarianism, and eccentric speculation is there in the effusions of some men who have written descriptions of Walton. 'The Horrors' came upon us suddenly not long since when, whilst referring to the pages of a local historian, we found that in describing Walton he began with Chaos and Old Night, got through the glacial period quietly, entered the epoch of the rhinocerous and the great bear complacently, shot calmly past the Roman era amid Latin roots and shadowy remnants of Caesar's commentaries, plunged into the civil turmoil of the seventeenth century learnedly, and ended contentedly with cotton and gospel.

Anthony Hewitson, *Our Country Churches and Chapels* (1872), p. 20.

T MIDNIGHT on 31 March 1974 Walton-le-Dale Urban District Council passed into oblivion. With it the district lost a degree of independence to manage its own affairs that it had enjoyed for over a thousand years. How this power was used, by whom, and to what effect, forms an important part of this essay. Each local history presents its own problems, and has its own characteristics. In this respect Walton-le-Dale is notable for an embarrassment of riches, for although individual episodes in the story are quite well known, comparatively little attention has been given to local considerations of community and landscape history. For example the spectacular Romano-British settlement, the Cuerdale Hoard, Cromwell's great victory of 1648, and the Bamber Bridge Tramway, have developed something approaching lives of their own, quite removed from their local context.

The area under consideration broadly accords with the extent of the old Urban District, with a number of highly opportunistic additions, coinciding broadly with both the ancient chapelry parish of St Leonard, and the Manor of Walton-le-Dale. Through time the balance of settlement in the district changed, with the rise of Bamber Bridge as the main centre of population and administration, and the emergence of Lostock Hall–Tardy Gate, and Higher Walton–Gregson Lane. The quite separate manor of Cuerdale has been included, and to the south Cuerden has been considered in the context of the growth of Bamber Bridge. The development of the early cotton industry was closely related to the exploitation of watermill sites on the rivers Darwen and Lostock, and in order to present a more balanced picture of these developments it has been necessary to stray into both Samlesbury and Cuerden.

Local history now enjoys an established position in the school curriculum, and a new generation of local historians is on the march. There remains a great deal of work for them to do! The publication of the report on the excavations on the Roman site along the Darwen is eagerly awaited, and a detailed analysis of the river deposits along the lower Darwen and Ribble might shed much light on the early settlement of the area. The discovery that the village of Walton had for a time been an island, came as a great, unnerving, and rather unwelcome surprise! My own interest in the history of the district was stimulated by Frank Coupe's book published in 1954, and was further developed by a school project undertaken in 1972. I am most grateful to Baxi Partnership and Alistair Hodge of Carnegie Publishing, for giving me the opportunity of bringing these many years of happy and interesting work into print. Local history is a pleasant and useful hobby, but for all those who develop an interest in the history of their own locality it is a joy for life.

Over the years a great number of people have taken the time to assist me in many ways, and it is impossible to mention them all. A general thank you will have to suffice. I was extremely fortunate that the late E. E. Pickering spent a lot of time explaining to me his far reaching ideas on the development of the district in general, and of the Roman site in particular. In the present study I am most grateful of the assistance or Robert Rushton and the staff of the Leyland Library, of Terry Shaw and the staff of the Harris Reference Library, and to the staff of the local studies section at library headquarters in Corporation Street, Preston. Particular thanks are due to Aidan Turner-Bishop at the library of the University of Central Lancashire for his efforts to trace the Walton colony in Australia, and to Jude Boxall and Zoe Lawson librarians of the Joseph Livesey Collection.

Among the staff of the University in Preston, I am most grateful for the help and encouragement of John Baker, Margaret Clark, Geoff Timmins, and Henry French. The latter advised me on early handwriting, and the former how to type it into a computer! My colleagues at South Ribble Borough Council have similarly helped in many ways, and particular thanks are due to Bill Morton and Donna McGaw. Particular thanks are due to the Friends of South Ribble Museum, and to those 'usual suspects' of the Leyland Historical Society, Bill Waring, Elizabeth Shorrock, Peter Barrow, and George Bolton. Specific contributors are thanked in the footnotes, but especial thanks are due to Derek Edmondson, Arnold Rigby, Colin Dickinson, Alan Hunt, Chris Aspin, Roy Bannistre-Parker, George Fletcher, Sylvia Birtles, Alan Crosby, Bob Burns, St Aidans Primary School, and all at Carnegie Publishing. Special thanks are due to Jack Lanigan and the people of the Rockhampton and Wowan districts in Queensland, Australia, who responded to Aidan Turner-Bishop's appeal for information about the Wowan Colony.

Along with all local historians working in Lancashire, I owe an enormous debt of gratitude to the staff – past and present – of the Lancashire Record

Office in Bow Lane, Preston. The search room staff, in particular, have not only borne virtually all of the materials on which this work is based from the distant recesses of the building, but as individuals have also contributed to its progress very significantly. Jeremy Parker (whose father wrote the preface to Frank Coupe's book) kindly made available his family papers, and assisted in many ways from the very start of the project. Particular thanks are also due to Howard Hammersley for his encouragement and enthusiasm, and to my wife (to whom the book is dedicated) for her support over a long period. Finally I am pleased to acknowledge the encouragement and financial sponsorship of Baxi Partnership of Bamber Bridge, for the wonderful opportunity of presenting an updated history of our district.

David Hunt

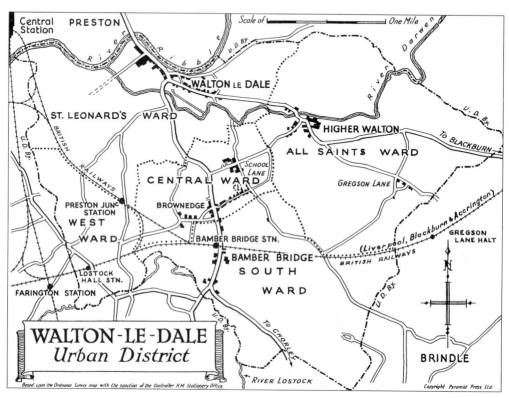

The Walton-le-Dale Urban District Council preserved until 1974 the distinct entity of the ancient manor and chapelry of Walton-le-Dale, whose history can thus be traced for upwards of 1,000 years.

CHAPTER ONE

Archaeology and Early History

The Walton landscape

HE ANCIENT MANOR of Walton-le-Dale consisted of two related units: the village of Walton overlooked by Walton Law (Cooper Hill) on a peninsula between the rivers Ribble and Darwen; and a great arc of townlands extending south from the Darwen to boundaries with Brindle, Cuerden and Penwortham. The latter comprised three principal sub-regions: the water meadows at Walton extending along the Ribble valley to Penwortham; the eastern rim of the West Lancashire mosses stretching from the river along the line of Leyland Road to Tardy Gate and Walton Moss; and the central belt of the Lancashire Plain proper dominated by modern-day Bamber Bridge. This area of relatively higher land, lying only between 100′ and 150′ above sea level, appears in marked contrast to the incised valleys of the Darwen and Ribble which are cut through it, and the mossland fringe of Walton Moss, Charnock Moss and Farington Moss in the south and west. It forms the largest landscape unit in the manor, rising from the edge of the moss along Brownedge Road to the gently hilly district approaching Brindle in the east, and the Ribble Valley to the north. Comparatively minor variations in altitude thus have a disproportionately large impact on the settlement geography.

The townlands are further distinguished by their soil types, and the history of their cultivation and land use. The light alluvial soils of the river valleys have proved capable of supporting intensive cultivation where their inherently acute problems of flooding could be alleviated, whilst the mosslands have been steadily drained and enclosed from at least early Tudor times, and have now disappeared. By contrast the heavier clay soils of the higher plain, whose steep scarp edges are encountered at Cinnamon Hill, the Forty Steps, and Kittlingbourne Brow, supported extensive forest resistant to settlement long into the medieval period. Up to the industrial revolution the pattern and sequence of the development of the townlands are broadly similar to that encountered throughout the region – woodland clearance, enclosure from waste, and moss reclamation. It is the rather unique location of the village itself which makes the earlier history of the district so distinctive, and of considerably greater than local interest.

The village of Walton occupies one of the key strategic points in the north of England. The first bridging point on the Ribble, at Ribble Bridge, carries the London road onto Walton Cop, where the road passes a short

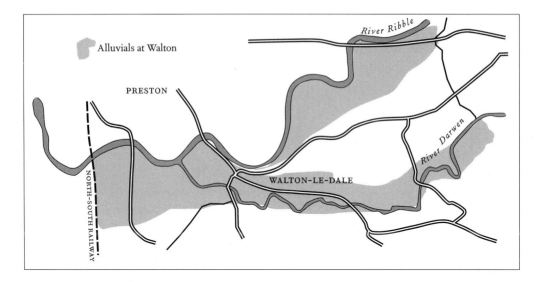

distance south through the village to the first bridge over the Darwen. Between the two bridges, Church Brow carried the Yorkshire road over Walton Law, branching at Knot Lane onto the Blackburn road. A short distance south from the Darwen bridge, the London road branched at Hennel End into Hennel Lane to meet the Croston road at Tardy Gate. This was the principal road running south along the eastern edge of the western mosses. Just before crossing the river Lostock over Bamber Bridge, the London road also branched by the Hob Inn for Chorley and the Manchester road. Thus the short stretch between the Ribble and Darwen bridges formed a key link in the north–south and east–west routeways, and from Roman times onwards the principal military movements along the west coast have had to pass along it.

The situation of the settlement itself, the micro-location, is similarly remarkable. It clusters along and around a narrow peninsula of higher ground which extends into the Ribble valley, separating it from that of the Darwen to the south. The ancient church stands astride the highest point of the ridge, and the two rivers meander together in the flat water meadows to the west. Alternatively, when seen from the Ribble, the church overlooks the junction of one of the system's principal tributary valleys, that of the Darwen extending deep into the heart of the ancient Blackburn Hundred.

The modern village sprawls over a range of quite distinct landscape forms, which in earlier times would have provided a variety of potentially rich resources – Walton flats, the Townfields along the Darwen, and Walton Law.

Walton flats, a low-lying tract of river and eroded post-glacial gravels lying to the west of Chorley Road, straddles the 25′ contour. Up to the early nineteenth century these deposits must have flooded very frequently, and even today the waters of the Ribble are only kept at bay during very wet weather by the great embankment under Victoria Road. Spot heights

The riverine aspect of early settlement at Walton. The broad alluvial flats formed at the confluence of the valleys of the Ribble and Darwen, overlooked by the steep bluff of Walton Law, were an important factor in the geography of early settlement here. The principal townfields of the medieval village, their fertile soils have long been cultivated intensively, and those along the river Darwen still support productive market gardens.

The view north-west from Cuerdale hill, looking across to Walton Flats. At this point the mass of Walton Law extends out into the Ribble valley. (Author)

here at Edward Street and by the Yew Tree Inn, are still only 27′ and 33′ respectively. The recurrent floods, and secondary flooding along Higher Walton Road and Chorley Road due to the waters of the Darwen 'backing up' from its confluence with the Ribble in flood, has meant that the cultivation and occupation of the flats is a comparatively recent phenomenon.

Up to the construction of the present embankment, even the preservation of the road along Walton Cop required a great and sustained effort on the part of the civil authorities, and the flats rarely seem to have been exploited for anything more intensive than seasonal pasture. Thus the system of medieval ridge and furrow cultivation in neat townfield strips, which one might have expected to have emerged on such light and fertile soils, is unlikely to have developed here. On the early nineteenth-century tithe map the feature is shown as heath or rough grazing. Without their encircling rampart of expensive modern flood defences most of the flats lie perilously close to the winter flood levels, whilst the Ribble is tidal to Walton Bottoms and the Darwen to just upstream of Darwen Bridge.

The 25′ contour is thus a major factor in the settlement of the valley bottom, and a variance of only + or − 5′ can be very important. Of central importance is the fact that the alluvials of the Darwen valley to the east of Chorley Road lie consistently above this line, allowing investment in buildings and agriculture in considerably greater security. The O.D. bench mark by the Unicorn Inn in Chorley Road indicates 30′, and Higher Walton Road gradually rises from 29′ at Princes Road, to 32′ by St Patrick's Church. The soils along this valley floor, extending from the eastern edge of the flats to Higher Walton, are extremely productive, and in the present century have been farmed as market gardens specialising in flowers.

The section from Chorley Road to Knot Lane end, formed the village's townfields, perhaps the longest exploited and the most valuable agricultural land in the ancient manor. Originally extending north from the Darwen to the rocky crags of Walton Law, these fields with their long cultivation strips, were so important that the direct road to Blackburn was only cut through them in the early years of the nineteenth century. Prior to this travellers from Preston had to take a long detour up Church Brow, passing St Leonard's Church, before turning down Knot Lane and continuing east along Higher Walton Road. The manor corn mill was located on the western edge of the townfields, and the manor house lay only a short distance to the south across the Darwen bridge. To the south of the river the edge of the Lancashire Plain rises steeply to over 100′ O.D. in Holland Wood, enclosing the dale from the south.

The third and most prominent feature in the village is Walton Law, the long belt of millstone grit which forms the Cuerdale escarpment, separating the valleys of the Darwen and Ribble, and protruding out into the valley of the latter from the south, to form the relatively narrow neck of the valley at this point. Once again subdued heights have a great impact on the landscape. The parish church is located at 100′ O.D., close to the highest point of the ridge, which falls away very steeply to the Ribble to the north, and down Church Brow to the west. Most of the buildings along the scarp, extending eastwards from Cooper Hill, are enclosed by the 75′ contour. On the south side the surface falls away steeply between 50′ and 75′, but at about 60′ O.D. it rolls into the edge of the wide townfield, most of which lies between 30′ and 50′ O.D. Although the land to the north of Higher Walton Road is now extensively built up, this critical break of

The broad vale of the Ribble at Cuerdale, looking towards Halfpenny Bridge, with the find spot of the Cuerdale Hoard in the middle distance. (*Author*)

slope can still be clearly seen at the top of Prince's Road and Queen's Road. Medieval references to the parish church frequently refer to it as 'The church on the Law' ('Capella Ecclesia de la Lawe' – thirteenth century; 'Le Lawe' – 1319), and it was known as 'Law church' ('The parish of ye Law' – 1526), well into the eighteenth century. 'Law' is derived from the Old English 'hlaw', meaning an isolated eminence or mound. The latter is the usual Lancashire usage 'Lowe', but the more pronounced Walton situation is much closer to the former, illustrated, for example, by the Law Hill which rises steeply above Dundee.

The site of Walton village is therefore a complicated but interesting one. The threat of flooding in the water meadows of the Ribble valley to the west was offset by the better drained, sheltered, and productive soils along the lower Darwen. The combination of the strategic higher ground of Walton Law, and the adjacent river crossings, gave the locality a strategic aspect of more than local significance. When the resources of the wider manor are included – the mosses, woodlands, fisheries, and ploughlands – the attraction and success of settlement here throughout the last 2,000 years can readily be appreciated.

'Darkness and Old Night'

If the strategic implications of the Walton site were first appreciated by the Romans, the exploitation of the agricultural potential of the district has a much longer history. Ice action has removed all trace of early man's activities in northern Britain, apart from isolated deposits preserved in caves, such as Victoria Cave at Settle. With the opening of the present warm period about 12,000 years ago, bands of hunters and gatherers ranged far and wide across the Pennine valleys of Northern England. At Poulton the discovery of the remains of an elk provided carbon-14-dated evidence of their hunting activities in the period 9500–10500 B.C. By 4000 B.C. farming communities had established themselves in most of the more favourable niches, and the settlement of the middle and lower reaches of the Ribble probably dates from this period. Though archaeological evidence is as yet typically limited, it is unlikely that the obvious attractions of the district were entirely overlooked.

Large numbers of Bronze Age burial cairns survive on the moorlands above Chorley and Burnley, but the more intensive land use has largely removed the lowland counterpart to the overall distribution and settlement pattern. Faint traces of this can be seen in the scatter of chance finds of stone axes and bronzes across the lowlands and at the sites at Bleasdale, Astley Hall, and in the bend of the Ribble across from Hacking Hall. The enormous timbers found at Bleasdale, the soils preserved beneath the cairn on Winter Hill, and pollen evidence from the region's peat mosses all attest to the extent and scale of the former forest cover. Settlement expanded outwards from particularly favourable points. In addition to its light soils the Walton district could offer access to the sea, fishing (particularly of salmon), wild fowling on the mosses and marshes, and hunting in the woodlands.

The district has produced a mixed assortment of prehistoric artefacts. The river gravels at Cuerdale and Samlesbury have produced Bronze Age axes and spearheads; a stone hammer was found to the west of the Black Bull on Station Road, Bamber Bridge; and before 1857 fragments of a bronze harness mount (750–650 B.C.) and the handle of a bronze mirror were found at Walton. The excavation of Preston dock in the 1880s produced a similarly wide assortment of unrelated and largely undateable items.

During the Iron Age, the period prior to the Roman conquest, evidence of the permanent settlement of the Ribble valley comes from the defended camps at Portfield above Whalley, and Castercliffe near Nelson. It is hard to accept that the marked strategic advantages of Walton Law were entirely overlooked during this period. It is perhaps significant that the only extensive archaeological excavations in the region, at the Roman sites at Ribchester and Walton, have produced evidence of earlier activity. At Walton the early settlement of the Flats area was indicated by a large assemblage of Mesolithic and Neolithic flint flakes recovered from the surface of the subsoil during the 1981–83 excavations. Ridge and furrows indicative of early farming practices, were sealed beneath the later Roman horizons, suggesting to the excavator evidence here of a prehistoric field system, or of farming activity very early in the Roman period. The attractive hypothesis that the Roman activity at Walton occurred in the context of pre-existing British settlement can only be tested by further discoveries, but the first workers on the Walton site, Charles Hardwick in the 1850s, and E. E. Pickering in the 1950s, were both firmly convinced that this was in fact the case.[1]

The Romano-British site

Roman activity on Walton Flats was confirmed by Charles Hardwick in the 1850s. A century later fragments of the site were ably explored by Richard (Dick) Livesey and members of the specially formed Walton-le-Dale Archaeological Society under the direction of E. E. (Ernie) Pickering. The report of their activities carried out over a decade in extremely trying and difficult conditions was to become something of a model of amateur achievement in the 1950s, and is notable for its clarity, lucidity and foresight. That Pickering was able to demonstrate the long chronology, and the extreme complexity of the structures on the site says much of the enormous abilities of this remarkable individual.

The excavations of 1981–83, and subsequent fieldwork on Walton Flats, have demonstrated the remarkable complexity of the low-lying alluvial deposits at Walton. Changes to the lower courses of the Ribble and Darwen,

The 1997 excavation of the Roman site on Walton Flats. A large area of the site was uncovered ahead of further building operations on the Flats. (*Author*)

flooding and human interference over 1,500 years have greatly reduced the area of the landscape surviving from Roman times, which is now restricted to the higher land above the 25′ contour. Accordingly the surviving archaeological deposits can provide only an indication of the extent and function of a site which 'is unique within the British archaeological record and is recognised as having international importance'. The early date of several coins found on the site perhaps indicates an early date for the establishment of the site, and its occupation seems to have continued throughout much of the Roman period in Britain.

Working on Pickering's site one (the 'Plump'), Adrian Olivier was able to demonstrate the existence of a subsequent series of rectangular timber buildings aligned at right angles to a metalled road which ran north–south across the Flats. Dating from the second century A.D., the regular layout and the associated hearths and pits indicated some form of industrial activity under military control. The earliest buildings were destroyed by fire and rebuilt on a number of occasions, but the essential features of the plan were maintained to the end of the second century. Early in the third century the buildings were reconstructed, and industrial activity in this part of the site at least seems to have ended, leading the excavator to conclude that the function of the site had changed from that of a 'military works depot' to a 'storage depot'. The latest Roman deposits at Walton are very shallow and have been greatly reduced by subsequent denudation, but indicate activity here into the early fourth century.

In addition to revealing the complexity of the function of the site, Olivier's excavations greatly revised assessments of its plan and wider geography. Pickering explored two locations, the orchard or 'Plump' on Winery Lane, and an area to the south-west in the market gardens (his 'site two'). Located on higher land, with a former course of the Darwen between them, they seemed to indicate the existence of two individual sites. Hardwick had noted in the 1850s that:

> The Darwen in its course from near the site of Walton Hall, towards its junction with the Ribble, made a deep indentation eastward of the present course of the Darwen is artificial. The remains of the old channel may yet be distinctly seen. The centre of the curve reaches nearly to the weaving shed lately erected by Mr Calvert.

Extensive excavations in the early part of 1997 on Pickering's second site, have revealed similar features to those found along Winery Lane, and located the former loop of the river Darwen, clearly revealed in section. This can now be shown to have cut through an enormous military-industrial complex and base, and it is probable that the site originally spread

The suggested former course of the river Darwen. This unique photograph was taken by E. E. Pickering in the 1950s, during the pioneering work of the Walton-le-Dale Archaeological Society on the site. The river Darwen can be seen top right, with the Ribble bottom right, and the line of Winery Lane running left to right. The square of trees below Winery Lane was the small orchard known as the 'Plump', and the principal site of the post-war excavations. The earlier course of the river Darwen is marked in white. The photograph also reveals the intensive pattern of rich market gardens for which the Flats were once famous. (*South Ribble Museum*)

A former bed of the river Darwen revealed during the 1997 excavations. (*Author*)

A fragment of a Roman amphora found in the 1997 excavations. (*Author*)

over a large proportion of the Ribble–Darwen lowlands at Walton. The site is clearly of incalculable historical interest, and much of the present understanding of the Roman era in the North West will have to be reappraised in the light of the discoveries.

The site at Walton must be seen in the context of Roman activity in the region, with the large fort and settlement upriver at Ribchester, and the site to the west at Carr Hill, Kirkham. All three sites seem to have been well established in the first century, and Walton and Ribchester were to be the foci of settlement for centuries. The Roman presence in the district, and the related settlement activity, must therefore have been very considerable, as the scatter of chance finds, such as the Worden and Kirkham hoards would seem to indicate. Much material of this type must also await discovery, or have gone unrecorded in the past. The first large-scale impact of settlement in the area, with its related effects on landscape evolution and woodland clearance, can therefore be securely dated from this period of Romano-British settlement.

It is hard not to see the Ribble valley as central to these activities, and the Roman surveyors clearly appreciated the remarkable topography of the valley at Walton. Here a large, level peninsula, bounded on three sides by the two rivers, which are here at their tidal limits, lay across the main routeways of North West England. A timber feature located in 1987, on Pickering's site two, to the south of Winery lane, may have been the remains of a timber wharf. Alternatively the potential of Walton Law to the east as a vantage point may have been exploited in the vicinity of the parish church site. This was thus no isolated outpost, but rather a very extensive industrial and storage complex supplying military operations in the North.

Antiquarians have long argued over the lines of the roads in the district, and the precise location of the river crossings. The excavations off Winery Lane revealed a large stretch of metalled road, which was also identified at site two. If this was the main throughway, it would cross the Darwen close by the London Way bridge, and the Ribble beside the Ribble bridge. Significantly this line makes best use of the slightly higher land. The passage east–west may also have been directed by the higher alluvials to the south of Victoria Road. This was suggested by Hardwick in his map of the site, whilst 'the workmen employed in the erection of Mr Calvert's weaving shed, which crosses its line, state that at some distance below the surface, they came across a compact mass of road material, so hard that a pick-axe could scarcely penetrate it'. Since the present line of Victoria Road is artificial, this feature could equally be the remains of the medieval line.[2]

The settlement of the Welsh

The evidence for the evolution of much of the present-day geography of the North West in the centuries between the collapse of Roman power and the imposition of Norman rule, has recently been brilliantly re-assessed by Denise Kenyon. Working largely from the evidence of early place-names she is able to demonstrate the complex sequence of settlement built up by the native British, the early Saxons, and successive waves of Norse free-booters and farmers. The region was a remote backwater on the fringes of Mercia to the south, Northumbria to the north-east, and Strathclyde to the north whilst the Irish Sea and its river estuaries penetrating deeply inland gave a window on to the world of the Norse.

During the period of Northumbrian control, both Saints Cuthbert and Wilfred acquired lands in the west, the latter obtaining lands along the Ribble in A.D. 678. The breakdown of Northumbrian authority in the ninth century was followed in the west by Norse raids and settlement. From this period also the Saxon kings began to push their authority northwards, and in the early 920s Edward the Elder strove to bring the Ribble under royal control, and the lands between the Ribble and the Mersey began for the first time to develop an identity of their own: 'Betwux Ribbel and Moerse'; the 'Inter Ripam et Mersham' of the Domesday book. The establishment of the castle at Penwortham may date from these efforts.

Throughout this period the boundaries between these linguistic and political groupings remained largely fluid, and the size and location of specific individual settlements are extremely difficult to assess. To overcome these problems Kenyon uses a very loose form of central place theory, based on resource territories and natural route centres. Particular importance is given to the Ribble crossings to the south of Preston, a strategic point utilised by the Romans at Walton, and subsequently an economic and strategic zone divided between three of the Saxon hundreds. It is hard to escape the conclusion that Walton continued to be a focus of settlement, a point strongly indicated by the etymology of the Walton placename. The system of land use, and the pattern of land ownership and ultimately political control which evolved throughout this period are unclear. Kenyon suggests that much of the region may have been divided into 'multi settlement estate groupings' (numbers of settlements grouped into estates), from about the sixth century. Control of these British estates is seen as passing into English hands towards the end of the seventh century, to form the basis of the Anglo Saxon hundreds in the tenth, in the wake of the push to the Ribble. By this time it is likely that the hundreds of Blackburn (including Walton), Leyland (including Leyland and Penwortham), Salford and West Derby, had emerged as the principal territorial units between the Ribble and the Mersey.[3]

Evidence of the origins of these communities can be obtained from the

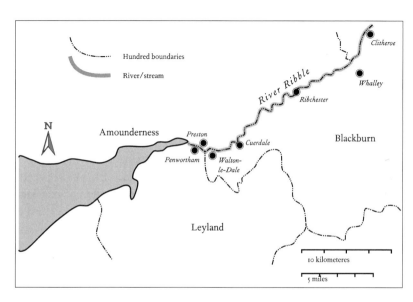

The early importance of the principal crossing points on the Ribble is suggested by the cluster of early settlements in the vicinity of the main crossing at Walton. Here three of the Saxon Hundreds converge, giving them access to, and some measure of control over, this important route centre. (*After Kenyon, 1991*)

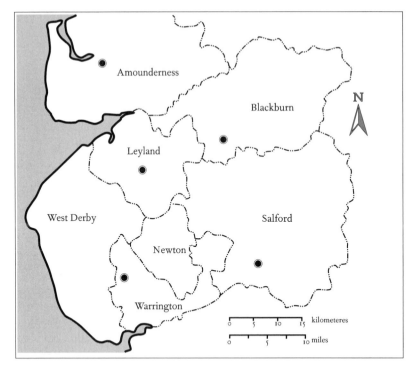

The Saxon Hundreds. Note how the boundary of the Blackburn Hundred extends westwards along the Ribble to take in Walton, and secure control over the lower valley of the Darwen. (*After Kenyon, 1991*)

analysis of their place-names. Survivals of the original British population are indicated by about 50 place-names in Lancashire, mostly south of the Ribble, such as Eccleston and Wigan, but also including Rossall, Preesall and Treales in the Fylde. A local example, Penwortham, comprises *penno* (Welsh for 'hill'), a confusing middle element which may have been *word* (Old English for 'enclosure'), and *ham* (Old English for 'village' or 'estate'). Much depends on the original pronunciation, and the way in which the early scribes spelled it out on paper. This could lead to variations in the spelling, so that Penwortham is recorded as *Peneverdant* (1086), *Penvertham* (1149), *Pendrecham* (1200), *Penwortham* (1201), and *Pennewortham* (1294). Thus in this instance the British placename of a settlement adjoining Walton, was adopted and adapted by English speakers.

A number of instances of the Walton placename occur in the North West, and the *walh* element has been much studied by scholars. Walton-le-Dale is recorded firstly in Domesday book as *Waletone* (1086), and subsequently as *Walaton* (1190, 1212), *Waletona in Ribbellesdale* (1210), *Waleton* (1213), *Walton in la dale* (1304), and *Walton in le dale* (1318). Notwithstanding Victorian interpretations as Wall-tun (the walled tun), and Weald-tun (the tun on the weald or hill), modern scholars consider the word to be an Anglian name used by the newcomers to designate a clearing, settlement or estate of the 'Wales' – that is 'Welsh' speaking native British population. Over time the word for Welsh (Walh, Walas, Wales) came to be applied to serf or slave, indicating the subjection of the British population by their English overlords. When these meanings changed is unclear, but it seems likely that such settlements were enclaves of Welsh speakers in a landscape dominated by English speakers. The probability, is therefore, that the estate on which the later manor of Walton-le-Dale became established has an extremely ancient origin.[4]

British names for prominent geographical features were often taken over by the Anglo Saxons, and the name of the river Ribble, though obscure, is probably British in origin. Almost uniquely it is recorded prior to the Domesday Book, which usually provides the first evidence of place names in the North West, *Rippel* (710), *Ribbel* (930), *Ripam* (1086), *Ribell* (1094), *Ribble* (1130), and *Rybel* (1246). The name of the river Darwen is possibly derived from the British word for oak, and is recorded as *Derewent* (1227), *Derwent* (1240), and *Derewent* (1277). Classical origins have been claimed for both rivers. The Ribble has been linked to Ptolemy's *Belisama Fluvia* ('Beautiful Stream'), and the Darwen to the Derventione of the *Antonine Itinerary*, and the Venerable Bede's Dervventionem. The river Lostock is recorded as *Lostoc* (1200), and *Lostok* (thirteenth century). Again very obscure, it could possibly be related to the Welsh word for beaver.

Many of the place-names of the Ribble valley, the Lancashire Plain, and the Manchester embayment thus have Anglo Saxon origins. To the west, in the Fylde, and in Cumbria, a further layer of Scandinavian names was superimposed onto this confusing linguistic pattern. Eilert Ekwall argued that in the North West this element was Norwegian.

The great Cuerdale treasure

It has been suggested that key elements of the territorial division and settlement pattern of Lancashire were a product of English resistance to the Norse in the early tenth century. Direct, if enigmatic, evidence from this period is provided by the Cuerdale hoard, discovered in the bend of the Ribble at Cuerdale in 1840. Estimated to contain over 8,500 pieces of silver, including 350 ingots, weighing 44 kg (88 lbs), this wonderful and varied trove is now split between over 170 collections. In present-day money its value has been estimated at £300,000. The latest coins, and therefore the clearest indication of the date of the burial of the hoard, are those of Louis the Blind, King of the West Franks, A.D. 901–5, suggesting deposition in the years around 905. The hoard contained about 5,000 Viking silver pennies minted at York *c.* 900, and about 1,000 Anglo Saxon silver pennies of King Alfred and Edward the Elder (899). Other individual specimens, originated from all over the known world. A broad selection of jewellery, perhaps used as bullion money, included silver neck rings from Russia and Irish broaches. Indeed much of the bullion, representing 75 per cent of the hoard, was probably Irish in origin. The coins were leather bagged, and placed with the bullion in a lead lined chest, hidden by a ford near the tidal limit of the Ribble early in the tenth century, and never recovered.[5]

The date and the Irish look of much of the silverwork are significant.

In 902 the Vikings were driven out of Dublin, and the bullion and money may have been a part of their attempt to establish themselves in the Ribble valley. In the event their Irish powerbase was restored in 917, and English control in Amounderness, Preston and south of the Ribble was established by A.D. 934. This enabled the Ribble to be closed to Viking ships. Modern research does not support the contention that the Cuerdale hoard was part of the war chest of participants at the battle of Brunanburgh, since this took place in A.D. 937.[6]

Nearly 200 years later the Domesday Book marked the assertion of Norman power in the district, and provided the first documentary record of the existence of Walton, Leyland and Penwortham. Yet, as has been seen, the main estate groupings, or parcels of manors – the Hundreds – were already centuries old by 1086. The boundaries of the hundreds of Amounderness, Leyland and Blackburn converge on the Ribble crossings between Penwortham and Walton. That between Leyland and Walton is particularly interesting, for as Denise Kenyon has noted, 'Walton lies on the extreme edge of Blackburn Hundred and the Hundred boundary actually snakes around here to include it'. The Walton outpost, down the valley of the Darwen, gave the king's estate at Blackburn control of the north–south routeway, and consolidated control of the east–west route along the Ribble–Aire gap down to the tidal limits of the Ribble. Thus although Walton, Preston and Penwortham are geographically neighbours, in economic, political and perhaps social terms they relate to quite different regional groupings. Critically, and for a thousand years, Preston was to look west to its market territory on the Fylde, whilst Walton looked east to Blackburn.[6]

After the establishment of the authority of the Saxon kings in the early tenth century, the lands between the Ribble and Mersey were retained as part of the Royal estate. Of the organisation and geography of the manor at Walton during this period we are completely ignorant, but the estate, perhaps already many centuries old, was notionally assessed as being worth two ploughlands in the time of Edward the Confessor. After the Conquest the hundred of Blackburn was granted to one of William's henchmen, Roger of Poitou, who in turn granted it to Roger de Busli and Albert Grelley. Thereafter the hundred passed to the Laceys of Pontefract, whose local stronghold was at Clitheroe castle. The individual history of the manor at Walton can be traced to the grant in *c.* 1165 by Henry de Lacy (1146–77), of Mellor, Eccleshill, Little Harwood, Over and Nether Darwen, and Walton, to Robert Banastre, Baron of Newton-in-Makerfield. On the death of Robert Banastre, *c.* 1291, the estate passed through the marriage of his daughter Alesia to John de Langton, whose descendants were lords of the manor until the death of Thomas Langton in 1605. The manor then passed to the Hoghtons in compensation for the death of Richard Hoghton at the hands of Thomas Langton at Lea in 1589. From the middle of the twelfth century, therefore, the manor has been held by just three families, the Banastres, Langtons and Hoghtons.

CHAPTER TWO

The early lords of Walton

N 17 February 1659 Christopher Towneley borrowed the Hoghton deeds from Sir Richard Hoghton. They were carefully transcribed and returned, and the original volume of transcripts can be seen in the Lancashire Record Office at Preston. Most of the original documents are now lost. The efforts of the worthy antiquary over 300 years ago thus allow a glimpse into the world of the medieval lords of Walton.[1]

The development of both society and landscape was closely related to the structure of medieval society. Most land, in theory at least, belonged to the king; its tenure was devolved downwards in return for military and other service. Just as the local lord held his lands through 'service' and 'homage' to his superior, so his tenants in turn owed him his dues. Once these relationships became established they frequently became hereditary. Alternatively the manor was the lord's principal unit of income, and was to be strenuously worked towards this end. Where the lord was absent, or held a number of manors, this task would rest with the stewards, in effect the landowner's agent, or farm bailiff. It was his job to know the precise details of everyone's tenure, the rents to be paid, the exact location of holdings in the open fields, and the days' service due from the smallholders and serfs. Walton Hall had its own large landholding carved out of the manor, and this would have been the bailiff's particular responsibility. Beyond the manor house's holding, or 'demesne', land was held in two principal forms, by freeholders paying rents for large holdings which often passed on for several generations in the same family, and free tenants paying smaller rents and owing days of service work to the lord for their small holdings.

The Banastres' manor at Walton was organised on familiar feudal lines, with the lord's own lands, the holdings of his freeholders, and his tenants clearly designated. All had to use his corn mill, and the estate was run from the manor house. Even from very early times this would seem to have been Walton Hall, a site which is very centrally located on the Walton Mains–Walton Flats–lower Darwen alluvials. The earliest known view of the hall can be glimpsed in S. and N. Buck's *The South Prospect of Preston in the County Palatine of Lancaster*, published in 1728. This appears to show the survival of a medieval tower house amidst the cluster of later buildings.

Most of the Banastre deeds (1130–*c*. 1292) relate to the lordship of Robert Banastre (1260–91), the last of the Banastre lords of Walton. In 1253 a dispute with Peter de Burnhull (Brindle) led to the formal fixing of the boundary between the townlands. Since Peter had been cutting down trees in Walton Wood, this would seem to indicate the survival of the ancient oakwoods in the eastern and perhaps northern parts of the manor. In 1283 a similar agreement with Alexander de Keurdale fixed the bounds of Walton and Cuerdale. Robert Banastre was similarly forthright in asserting his rights at the corn mill, prosecuting freeholders who challenged his monopoly in 1278.[2]

References to the boundaries of land holdings in the early Walton deeds are extremely enigmatic. In 1240 Henry (the) Clerk 'Granted to Henry Bannastre lands in Walton called Suthale within these bounds – beginning at the hedge which goes down to Suthalebroc following that hedge westwards to the land of Yarfrit, going along that land to a streamlet, following the streamlet to the Darwent, up the river to Suchalebroc and then to the starting point'.[3] Robert Banastre granted land to Henry, son of Robert de Camera, 'Beginning at Le Menegate which leds to Ladrigate, following Menegate to Le Eustbroc, along le Eusbroc southwards to a ditch, along the ditch to le outlone which leads to le Holmesnape, and along the outlone to the starting place'.[4] In 1291 Robert son of Emma de Walton granted to Roger son of Bimma de Walton, 'for homage and service to Sir Robert

The Ribble bridge seen from near the top of Swillbrook, c.1900. Swillbrook was one of a number of ancient pathways which originally led from the old Ribble bridge up the Frenchwood escarpment and across the open fields to Preston. The graceful lines of the bridge before it was widened in the mid-twentieth century can clearly be seen.
(*South Ribble Museum*)

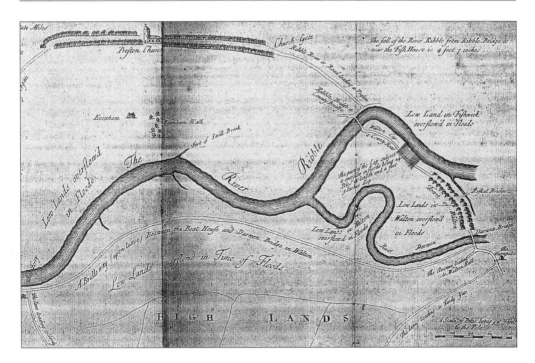

A detail of Robert Porter's map, 1738, the earliest known detailed map of Walton village. This reveals many interesting features: the ancient Ribble bridge; the Darwen's meander; the areas along Walton Cop most susceptible to flooding; the mill stream; 'Boskal Bridge' (Burscough Bridge); and the Darwen bridge. It is particularly noteworthy that the section of the Cop then 'subject to the overflow of the floods' flooded in 1935 and subsequently during periods of heavy rain in the upper Ribble Valley. (LRO, DP256, by courtesy of the County Archivist)

Bannester ... Land in Walton within these bounds ... from the North of Burnilgate [Brindle Road] between the old dyke and the land of Bovatis of which one head goes into le Henesbroke and the other into the dyke towards the house of Roger son of Huttemon on the west' (pre-1291).[5] Other lands referred to in the earliest deeds include 'le Wodeleye', the 'Blakelowe', Hulcroft and Blakecroft, 'Lands next le Houtlone from Walton to Lostock' (Hennel Lane), 'Brocktonbonke', the 'Houtlones [trackway] from Walton to the Haukeserd' and from Walton to Mucklehurst', Bradelegh and Clossebroc, Bradelegbroc and Edolfsacris, Wyggeschawebroc, Closs Broc, 'Le Dedelie', Longeleye, and 'The smithystead next the highway'.[6]

Robert Banastre's son James died in his father's lifetime, leaving a daughter Alesia (Alice), who on her father's death became heiress. On her marriage the manor passed into the Langton family. Yet Robert, though last of the Banastre lords, was to have a profound influence on the development of the manor; he granted further lands to the monks of Stanlaw Abbey in 1283 before their move to Whalley, and he created the 'many free tenancies' which according to Farrer 'distinguish this township'. The break-up of the feudal lands, and the establishment of free tenants holding leases for their lands, was thus well under way here before 1300.[7]

The process of fragmentation was already long established, and the important estates at Bannister (or Darwen) Hall, Little Walton (subsequently Bamber Bridge), and Lostock Hall, may have been established as grants by the very early lords of Walton, in the newly cleared woodlands. The main units of land holdings thus came to comprise the lord's own large estate on the manor's best soils (Walton Mains, Walton Hall, Walton

Flats, and the Townfield), a number of relatively large holdings along the Darwen and in the once extensively wooded upland to the south and east of the Ribble, and a large number of farms and small holdings. Related economic units included the Ribble fisheries, the manor corn mill, Brown-edge Common, and the seasonal pasture and the turf diggings for fuel ('peat') on Walton Moss. Although the balance of land ownership shifted away from the lords of the manor, this pattern was not fundamentally challenged until the industrial revolution.

On the payment of 250 marks, Edward Earl of Lancaster, future King Edward I, consented to the marriage of Alesia Banastre and John Langton. The Langtons were to be lords of the manor for the next three centuries. The rising prosperity of the district, so apparent in Preston at this time, was marked at Walton by the granting of the right to hold markets and fairs. Smith has suggested that this followed an earlier grant made in 1221.[8] The market was held on Thursdays to avoid the Preston market days, and the fair was held on 'the eve, day, and morrow of St Luke the Evangelist', that is 17, 18, and 19 October.

A taxation of 1332 lists the principal freeholders. Walton was ordered to pay 46 shillings, of which John Langton had to pay almost one third:[9]

John de Langton	14s.	Walton Hall.
Henry Banastre	3s.	Bannister Hall. This, and subsequent Banastre land holdings were probably made to kinsmen by the earlier lords.
William Banastre	3s.	
Geoffrey Banastre	3s.	

A section of S. and N. Buck's celebrated *Prospect of Preston* in 1728. The ancient five-arched Ribble bridge, and the posts-and-rails erected along Walton Cop as the only practical means of preventing travellers being swept away by floods, can clearly be seen. The drawing of Walton Hall is particularly important since, as E. E. Pickering suggested, it may reveal evidence of an original defended tower on the site – shown as a higher square block at the far end of the range of buildings.

Walton Hall, c.1820. Rebuilt on a number of occasions, Walton Hall was the site of the manor house, and for centuries the administrative centre of the district. The last structure on this site – which was located between St Leonard's Primary School and Walton Hall Farm – was removed in the 1940s.

John de Walton	3s.	Little Walton, Bamber Bridge.
James de Lostok	3s.	Lostock Hall.
Adam de Balshagh	3s.	The Balshagh lay off Wateringpool Lane.
William de Colville	2s.	Early tenants of the Banastres, a descendant owned the Shuttlingfields – Schetylyngfeld – in 1536.
Alexander de Langley	2s.	Lands in the Longliegh are mentioned in 1391.
John de Redding	2s.	Riding House, off Hennel Lane.
Adam de Windybank	1s. 6d.	'A place in Walton called Wyndebonkfelt' is mentioned in 1384.
William Garston	1s. 6d.	
Hugh de Haydock	12d.	Haydocks was part of the Legh estate in the sixteenth century.
John de Blackburn	12d.	Henry Blackburn was granted lands in Wode-leye before 1291. 'Le Woddelegh in Walton' is mentioned in deeds in 1349.
John de Grendon	12d.	
John de Hanshaw	12d.	Hanshaw Hall, off Hennel Lane.
Henry son of Henry Laghman	12d.	The lawmen of Walton-le-Dale, subsequently spelled Lemon. Lemon House, off Kellet Lane.

A subsequent deed of 1342 lists 36 freeholders, and 32 tenants, separately.[10] Walton was the largest contributor in the Blackburn Hundred to the Poll Tax of 1377/9. Here 73 heads of houses paid 54s.; 48s. was paid by the 49 heads in Samlesbury, and 15s. 6d. was paid by Cuerdale. By contrast the inhabitants of Blackburn paid only 30s., and Burnley 26s.[11]

Economic growth in the first part of the fourteenth century was checked by the Scottish raids, and the ravages of the Black Death. In 1322 the Scots raided deeply into Lancashire, burning Preston, and stealing items from

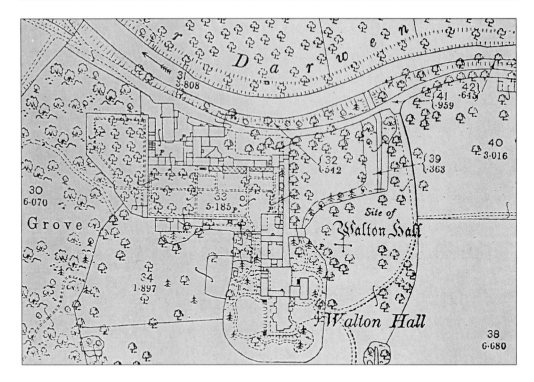

the church at Samlesbury worth, it was later claimed, £18 6s. 8d. Walton seems to have escaped, for the following year a number of locals were prosecuted for stealing from people fleeing the Scots at Lostock Bridge. Ellen de Pleasington lost goods worth £10, and others lost cattle and livestock of similar value. As late as 1347 the priests in Preston claimed that there were lands lying uncultivated and waste due to the ravages of the Scots.[12]

Robert de Langton died in September 1361. His 'inquest post mortem' reveals him to have been lord of the manor of Newton, and of the manor of Walton, where he held 1 capital messuage (Walton Hall), with 80 acres worth 15d. per acre p.a., and 20 acres worth £1, in his demesne, and 2 water mills and a fishery worth £4 a year. The rents of the free tenants were worth £5 4s. 9d., and the tenants at will £9 17s. 4d. In all, Walton was reckoned to be worth £24 2s. 1d. a year, and Newton £17 16s. 9d.[13] The inquest into the affairs of Henry de Langton, who died in September 1419, revealed that he had given to his son Henry and his wife Agnes, 15 messuages, 160 acres of arable land, 20 acres of meadow, 20 acres of woodland, 20 acres of moor and 100 acres of pasture in the manor.[14]

By the middle of the next century the Langtons had assembled a great estate, of which their lands at Walton were only one part. The will of Sir Thomas Langton, made on 4 April 1569, reveals an enormous estate, comprising 'the manors of Newton, Wigan, Walton in le dale, Mellor, Darwyn, Nether Darwyne, Cuerden, Makerfield, and Little Harwood, together with the advowson of Wigan church and 600 messuages, 200

The ancient site of the lord's hall, the nineteenth-century Walton Hall, and Walton Hall Farm, at the centre of the Walton Hall Estate. (*Ordnance Survey, by courtesy of the County Archivist, LRO*) tofte, 12 mills, 20 dove houses, 600 gardeyns, 600 orchards, 6,000 acres of lande [arable], 2,000 acres of meadow, 5,000 acres of pasture, 1,000 acres of wodde, 6,000 acres of heath, 600 acres of more, 1,000 acres of mossys, three score pound of rentes ... and the free fisheries in the waters of Darwyn and Ribble in Walton, Ffishewicke and Preston'. Walton Hall was the great Baron Langton's main residence; he left sums of money to his servants, and took care to stipulate that 'I will my body be buried in the ... side of the chancell in the parisshe churche of Lawe amonge my ancestors there lying and I will that the church shall have all yt rightes and duties as towchinge my funeralle'.[15]

Since his six sons died in his own lifetime Baron Langton was succeeded by his grandson Thomas, who, having no children, was to be the last of the Langton lords of Walton. In 1596, heavily indebted, he obtained a mortgage of £14,000 for the manor from a group of 'London Citizens and Cloothewoorkers'. It was thus a heavily mortgaged property which passed to the Hoghtons in settlement of the dispute arising from Thomas Hoghton's death at Langton's hands at Lea in 1589. An inscription found in Wigan church provides an interesting memorial, 'To oblivion and ye true bones of Sir Thomas Langton of ye Hon'ble Order of ye Bathe Knight, Baron of Newton Makerfield ye last of his name and ye undoubted patron of this church descended from a most antient famous and farre renowned family of Langton in Leicestershire who some times were of great authority both in ye church and Commonwealth of this Kingdome and for ye space of 300 yeares have flourished in this County. A gentleman yt many times tugged with extremityes and made warre with ye worst of misfortues etc. He departed this lief in ye Citty of Westminster 20 Feby 1604 when he had lyved 44 yeres and lyes buried nere ye high alter in St Peters adjoining to ye Abbay.'[16]

Saint Leonard's Church: the church on the Law

The site of the parish church of St Leonard, overlooking the village of Walton, yet at the extreme north end of the parish, is a most remarkable one. As Anthony Hewitson noted in the 1870s, 'A small, strongly built, venerable looking pile ... not one modern church out of 10,000 occupies a site so prominent'. A site was chosen close to the crest of Walton Law, with the Ribble valley falling steeply away to the north, and the sheltered village and townfields along the Darwen to the south. Prior to the construction of Higher Walton road in the early nineteenth century, the church lay on the line of the main road into both Blackburnshire and Yorkshire. Fine, if increasingly interrupted, views of the church can be had from the village, Walton Hall, the flats, and the Darwen lowlands, whilst the roof of the tower affords clear views over much of mid-Lancashire.[17]

In common with the neighbouring parishes, little of the pre-Reformation building survives away from the chancel and the tower. The nave, or body

The prominent position of the parish church of St Leonard, seen from Walton Cop. (*Author*)

of the church, has been rebuilt on a number of occasions. As early as 1503 Ralph Langton bequeathed 20 marks towards its rebuilding. In 1798 it was pulled down; transepts were added in 1816, with further work undertaken in 1855, before a very extensive rebuild in 1906. In 1855 the parish records record that, 'the ancient entrance into the church through the tower was opened, deformities were thrown down, and sundry unsightly objects removed. The pews, many of them like unto loose boxes for cattle others

St Leonard's Church from the south. The low lines of the ancient chancel, in contrast to the modern nave, can clearly be seen. (*Author*)

The coat of arms of the Asshetons, lords of Cuerdale, on the inside wall of the chancel. (*Author*)

The coat of arms and memorial of Sir Charles Hoghton. (*Author*)

of them similar in their filth to the styes of swine, were demolished and handsome pews erected ... The handsome reading desk and a commodious pulpit were erected on each side of the chancel arch, in place of the huge three-storied monster in the middle of the church ... The church at the same time was re-warmed, by introducing pipes of hot water throughout the building. Formerly a small stove pretended (for it was only pretence) to heat St Leonards; two things did that wretched stove do – it caused immense draught, and it tried to suffocate the minister with sulphur ... The whole of these alterations were made with the full approval of the parishioners with the exception of perhaps three, which seemeth very little out of three or four thousand'.[18]

This church contained steep galleries above the north and south transepts supported by iron pillars, cast at Thomas Whittaker's foundry at Higher Walton. Hewitson found the overall effect curious: 'The pulpit and reading desk, which stand on each side of the chancel arch, are tall and good looking. In design they are gothic and octagonal, are approached by elaborate brass-railed geometric stairs, and seem to rest on nothing. Like Mahomet in his coffin, the incumbent and his curate, when alternatively in them, are suspended between heaven and earth. An iron bracket, bolted into the angle of the wall, with cross bars to support the flooring, obviate the necessity of a pedestal for both the pulpit and the reading desk'.[19]

The millstone grit chancel is the oldest surviving part of the present building. Small, and quite low, it measures just 27′ by 18′, the south side contains the remains of an Early English doorway which Pevsner dates to the thirteenth century. Historically it belonged to the Assheton of Cuerdale and Hoghton families, and contains a number of interesting memorials to various of their members, including the long inscription to Cordelia Hoghton, 'A pure virgin espoused to the man Ct. Jesus', and Sir Charles Hoghton's injunction of 1710 that 'This plate of brass is here fixed to intimate to all persons whatsoever that it was his desire nobody for time to come should be buried under the seat or pew, belonging to the Hoghtons, where his remains are interred except the Lady Hoghton, his relict, if she so desire'. The chancel may well still contain the burials of the early lords of Walton, in deposits

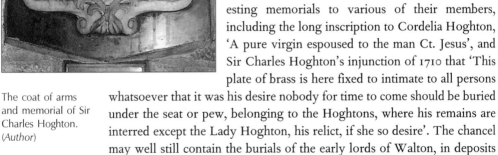

which have survived the various rebuildings. Sir Thomas Langton desired in 1569 to be buried here amongst his ancestors. More curiously, the chancel also contains the grave of Samuel Crook, killed in a fight-cum-duel with Mr William Buckley in Knot Lane in 1722.

The church tower stands 66′ high, has three storeys, and measures 13′ square in internal plan. Like the chancel, it is constructed of millstone grit, which Coupe suggested originated from the Hoghton district. The corner buttresses are very pronounced, reaching up to 50′, and give the tower a great impression of strength. Dating of the structure is again very speculative, but there seems to have been considerable interest locally in tower rebuilding at the end of the fifteenth and beginning of the sixteenth centuries, and the present tower may date from the time of Ralph Langton's bequest in 1503.

St Leonard's tower is notable for its fine tradition of bellringing, and the saga of the parish clock. In 1552 the tower possessed 'fower bells, one of them broken', and the subsequent parish papers contain many references to the bells. Here the campanologist's art has frequently risen to high levels, the fine tone of the bells being enhanced by the tower's very prominent position. In 1761 a peal of 6 bells replaced the 4 old bells, and the founders, Lester and Pack of Whitechapel, graciously allowed the ringers 12s. for drink at the first ringing. Repairs were carried out in 1832, and in 1947 two further bells were added.[20]

Above the ringer's room, but below the bell chamber, is the clock chamber. Writing in the 1830s, Edward Baines remarked that the appearance of the tower was spoiled by a ludicrously large face, which seems to have replaced an even larger one. This monster had been 16′ in diameter and seems to have been painted on to the wall of the tower. The clock had only one hand, and had to be wound daily. In the 1870s Hewitson could still see the date, 1808, cut into the wall below it. The door of the clock chamber comprises a piece cut from a very large wooden clock face, and may be the remains of the subsequent timekeeper noted by Baines, and put into place in 1826.[21]

Up to the nineteenth century virtually all local people, Protestant or Catholic, were interred in the ancient churchyard, which seems to have been confined to the north and east of the church. 'Towards the end of the eighteenth century whenever a Protestant died the funeral took place in the afternoon and the passing bell was slowly tolled prior to the burial: but whenever a Catholic died the interment took place towards the evening and a full peal of bells was rung upon the bells immediately before

A fragment of the enormous nineteenth-century church clock face, remarkably surviving as a door in the church tower. (*Alan Hunt*)

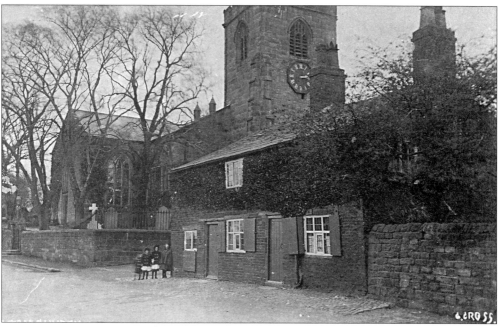

The church and cottages before the extensive rebuilding of 1905. The steady encroachment of the river Ribble into Church Brow has been a problem since the eighteenth century, and may have been exacerbated by the straightening and raising of Walton Cop in the early nineteenth century. The extent of this erosion is indicated by the disappearance of cottages which once stood to the *north* of the road. Prior to the construction of Higher Walton Road ('New Road') in the early nineteenth century, the Blackburn turnpike was routed up Church Brow, past these cottages and the church, before turning down Knot Lane, and along to Higher Walton. (*R. Burns*)

the ceremony'.[22] Walton churchyard is the setting for the old story of the alchemist Edward Kelley, who with Paul Waring is supposed to have brought the dead back to life here in 1560. Versions of this nonsense differ: one has the deceased revealing lost cash; in another the freshly animated cadaver delivers strange predictions of the future.

The remarkably consistent quality of English local history derives at least in part from the central role in everyday life played by the parish. From Tudor times much of what has come to be recognised as local government was undertaken by the parish officials on behalf of the community, and can be traced to the officers appointed to remove refuse, repair the roads, persecute wrongdoers, and look after the poor. The church provided a natural forum for the necessary meetings, which were often held after the service on a Sunday. In short the church was the centre of local life: 'In those times there were queer customs at the church: for instance after each service, the clerk announced at the door to the congregation standing in the churchyard all forthcoming sales by auction, cases for charity when anybody had met with an accident, and other things considered to be either interesting or requiring the attention of the parishioners'.[23]

The ecclesiastical history of the district, like that of the manor, is firmly set within the context of the Blackburn Hundred. Around 1160 Henry de Lacey granted the church at Blackburn – and the chapel which belonged to it at Walton – to Henry the clerk of Blackburn. By 1228 Walton Church possessed its own lands and tithes, and had many of the trappings of a parish church, though technically it was only to be created an individual parish in its own right in 1837. The chapel at Samlesbury is mentioned in 1238 when Blackburn parish was granted to the Cistercian monks of Stanlaw Abbey, prior to their move to Whalley. Both of the district's churches were thus well established by 1150. The lord of Samlesbury and the local people, however, attended the church at Walton on the main festivals. In 1283 Robert Banastre extended the monk's lands at Walton, granting them '10 acres of land adjoining Law chapel and the right to have common of pasture throughout the township, to run 30 swine in Walton woods ... and to take timber and wood for building and burning, and for making houses, heys, and hedges, and repairing the same', in addition to their house. The property was subsequently developed, and is sometimes referred to as a grange and manor. By 1347 John de Langton and four others were paying the abbey £40 a year to work the church lands in Walton. The pastoral work seems to have been undertaken here by chaplains, and 'Adam Chaplain de le Lawe' is mentioned in 1280.[24]

Robert Banastre's son-in-law, and successor as lord of Walton, contested the grant in 1324, eager to recover these lost lands. The monks successfully upheld their claims, despite having misplaced and lost their Walton deeds. These papers, which potentially could have shed much light on the contemporary landscape and system of agriculture, could not therefore be incorporated in the great *Coucher Book of Whalley Abbey*. In 1296 the monks of Stanlaw moved to Whalley Abbey, to whom the parish was thus subservient until the Reformation. At the dissolution of Whalley Abbey in 1537, the chapel with its tithes was valued at £27 11s. 2d.[25]

CHAPTER THREE

The making of the Walton landscape

 P TO THE END of the eighteenth century agriculture was the principal activity in the district, and accordingly the pattern of settlement was closely related to the local types of soil, and the history of their cultivation. Leyland's medieval townfield developed on the well-drained, light and sandy soils adjacent to Towngate, whilst at Longton settlement was closely related to the long belt of slightly higher boulder clays along the line of Chapel Lane and Marsh Lane. At Walton the main emphasis was on the low-lying sandy soils along the floors of the Ribble and Darwen valleys, which probably comprised the ancient 'oxgang' lands mentioned in the Domesday Book. From this focus of very early farming activity, woodland clearance for arable and pasture began to encroach onto the higher plateau lands to the south, and by the sixteenth century had begun to extend onto the mosses in the extreme south and west. Although the manor's economic and social functions (the lord's hall and corn mill, and the church) were centred on Walton village through-out the Middle Ages, this does not mean that the settlement pattern was nucleated in any meaningful sense. For up to the expansion of the textile hamlets in the early nineteenth century, population was only thinly spread across the landscape.

The alluvial soils along the Ribble and Darwen are, therefore, the key to the early settlement pattern. The Ribble lowlands were the most valuable lands in the manors of Walton and Cuerdale, and the Darwen lowlands formed a long belt of rich arable farmland which extended eastwards to the early intake at Bannister Hall. That the lord of the manor held the greatest share of these lands is indicated by a deed of 1624, which describes, 'the Manor of Walton in le Dale, and Walton Hall, Walton Parke, Walton Millne, and manorial rights, properties and lands, including the Copy, the townfeild, the flatt and Worlings, the StoneRiding, the Barneflat, the Cunnygreve, the intake, the Hey etc.'[1] The Walton Hall estate was central to these lands, and lay within its own park, to the west of Chorley Road, between the river Darwen and Hennel Lane. To the west of the park, on the broad alluvial flats of the river approaching Penwortham lay Walton Mains, which had been purchased by the Faringtons of Worden the previous year for £400, and was long regarded by them as a particularly valuable asset.[2] To the east of Chorley Road, the Cinnamon Hill escarpment cuts off the Darwen lowlands on the south side of the

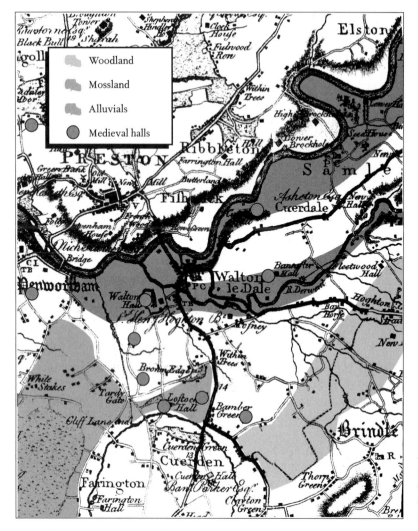

The principal landscape units of the district in the early Norman period.

river, but along the gently shelving vale to the north extends the Walton townfield.

The Walton Townfields

Lying between the river Darwen and the break of slope of Walton Law ('Cooper Hill') to the north, the water meadows beyond Chorley Road in the west, and Knot Lane in the east, the townfields were among the most fertile lands in the district, and were not subject to the flooding constraints which restricted the exploitation of Walton Flats. The advantages of this superb natural location can be very clearly appreciated when viewed from a point just to the west of the 'Forty Steps'. The medieval origin of the field plan can be seen in the tendency towards long rectangular fields extending from the low ridge to the river, which are indicative of the consolidation of the individual cultivated field strips which typify the

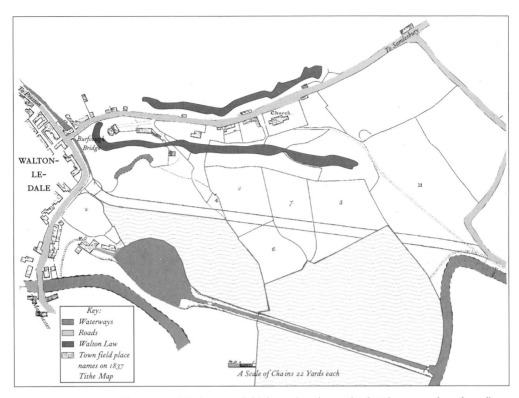

The principal Walton townfield, located to the south of Walton Law, along the valley of the river Darwen. The remains of the mill goit, Burscough Bridge, and the site of the early nineteenth-century corn mills can be seen on this 1808 plan for the new road. As late as the 1840s several of the fields which today form the recreation ground had the field name 'Townfield'. The sharp break of slope which marked the edge of the fields can still be seen to the north of Higher Walton Road ('New Road'), between Walton corner and the bottom of Knot Lane. (Map based on LRO, PDS 17)

agriculture of the period. As late as the 1840s the name 'Townfield' was applied to six of the fragments of the former 'open' field, the remainder being described as 'gardens'. The name is frequently encountered in the Hoghton estate records. In 1791, for example, the townfield was let accordingly:[3]

Near Town Field, Rent £9 9s. od.   Mr Richard Martin.
Salmon Holes, Rent £11 11s. od.   Joseph Hilton.
Far Town Field in two parts, Rent £28.   John Bibby.

At Cuerdale the townfield strips were held by a number of people. The *Coucher Book of Whalley Abbey* notes that 'Thomas le Molyneux held of the abbey for his life ... 6 acres 1 rod of arable in divers parts of the Townfield of Kyuerdale'.[4] The situation in Walton is less clear: early references to individual holdings may be masked in the fair number of early and still obscure field names, or alternatively, and perhaps more likely, the townfield here was held and cultivated directly as a part of the Walton Hall estate.

The ancient Walton townfield seen from the edge of the churchyard on the top of Walton Law. The prominent position of the corn mills remains after 700 years a major feature of the landscape. In the distance the edge of the Lancashire Plain can clearly be seen at Cinnamon Hill, and the enclosed and sheltered aspect of the fields is very apparent. (*Author*)

Walton Flats, a peninsula formed between the two rivers, to the west of Chorley Road, forms a large expanse of flat alluvial soils almost comparable in size to Walton Mains. Their exploitation was, however, closely controlled by the threat of flooding, which up to the early nineteenth century was an annual problem, and is still a threat today. In the old usage of the 1624 deed a 'flatt' or 'flattes' was the low ground through which a river flows, and 'worlings' were nearly level tidal tracts (taking their name from the woven hurdles used to preserve their banks). The regular system of medieval allotment which might be expected to have developed, thus does not appear to have been present here. Indeed, encroachment came quite late. An early intake is dated 1691; 'Lease ... by Sir Charles Hoghton to Thos Ellison of Upper Darren, mercer, of 30 falls of land out of The Flat, a house to be built on the land and yearly rental of 11s. 3d. to be paid. The lessee is to pay £1 2s. 6d. at the marriage of one of Sir Charles's daughters ... and to grind his corn at the lord's mill in Walton'.[5] A deed of 1750 describes a close of ground 2r 36p, 'ditched out of the flats'.[6] On the tithe map of the 1840s most of the flats remained 'rough pasture'. Coupe states that the stone retaining wall along the Ribble was built, and the level of 'Victoria Road' raised in 1822. Only when this was in place was the village free to spread across the flats to the Ribble bridge. The flood threat was thus a very real factor in restricting the development of the village plan.[7]

The Darwen alluvials extend a mile upstream from the townfields, broadening out at Bannister Hall. Farrer suggests that the latter estate 'probably represents a feoffment to a kinsman by one of the early lords of Walton'. The Banastres were established here by the first half of the thirteenth century, and the estate is one of a number of early holdings established away from the immediate environs of Walton Hall and the direct control of the lords of the manor. In 1567 the family is described as 'Banester of Darwin Hall alias Bannister in Walton'. The estate of Lawrence Bannister, who died in 1558, contained '9 messuages, 4 cottages, 200 acres of land [i.e. arable], 60 acres of meadow, 10 acres of woods, and 100 acres of turbary in Walton'.[8]

Cuerdale

Although within the parish of Walton-le-Dale, Cuerdale was a distinct manor in its own right, which included a large tract of the Ribble valley. In the possession of the de Kiurdale family from the twelfth century, early land deeds reveal something of the changing landscape and the related system of agriculture here. The manor house, destroyed by fire in 1346, stood on the present site of Cuerdale Hall farm; there was a manor corn mill probably on the river Darwen; woodland clearance was continuing; and the open field system of agriculture was practised. The following fields and field strips are described in a series of gifts of lands to Whalley Abbey:[9]

—Land in the Eghes [arable fields] of Kyuerdale near the Pullebridge,
    1a 2½ falls.
—In the Eghecroft ½a 12 falls.
—In the Chapelcroft ½a ½rod.
—In the Swannes Ridding ½a 1 rod 6 falls.
—In the Kerr of Kyuerdale 1a 1 rod 25 falls of meadow.

In 1614 Ralph Assheton acquired the manor, which then contained 'a water mill, a fulling mill, 20 messuages, 800 acres of land, meadow and pasture, 200 acres of wood, heath and moss, and a free fishery in the Ribble and Darwen'.[10]

A series of grants of land 'To God and Saint Mary of Cockersand' reveal a similar system of land use at Cuerden to the south. Before 1250 Henry de Cuerden's son, Thomas, granted to Cockersand Abbey 'a portion of his land in Cuerden, within these bounds, beginning at Lostock, following a certain meangate unto the hedge of Ughtred Ball, following the same to the ends of the strips in Aldfield, along the same unto a ditch, where the entire headland runs down'.[11] That a similar system of land holding and cultivation pertained along the Ribble and Darwen at Walton is indicated by a memorandum attached to a deed in the Whalley Abbey papers concerning William de Boghier's lands in Walton. These comprised 'a messuage and 6 acres lying on the banks of Ribble Water next the Fishyerd Kerr [Fishgarth Carr] also in the field called Merstalknoll 1½ rods, 9 falls of arable; in the field called Flathgel near the water of Ribble 2½ a 1 rod 3 falls; in the bankes above the house of said Wm below the vill of Walton 5a 24 falls'.[12]

Kittlingbourne and the Shuttlingfield

The early Walton deeds are largely concerned with land transfers, and contain interesting if enigmatic detail of the contemporary countryside, but only rarely can features be identified with any certainty. A number of brooks are mentioned, all of which would appear to be tributaries of the Darwen. Suthale Broc, Eustbroc, Bradelebroch, Wyggeshawbrock, Closbrooke, Henesbroc and Le Dene broke are mentioned between c. 1240 and 1306, to locate specific holdings. Today, with the exception of Hennel Brook (which flows from close by the Withy Trees in the centre of Bamber Bridge via Cockshutt Brook, to enter the Darwen near Walton Hall), all the significant tributaries are in the east of the district, and flow from Brindle. These include Beeston Brook above Red Rocks, and the Kittlingbourne system which comprises the Black Brook, Drum Head Brook, Bank Head Brook, and Fowler's Brook. With the exception of the references to 'Le Dene broc', which significantly includes the Browne-Egge (Brownedge), and so perhaps relates to Cockshutt Brook, the majority of the references to brooks would seem to refer to the Kittlingbourne system, whose principal stream is the Drum Head. A deed of 1367 describes a grant of land 'lying in parcels in Carthall and Shuttlingfield'. The Shuttlingfields lie along Fowler Brook, which enters the Drum Head just south of Gregson Lane. In 1536 Thomas Langton purchased the 'Schetylyngfeld and Broadfeld. The Brodfeld is mentioned in a deed of 1479, and a Broadfield is located on the Tithe Map to the south of Gregson Lane, by the lane leading from Lower, Middle and Upper Shuttlingfield farms. Such evidence would thus appear to indicate that the early penetration of the heavily wooded upland south of the Ribble valley lay along the tributaries of the Darwen.[13]

Little Walton and Hennel

Settlement of the central part of the manor, the uplands to the west of the Shuttlingfields, is indicated by the establishment of a number of distinct land holdings. At Bamber Bridge, the estate of Little Walton Hall probably shared similar origins to Bannister Hall, as a holding created by one of the early lords of Walton. William de Walton was living here in 1253, and the estate remained in the Walton family until 1682. The house survived into the early twentieth century, when Farrer described it: 'The house at Little Walton or Bamber Bridge is an ancient structure with central porch and gabled wings, the walls showing traces of timber framework. On the entrance post is the date 1675'.[14] In 1367 William Walton held lands in Walton 'with a house on the bridge over the Darwen'. A prosperous Preston mercer, he was mayor of that place in 1378–86 and 1389, and two years later Ralph de Longton granted him 'Lands in Walton in le Holme on the water of Lostoke and le Houtlone cum le Bent'.[15]

Lemon House, towards the south-east corner of the manor, was the home of the Laghmon (Lawman) family. Farrer suggests that they were the hereditary judges, or Lawmen, of the manor court. Adam, 'son of the Laghmon', is mentioned in 1248. The spelling of the name changed to 'Lemon' in the early sixteenth century, and William Lemon sold the Lemon House estate in 1663. Located in the rolling and empty country to the north of old Kellet Lane, the first edition of the OS map reveals a trackway connecting both Lemon House and Bradkirk Hall to the vicinity of the Withy Trees to the north. In the fenland environment to the west of Little Walton Hall, and to the south of the Brown-edge, Lostock Hall had become the home of the de Lostock family by the middle of the thirteenth century.[16]

The penetration of the upland in the east along the Kittlingbourne tributaries is matched in the west by a series of early farm estates along 'le houtlone from Walton to Lostock' – Hennel Lane. Riding House was located to the west of the line of Hennel Lane and Wateringpool Lane, between what are now Vernon's mill lodge and Carr Wood farm. The ancient home of the Riding family, a John del Riding is mentioned during the late thirteenth century. John Riding and William Ryding sold their lands here in 1582.[17] Half a mile to the south-east, on a site obliterated by the gas works, stood Hanshaw Hall. This estate, like most of the others, was held of the lord of the manor. John de Hanneshagh and Richard de Hanneshawe are mentioned in 1332 and 1350 respectively. Hanshaghhall appears in 1514, and Hanshaw Halle in 1648. On the first edition of the OS map the site is shown as Hanshaw Hillocks.[18]

Between Wateringpool Lane and Todd Lane, to the north of Doodstone Nook, the Tithe Map reveals a group of nine fields with the name 'Balshaw', which may originally have formed parts of one of the great open fields or ploughlands. The name 'Balshaw' is derived from the Old English 'Round Wood'. A family taking the name Balshagh held lands here from the thirteenth century, for Henry de Balshagh is mentioned in 1283, and lands 'in le Balshagh' are described in 1334.

Brownedge Common and Walton Moss

The mosslands formed a landscape quite distinct from the fertile valley floor alluvials, and the heavily wooded clays of the Lancashire Plain. Most of the manor's boundary on the east and south was formed by the northern edge of the West Lancashire mosses, that is south from Middleforth Green along the line of Leyland Road to Tardy Gate, then due east along Brownedge Road to Brownedge Lane. The physical change in the landscape, as the slightly higher plain gives way to the low, very flat lands of the former mosses, can be very clearly seen along Brownedge Road by Brownedge Church. As the road from Withy Trees bends around the very deep pit in the grounds of the Baxi factory, it actually runs down the slope onto the moss level.

Attempts to pump dry the Baxi pit, a feature clearly shown on the earliest OS map, have always failed, leading to the local belief that it is 'bottomless'. In fact the pit is an integral part of the hydrographic system under a large area of Bamber Bridge south of Brownedge Road. Changes in the level of the water surface in the pit indicate much broader fluctuations in the water table. Since the lowland mosses had their origin in the higher water tables resulting from poor drainage, the pit is, therefore, a rather unique survivor and indication of the processes which brought Walton Moss, and to the east Charnock Moss, into existence in prehistoric times. As late as the early sixteenth century much of modern-day Bamber Bridge west of Station Road, and extending in a belt through Lostock Hall and Tardy Gate, may thus have been mossland.

The process of the drainage and reclamation of the local mosslands (artificially subdivided by the parish boundaries into Leyland, Longton, Farington, Charnock and Walton mosses) has been under way from early medieval times. As turf was removed for fuel, and the peats were drained for farming, any trace of prehistoric trackways, moss-side settlements and 'bog burials' will have been lost. In 1246 Adam Laweman and Richard Banastre prosecuted the Abbot of Evesham and others who had broken up and enclosed 100 acres of Walton Moss. By the middle of the sixteenth

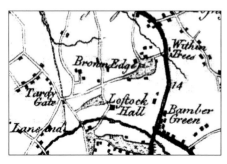

The Brown Edge: an area of unenclosed mossland is shown at the junction of Duddle Lane, Brownedge Road and Brownedge Lane. A second parcel of moss survived to the west of present-day Todd Lane South, and is marked as 'Walton Moss' on the first OS map of the 1840s. These two fragments were the remnants of the once extensive mosses revealed by the medieval land deeds, which had once formed the northern edge of the great wetlands of the west. Long into the eighteenth century local people clung to their right to cut peat ('turf') for fuel on the moss.

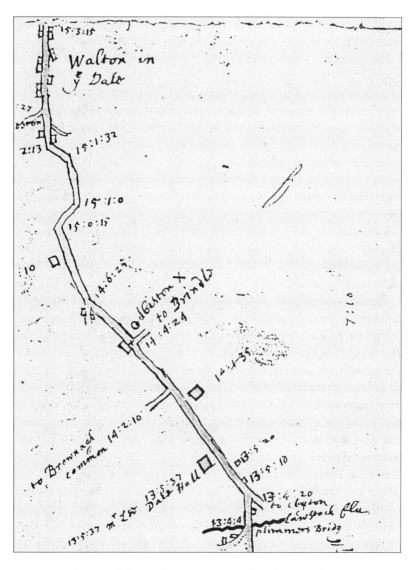

The map attributed to Dr Kuerden of the road through Walton and Cuerden, c. 1680. The track 'to Brownach common' is clearly shown (bottom left), and the site of the ancient Osbaldeston Cross is marked at the end of School Lane – the way to Brindle. (LRO, DDX 194/23, by courtesy of the County Archivist)

century enclosure of the local mosses was well under way, leading to many disputes as to rights on the former common lands. In 1551 William Charnock brought a case before the Chancery Court of the Duchy of Lancaster against Sir Thomas Langton 'in an action as to disputed title to common of pasture, turbary, and Housebote and Heybote to waste grounds called Walton Wood [Walton Wode], Blacke Lowe [Blac Lawe], Brownedge [Browne egge], and Walton Moss, in Walton-le-dale, and Cuerden [Kuerdon Common]'.[20]

The Brownedge was an integral part of this system of land use. A grant of 1306 defines lands bounded by le Browne Egge and le Denebroke (Cockshutt Brook?), and one of 1313 mentions Le Brounege, the water of Lostok and Swardifall.[21] Precisely what the Brown Edge was is unclear. Farrer suggested that it was a dyke extending to Dene Brook. The edge

could well have been the sharp boundary of higher land to the north of
Brownedge Road and Lane, with the flatter mossland to the south. Dr
Kuerden's map of *c.* 1680 clearly marks the Brownedge Lane–Station Road
junction at Withy Trees, as the way 'To Brownach common'. The Yates
map of 1786 shows Brownedge Lane, Duddle Lane, and Brownedge Road
leading onto the mossland. Lying adjacent to the main road from Preston
(Station Road), and readily accessible from it (via Duddle Lane and Brownedge Lane), the Brownedge was thus perhaps the first of the local mosses
to be brought into agricultural use.[22]

This line of reasoning raises the question of the size of the common,
which may have been very extensive, extending from the line of Brownedge
Road–Lane in the north to the River Lostock in the south, and from Station
Road in the east to the Lostock Hall estate along Moss Lane in the west.
The lands to the west of Moss Lane are clearly marked 'Walton Moss' on
the 1840s' OS map. The field pattern shown on this map suggests a
conservative extent, with the moss extending from the line of the junction
of Brownedge Lane and St Marys Road in the east. Both Meanygate (a
'meanygate' was a straight road onto a moss) and the stretch of Brownedge
Lane from St Marys Road to Duddle Lane have the appearance of comprising fairly modern enclosure roads. The Brownedge noted in the early
deeds would thus appear to have been the boundary or mossland rim of
the higher, better drained and longer-cultivated land. Once the mosses
were drained, the resulting rough pasture was utilised as rough pasture to
which common rights of grazing were attached. To the west of Moss Lane,
at the Tardy Gate end of the system, 'Walton Moss' survived into the
nineteenth century.

In 1588 Thomas Langton granted a lease to run for three lives at 9*s.* 6*d.*
per year to Roger Cowper of Cuerden for £16 5*s.* 0*d.* It included a small
parcel 'to be enclosed from Walton Mosse between the moss dale belonging
to Lostock Hall on the south side and a common highway leading from

The scene at the
end of Brownedge
Road, *c.* 1905.
Pilkington's Foundry
can be seen in the
distance,
overlooked by the
higher site of the
church of St Mary,
Brownedge. This
minor
differentiation in
land heights along
Brownedge Road
indicates the
boundary line of
the original
mossland, literally
the brown edge. By
this date much of
the flat lands to the
south of Brownedge
Road had been
developed as
sidings by the
Lancashire &
Yorkshire Railway
Company. (*R. Burns*)

Tardie Gate in Penwortham to Brounedge Common in Walton on the north side, and a highway from the stone bridge of Lostock to the town of Walton on the east side, and an Inclosure lately improved by James Werden deceased, from Walton Mosse on the west side'.[23]

The moss provided a valuable source of fuel – peat – or 'turf' as it called in Lancashire, and summer grazing. These rights, usually held to some extent in common, were carefully supervised on the community's behalf by the manor court. In 1631 the Walton Manor Court decreed that 'Any p[er]son [who] delve[s] or get any matter or soil from ye Lords waste or Common of Walton (except clods, sodds, clay and sands, such as only shall be cast out of their ditch or ditches) without the special lease and Lycense of the Lord of this mannor upon paine of every one of them making default as aforesaid to the Lord of this Mannor the summe of 6s. 8d.' [24]

Grazing rights were supervised by the court's officers, which annually appointed pinders to pound stray animals on Brownedge and Walton Moss. Thomas Shorrock and Roger Brewer were appointed in 1673. A year previously an enquiry into turf rights led Alice Martin (78) and Robert Sharrocke (75), to recall that 60 years previously Katherine Burscoe, a widow living at Lostock Hall, would only allow fuel to be cut there by her consent. Where this had not been duly obtained she would attack the stacks of drying peats with her 'speide', leaving them, 'cutt and soe utterly despoiled'.[25] From time to time the court ordered people living along the edges of Brownedge common and the moss to clean out the drainage ditches: John Woodcock was ordered to clean the watercourse from Wadkin Hey to Richard Sherdley's house hey, 'being the usual current or watercourse from Walton Mosse to Lostock'. The edges of the moss were also carefully watched for signs of land taking. In 1667 John Woodcock had stolen 23 falls of ground 'from the boundaries of waste', and was to be punished accordingly.[26]

In 1661 'Broune Edge' was carefully surveyed and 'the number of acres as nere as can be adjudged by Comon Estimacon will amount to 17' [customary acres]'.[27] Repairs of 'the highway over the brownedge' were ordered by the county magistrates in 1694, and in 1697 the 'repairinge of Walton Moss' required '30 loade small brick and 14 loade gravel 14s. 6d. ... 5 loades small witheringe Wood, 1 loade windeings, about 70 piles 10 foot long, and saplings 11s. 9d. ... Carts and men for loading ye brick, gravel and piles of wood 6s.'.[28] Notwithstanding the lateness of the season the road was to be repaired in 'several foule places' at an overall cost of £2 6s. 0d. By 1820 the common had become the property of the churchwardens and overseers of the poor of the parish, and was known as the 'Walton Poor Land'. Brownedge Farm, on the site of the Baxi car park on Brown-edge road, was estimated to contain 26 acres in the 1880s.[29] The pleasantly rural aspect of Brownedge was to survive into the early twentieth century, and in the 1870s Anthony Hewitson had found that the inhabitants to be 'comely and kindhearted'.[30]

Walton Cop and the Bridges of 'Rybill and Derwent'

The passage across the rivers Darwen and Ribble at Walton was as perilous as it was strategic, for the short length of road between the rivers was prone to flooding in both summer and winter. The courses of both rivers and their junction were also liable to move in the shifting alluvial sands. In response, the line of the road across Walton Cop also changed, and may have taken a line on the slightly higher river deposits to the south of the present Victoria Road prior to the raising of the Cop and the formal definition of the line of the road in the sixteenth century. To greatly complicate matters, an ancient mill race ran from the vicinity of the old Police Station on Victoria Road to close by the Darwen Bridge, and effectively made Walton Flats and the land to the west of Chorley road an island.

The origins of the Darwen and Ribble bridges are ancient, if uncertain. In 1302 the locals were granted the right to levy tolls on goods passing over or under them in exchange for building or repair work. Subsequently this duty passed to Blackburn hundred, and ultimately the county authorities, being units of local government more able to afford the upkeep.[31] A deed of 1383 describes the 'Chapel on Ribbill bridge', which was leased to Ralph de Langton and Thomas de Clayton, 'chaplain', for 3s. 4d. per year. In return they were to receive 'the oblates coming from the chapel' and 'vestments on the altar, chalice, images, relics, wax and all other profits, utensils and appurtenances for 30 years'. If the chaplain, after deducting reasonable expenses from the alms, did not use the remainder to repair and maintain the bridge, 'Ralph and Thomas will resign the vestments, etc. without delay'.[32]

In 1403 a new stone bridge was ordered to be built alongside the old one, which had been damaged by ice and floods.[33] Much repaired, this was probably the structure alluded to by Leyland in the 1540s: 'Within a mile of Preston I cam over Darwent River, the which at Penwardine paroche, a celle to Evesham, goith into Ribil ... Half a mile beyond Darwent I passid over the great stone bridge of Rybill having a V [5] great arches'.[34] Dr Kuerden, writing in the 1680s, described the bridge and road complex at Walton, 'Passing the Lostoc Water at a fair stone bridge parting Leyland from Blackburn Hundred you meet with the other road from Chorley to Preston ... About a mile further is another road from Brindle to Preston and shortly after you come to Walton, and leaving Walton Hall on your left ... you cross the Derwent at a large bridge which is 20 yds between the springers, then enter Walton Cop for half a mile well rampyred with stone. On the right is a great road from Blackburn to Preston. At the end of the Cop you pass over a stone bridge ... one of the statelyest stone bridges in the north of England'.[35]

From an early date the locals strenuously opposed the enormous expense of maintaining the passage through the manor, which the bridges and cop

entailed, but by the middle of the sixteenth century had successfully transferred the responsibility on to the county magistrates. In addition to the
two great bridges, crossings at Manybrooks (ordered to be repaired in
1640), Cann Bridge (rebuilt 1642), Bamber Bridge (repaired 1661), and
Lower Bridge (probably at Lostock Hall, repaired 1677), still had to be
maintained.[36] The 'Return of the bridges maintained by the township of
Walton-le-Dale, made in November 1801 by Richard Haydock, parish
constable' lists bridges at Cockshutt, Many Brooks, Kittlingbourne, Bank
Head, Hennel, Mosney Wood, Lower Hennel, Resolution Bridge (between
Walton and Cuerden), and Common wood.[37]

The good repair of the Darwen and Ribble bridges was, however, only
one aspect of the problem of maintaining a permanent way through Walton,
for the crossing of the water meadows between the bridges could be a
much more perilous enterprise. The very frequent floods meant that the
line of the road was frequently changing, as whole sections of the river
banks were swept away. During the floods there was a very real threat of
death for the unwary traveller. When the Ribble broke out of its course,
the Ribble bridge could be left high and dry, and getting across the new
course could be highly dangerous. Accordingly great efforts were made to
keep the river in place in the channel under the bridge, and to stabilise the
line of the road. From the early seventeenth century the line of the road
between the Ribble Bridge and the bottom of Church Brow was gradually
embanked by a sort of Ribble rampart. This became known as Walton
Banke, or the Town Banke, but more generally as Walton Cop.

In 1634 the county magistrates agreed to the 'repair and amendment of
the bank or Copp in Walton ... lying between Rible Bridge and Darwen
Bridge called Walton bank or the Copp, and a fair and sound way to be
made upon the said Copp for all maner of passages with carts, carriages,
and all other arrangements for a convenient way to passe', providing that
Sir Gilbert Hoghton would give them the land on which this road was to
pass.[38] Before anything could be done Sir Gilbert died. Richard Shawe
tried to persuade Richard Hoghton to agree to the project. Great sums of
money had been spent, and large quantities of 'underwood and brushwood'
used to preserve the river bank. 'If the work is not done then within a few
years the whole land will bee lost, and the current now under the Bridge
will run abroad over the land, and the Bridge found dry'. His argument
was ultimately persuasive. 'You know in what grait danger of overflowing
all the lande beetweene Walton Bridge and Ribble bridg along the Copp,
have continued many yeares, and what great charges Sir Gilb[er]t Hoghton
your father hath been att'. The cost to the county for the repairs would be
£500, and the value of the land negligible in comparison.[39]

Acting on Shawe's advice, the Hoghtons duly rid the manor of a costly
expense. Accordingly the level of the road was considerably raised, but
only two years later the condition of the road and bridges caused the county
magistrates to order £20 'att the least', for the locals 'and workmen of skill'

to undertake repairs 'with all convenient speede'.[40] The ravages of the Ribble, sweeping down the valley in flood, and bursting out over the water meadows, continued unabated as they had done for centuries. In 1664 the Ribble Bridge and Walton Cop were 'in very great decay by reason of the late great inundation of water ... in regard of the iminent danger that may happen to such people that have cause to pass that way by reason of the breaches and decays thereof' £315 14s. od. was to be set aside for 'experienced workmen', timber piles and stones.[41]

Ten years later a great breach was torn through the Cop, making the road impassable. Passers-by made their way through the flats as best they could, trampling crops and disturbing the cattle. Further damage was done when the county's workmen dug away great quantities of earth and gravel to effect the repairs. This seems to have provoked Sir Richard Hoghton into charging the public for passing through what were still in effect the grounds of Walton Hall. Of course a great row ensued. The 'learned advice' of Creswell Levin was sought: if the road flooded people were entitled to made their way around the obstruction 'if there be no other way for the King's people to pass', but any damage done by the workmen must be made good. Sir Richard made further claims from this settlement, that the county should carefully fence the road 'not only by quick wood and staffe hedge but also by stoops of wood and railes ... from the Ribble Bridge to ye kilne [Walton corn mill]', and that if repairs were not in future made to the Cop six months after he had given the Sheriff due notice, he could close the road. These efforts had little effect in preventing the flooding, for in 1678 the Sheriff ordered John Leigh (81) to be given relief following his 'loss from floods'.[42]

Central to the problem of flooding on Walton Cop was the location of the Walton corn mills, and the arrangement of the mill races. These had important consequences for the developing village plan. The best pre-industrial plan is contained in Yates map of 1786. This clearly shows three mills along a race running in a line, north to south, between the Ribble and the Darwen. A pair of mills occupy the site of the modern corn mill a short distance from the Darwen, whilst the third is located close by the Ribble, behind the site of the present White Bull public house, at the foot of Church Brow. This may have been a comparatively modern, and short-lived, textile mill. The mill race thus made Walton, in effect, an island.

Although the direction of the flow of water in the race must have been affected by the tides, the predominant flow (according to the Environment Agency) would be from the Darwen to the Ribble. The line of the race would thus have powered the pair of corn mills on the present-day Dalgetty site, then passed north under Burscough Bridge (carrying the Blackburn road across to Church Brow), to power the textile mill close by the Ribble outfall. The Coroners' records contain several references to fatalities in the 'mill floam [stream] issuing out of, and running from, a certain river called the Derwent' (1741), by 'the bankes of the mill pool' (1782), and by the mill dam (1760). Alternatively, since both outlets are by the tidal limits of their respective rivers, it is possible that at one time the mill pool could have been filled from both sources. The straightening of the 'Burscough Bridge to Blackburn Turnpike Road', planned in 1807 but seemingly only effected after 1814, resulted in Higher Walton Road being constructed through the Townfields, and the filling-in of this mill race. In 1809 the present extensive weir and associated race were under construction on the Darwen.[43]

Burscough's Bridge and the Walton Corn Mills

The earliest reference to the corn mill at Walton is found in a series of grants made in 1213–19 to the monks of Cockersand Abbey: 'Grant in Frankalmaign from Thurstan Banastre to God (and the Canons of Cockersand), of half a mark of silver, to be paid yearly at the feast of St Giles out of his new mill in Walton-le-Dale, situated by Westbrook'. In a further deed he added the tithe from the new mill, 'which he had erected, and of the fishery belonging to that mill'. This was clearly not the first mill at Walton. It does not appear to have been on either the Ribble or the Darwen, and the Westbrook appears on a number of early deeds (le Euestbroc c. 1260–91), though its precise modern-day identification is uncertain.[44]

'Thomas the miller' is mentioned in deeds around 1290, and his son Geoffrey occurs in 1323.[45] Most celebrated of the Walton millers is Robert Smalbrid ('Small bread' – probably a nickname), the 'milner of Walton-le-dale fugitive for theft', the subject of an inquest in 1376. He fled the district, with 'goods on the day he fled to the value of 23s. 4d.', these

The foot of Church Brow, c.1895. Presumably unknown to him, the cyclist is standing on the line of Burscough Bridge, which crossed the mill stream at this point. Stonework in the footings to the wall to his left may have been taken from the remains of the bridge and its approaches. Other notable features are the side entrance to the White Bull Inn juxtaposed to the Methodist chapel, with the splendid structure of the Walton-le-Dale Working Men's Institute on the bend of the hill, near to the site of the old turnpike gate. (R. Burns)

included 2 casks of oil (40d.), 2 pigs (40d.), 3 little pigs (40d.), and other household goods (40d.). The indictment also reveals that he had two mills on 17 years lease in Walton, worth 20s. per year, and includes the following note: 'Item there used to be a highway in Walton through the middle of the field of Ralph de Longton called Waltonheghes to a bridge over the water of Derwent which highway has been obstructed and changed by him and Ralph de Longton to the injury of the customary tenants without licence of the King'.[46] From the field name – Waltonheghes (Walton Hays) – and its size, location by the River Darwen, and value (2s. per acre per year), this was probably one of the townfields. It is possible that changes in the line of the road may have been due to changes in the line of the mill race, or perhaps the development of the present site at this time. The two mills are also listed in the Inquest into the estates of Robert Langton, who died in 1361. The precise location of the early Walton mills is uncertain, the present central location in the village can be identified early in the seventeenth century, and may account for one of the mills, whilst another may have been sited higher up the Darwen in the vicinity of Higher Walton. Alternatively, an estate mortgage of 1674 clearly lists 'the Demesne of Walton and Walton Mill and the mill near it'.[47]

The physical geography of the river deposits at Walton appears to have changed markedly in recent centuries. The rebuilding of Walton Cop in the 1820s appears to have altered the flow of the Ribble quite markedly, by accentuating erosion along the Church Deeps, and in the vicinity of Kings Croft, whilst the houses which formerly stood opposite St Leonard's Church have long since been swept away, and the road continues to suffer problems of erosion. It is unclear to what extent erosion has affected the length of river from Kings Croft to the old Police Station – the location of the entrance to the mill stream which ran south into the Darwen, although Robert Porter's map would seem to indicate that erosion here has also been extensive. This millstream clearly existed by the early seventeenth century, for Peter Burscough left monies in his will for the construction of a bridge over it. Known as Burscough Bridge, it seems to have been removed in the early nineteenth century, when the mill race from the Darwen was reconstructed. It is frequently referred to in the county papers, and a fine line drawing of it is preserved in one of the county 'bridge books'. It crossed the mill brook almost precisely on the line of the present pedestrian crossing island at the bottom of Church Brow, immediately adjacent to the White Bull public house.

The millstream's outlet into the Ribble, cutting through the river bank and flood defences, presented an obvious point of weakness during periods of high water. It may have utilised a former channel or some similar natural feature such as a cut-off ox-bow, whilst the exploitation of the natural fall between two independent rivers to power machinery must have been a novel and rare engineering feat at this time. As the Cop was raised, and the 'Town Bank' was built up, this point of weakness must have become

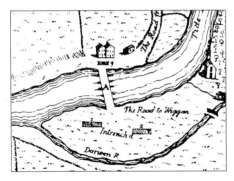

A detail from 'An Exact Plan of the Town of Preston' published following the Battle of Preston in 1715. Although very inexact, the line of the mill stream, and the mill itself, can be seen to the east of Darwen bridge.

exaggerated, and to preserve the millstream from damage a caul was constructed along the river. The stream itself was also a hazard, as the road to Blackburn had to cross it at the foot of Church Brow.

Peter Burscough left monies in his will of 1624 for a range of public utilities. The inventory of his goods totals a massive £1,477 1s. 0d., and lists 24 lots of debts and cash bills owing to him. William Osbaldeston of Walton alone owed him £214 16s. 6d. He left grants of £100 for 'shirtings and cloths' for the poor of Walton, Cuerden and Whittle-le-Woods, £100 to the Free Grammar School at Leyland, and a similar sum 'for the erecting and maintenance of one free school att the Lawe Church in Walton-le-Dale'. He seems to have had a particular interest in the highways, for he left £40 for repairs and improvements to the 'Cop between Ribble bridge and the town of Walton'. He also left funds for the construction of the stone bridge over the mill stream: 'I give and bequeath for and toward the erecting and mainteyning of one stone bridge at the end of Duddels Lane [not the present Duddle Lane, but presumably the contemporary name for Church Brow] between the Lawe Church and Ribble Bridge – the sum of £20, for footemen and horsemen to pass over the same'.[48]

A further £40 was left for the remaining roads in the manor. This money was invested in land which produced an annual income of £3. It was decided to expend it as follows:[49]

Betw. Tardie Yate and the towne of Walton	6s. 8d.
Lemon House and the towne of Walton	6s. 8d.
Cleton Grine and the towne bancke	20s.
Brindle Yate and Osbaldeston cross	7s.
Brindle Stups and the Many brook	3s.
Meare Yate by Popes and Can Bridge	6s. 8d.
Smithie Crosse and The High Gate lane	6s. 8d.
Curdall and Atkinson Yate	3s. 4d.

Throughout the seventeenth and eighteenth centuries the mills and various waterways at Walton continued to be the cause of much expensive concern. In 1637 it was found that money intended to be spent on repairs to 'Burscow Bridge' had been 'retained' by the Sheriff's officers, who were ordered 'to be arrested and conveyed to Lancaster Jail'. Extensive repairs were carried out in October 1662, employing 24 men each day. Out of a total cost of £95 8s. 0d., Thomas Watson was to be paid £26 13s. 4d. 'for his work building and finishing the Bridge'. Further repairs followed in 1702.[50]

The Blackburn Hundred Bridge Book (1803–5) is a major source for the study of the local bridges, and contains much interesting detail, including

The site of the Ribble end of the mill stream, behind the White Bull Inn. Extensive defence works ('the groin') were constructed here to protect the stream from the seasonal floods which frequently burst through at this point. They can be seen on Robert Porter's map of the Ribble and its fisheries produced in 1756. (S. Cook)

a detailed drawing of 'Burskow Bridge' which crossed the 'mill goit' on an arch 8' high and 24' across. By comparison 'Bamber Bridge' was 8' 3" and 29', and the old Darwen Bridge 16' and 60' respectively.[51] The wholesale disappearance of Burscough Bridge is one of the more remarkable aspects of the changing plan of Walton village. It does not appear on the first OS map of the 1840s, but a detailed plan of its position is preserved in a Hoghton Estate plan of 1890. Most of the other manor bridges have been rebuilt on, or close by, their ancient sites.[52]

In the 1650s the line of the mill race was changed after a woman was drowned in the floods, 'for ther was so little ffall into the River Daren the ground lying so upon the level, that the King's Highway in Walton town was sooner overflown than now it is (1693), and in those times they were often forced to fetch a fish boat between Walton Kilne [the corn mill] and Darwen Bridge'.[53] The mill also had its troubles, for in 1682 'severall credible persons and people of Good Qualitie' complained that the miller John Tipping '. . . is not of good name nor of honest conversation amongst his neighbours, but an evil doer, a quarriller and perturber of the peace of our Soveraign Lord the King'. He was ordered to attend the next Assizes at Preston, and explain himself.[54]

Floods in 1689 again breached the Cop. In 1691 the mill stream broke out of its channel; £2 had to be spent 'for cleansing the old watercourse stopping up the new one', and £54 6s. od. on strengthening Burscough Bridge by adding 'battlements and wing walls'. A major inquiry followed in 1693 into the flood of 1689 and the subsequent management. It reported 'that part of the Copp next the mill streame as also the land opposite was much shaken and by the many floods since, those shaken places not being repaired are much worse'.[55]

Despite the effort of centuries nothing much had been achieved in the face of the Ribble floods. To lessen the danger stone posts and rails were provided along Walton Cop to prevent passers-by from being washed away. Although a prominent feature of Buck's engraving of the Cop, they could not prevent the death of Robert Heath of Preston in December 1737. The coroner found that 'the waters of the Ribble being by the excessive rains and melting of snow upon the hills swoln to a great height and having overflown the banks of the said river ran out of the current of the said river over Walton Cop into a close of ground called the Flatts in Walton with a high strong current at a place there betwixt the houses of George Walmsley and John Seddon that the deceased was on horseback and attempted to ride through the said current'. Heath's horse bucked, he dismounted and tried to walk through the current: '... body found this morning washed into the old stream of the Darwen. Driven through the rails of the Cop'.[56]

At the Assizes of 1749 Sir Henry Hoghton was sensationally accused by his enemies of serious misconduct in appropriating materials provided by the county for the repair of the Cop. Angry at this afront, he denounced his accusers for 'Affecting popularity without bringing these pretended grievances upon the carpet', and drew up a long document in his defence, threatening to close the road through the Cop and, more pointedly, to enquire into the recent repairs at Lancaster Castle. The matter was cleared up to Sir Henry's satisfaction, and his report sheds much light on the evolution of the Cop, the mill stream, and ultimately the development of the village in the early industrial revolution.[57]

Sir Henry recites the history of the Cop from Sir Richard's agreement with the county. In recent years houses had begun to be built on the west side of the Cop road, and the approaches to the Ribble Bridge had been strengthened. The central section of the Cop had deliberately not been built up by his ancestors 'for the River Ribble to spend itself in High Floods over my grounds, sometimes to the great damage thereof'. This section can still be seen in the slight fall of the road by the traffic lights adjacent to the Capitol Centre. He describes the weir or 'Cawls' on the Ribble, but was not sure when they were built. Around 1720 it had been found that the river 'was got to the foundation of the wall at the foot of the mill fleam next the river, and was very near undermining the same', and was about to break through and destroy the Cop and the road. The cawl was repaired 'so as to arrest the course of the River which about the Cawl points upon the Cop'. The sides of the mill stream had been lined with stonework and built higher, 'to prevent the water flowing over the Cop when the Rivers Ribble and Darwen meet'. Two mills are mentioned (1749), the 'Blue Stone Mills'. Access to them was by way of Burscough Bridge, and one was a corn mill, the other an oil mill. These would seem to be the pair of mills shown on Yates map (1786), on the site of the present corn mill, and frequently occur in the estate accounts. In 1791, for example, Mr Winstanley and Richard Cooper rented the corn and oil mill respectively for £45 each.[58]

In the years 1807–9 considerable investment was put into the Walton mills, including the construction of the weir on the Darwen and the cutting, or alteration, of the mill race. Perhaps at this time, if not before, the Darwen–Ribble race fell out of use, and began to be filled in. In 1807 George Darwen was to be paid 4*d.* per cubic yard 'to cut the mill race through the mill croft into Darwen above the bridge'. In May 1809 the new mill was let to Mr Roger Haworth, 'together with the drying kilns, house, warehouses, school cottage, shippons, stable, and the mill croft for the term of 14 years ... at the clear annual rent of £500 ... the stone weir to be kept in repair by Sir H. P. Hoghton, and all falling necessary to turn the water to the mill to be completed by Sir H. P. Hoghton'.[59]

The Walton Mill Papers provide a great deal of information on the operation of the mills in the early nineteenth century.[60] That two mills still operated on the site, or in close proximity to it, is indicated by a valuation of 1831. In 1845 plans were made for the installation of a new water wheel, to be constructed at Moons Mill Foundry. It was to be 16′ in diameter, and 8′ wide, with 40 buckets and a cast iron shaft. In 1848 a careful estimate was made by Mr Knowles of the capacity of the Walton mills, given 'plenty of water and plenty of work'. The 'old mill' could gross £1,766 13*s.* 4*d.*, and the 'new mill' £875, under these conditions. The costs for the 'old mill' would include 4 millers £208, 2 dryers £70, cinders for drying £50, fire for engines £80, bookkeeper £50, wear and tear £50, to mill 10,000 loads of meal and 5,000 windles of wheat. The mill estate was described in a lease agreement of 1852: 'All that water Corn Mill situate in Walton-le-Dale ... called Walton Mill together with the reservoir, drying kilns, dwelling house, cottages, gardens, mill croft, the two townfields, and the Salmon Holes [fields alongside the Darwen], subject to a right of road through the said mill croft to the garden and lands beyond the same'. The wear and tear on the four pairs of valuable mill stones was to be paid for, 'The depth of the Greet upon the Trench stones was to be measured and the number taken at the commencement and again at the end ... of the said term, and the sum of one Guinea per inch to be paid or received'.

In the twentieth century the mill wheel was replaced by an electric turbine, and although the Darwen no longer powers the site, the mill continues in production at the end of the century. One of the oldest continuously used industrial sites in the North West, its story is a remarkable testimony to industrial survival and adaptability.

Trouble and strife

HE SIXTEENTH CENTURY was a period of great and sustained economic and social change, although as late as the middle of the seventeenth century Samuel Pepys could be convinced that the remote borders of Lancashire were roamed by great lizards able to shoot down passing birds! In particular, the changes in the state religion unfolding from the attempt of Henry VIII to divorce Catherine of Aragon in 1527, and the seizure and privatisation of church assets in the 1530s and 1540s, led to widespread and largely unforeseen developments in everyday life.

In 1525, on the eve of these events, the parishioners at St Leonard's were in open dispute with John Paslew, the abbot of Whalley Abbey. Thomas Langton denied his right to nominate the clergy at the chapel, and two years later his claim to the customary payments to be made when a person died were denied. Twenty men 'of Walton within the parish of Lawe', and two each from 'Keurden', and 'Keuerdale' (the 'twenty four' of the 'parish council'), swore that they 'never herd tell' of any such 'ded corse [dead corpse] presaunts or mortuaryes', being paid, and requested that Thomas Langton as lord of the manor add his seal to the document. The end of Whalley Abbey quickly followed the failure of the Pilgrimage of Grace, and John Paslew was executed at Lancaster castle in 1537.[1]

At the suppression the 'Chappill of Law, with the tieth belonging to the same by year' was valued at £27 11s. 2d., and the attached lands were acquired by the Asshetons of Cuerdale.[2] If the Lancashire gentry families were prepared to profit financially from the new opportunities, they were firmly opposed to the doctrinal changes, which were often simply ignored or avoided: 'Whereas Sir Thomas Langton and Anne his wife have built a chapel or oratory in their manor house at Walton, John [Bird] Bishop of Chester sanctions matins, vespers, and other divine offices and the Eucharist within the chapel for their family and servants providing that nothing is done to the prejudice of the mother church'.[3]

At Preston the rapid restoration of Catholicism under Mary (1553–58) suggests that little change had in fact ever been made. Under Elizabeth the Anglican Settlement also met with little enthusiasm, and at Walton the suppression of the mass led to immediate trouble. In 1559 the Privy Council ordered the Earl of Derby to arrest the curate Thomas Heavenson (a nickname or alias? – this may have been Thomas French), for openly saying mass 'aided and abetted' by nearly 50 locals. Thomas Clayton had been driven to inform by his 'mislike of theise lewde doynges', and was ordered

to be given protection from them. Although the curate signed the Act of Supremacy in 1563, he had to be disciplined further by the earl in 1568. How the church was served in the following 30 years is unclear. In 1578 it was reported that the church bells were still being tolled for the dead, and it was later claimed that two of the old clergy, having become recusants (people who refused to attend Anglican services), were not only still serving their former district, but sometimes occupied their old rooms in Walton.[4]

The county's remoteness, the hostility of the gentry to any of the dictates of central government, and the weakness of the new diocese of Chester, meant that it was very difficult to impose the new order from above. Yet pressure could be brought on the heads of the leading families. Thomas Langton (1497–1569) had his own private chapel away from prying eyes in Walton Hall, and left careful instructions for his burial in the parish church. His grandson Thomas (1561–1604) was ostensibly receptive to the new order, but in 1592 the government spy Dingley told a different story. Appointed to watch the homes of the Hoghtons, Southworths and Langtons, he reported that Thomas Langton had been restored to Catholicism by a priest named 'Griesley'. 'He was reconciled in London about Mydsomer before Babington and the rest were apprehended (1586). And the prieste was with him the same sommer in Lancashire at his owne house, as the priest him selfe told me.' Elizabeth's great minister, Lord Burghley, commented on these reports that Thomas Langton 'would be more determined than any to take Dingley's life if only he knew what our informer had said of him'. A short distance across the Ribble, the Molyneuxs of Fishwick were leading Catholics, and a chapel at the hall seems to have been served by priests throughout this period.[5]

Members of the district's large Catholic community in procession along Station Road, Bamber Bridge, c. 1905. Hornby's shoe shop, and the stone cottages adjacent to Greenwood Street can be seen in the background. A number of similar stone cottages survive along Station Road, giving a fair impression of the restricted extent of urban development here in the early years of the nineteenth century. (R. Burns)

The Southworths of Samlesbury Hall were carefully watched, and the hall was raided on 21 November 1592. Books containing 'much papistrie' were found, along with 'a frize gown without a pocked and yet devises secretlye to keepe letteres in'. In the roof they discovered 'a secrett vawlte over the dyninge chamber and another chamber', containing 'one canabie to hang over the alter ... two candlesticks of brasse of the fashion used in the tyme of Superstition ... fourteene images of divers fashions'. After several imprisonments and repeated fines, John Southworth was forced to conform.[6]

Thomas Hoghton of Lea Hall experienced similar difficulties. Celebrated as the builder of Hoghton Tower, he fled persecution in 1569, and remained in exile until his death at Liege in 1580. In 1576 his brother Richard of Park Hall, was allowed to 'depart out of our Realme of Englande ... unto the towne of Antwerpe ... To th'intent to advise, pursuade, and counsell Thomas Hoghton ... who as we are informed, by occasion of synister and evill counsell, is departed out of our Realme, without our lycence, to retorne unto this our Realme, and to submitt himselfe unto us and our Lawes'. Further attempts to get him to return failed two years later: 'To Thomas Hoghton esquire being beyond the seas for religion he is advertised that upon ernest sute made in his behalf for his return home into th country her Highness is pleased that he should doe so (upon conditions such as his servants shall declare unto him) and shall enjoye his owne as any other good subject of her realme'. In his absence the estate was run by his brother Alexander, and Thomas Campion SJ stayed at the tower in 1580. Practising Catholics themselves, and leading magistrates, the Langtons, Hoghtons, and Southworths were thus clearly unwilling to coerce tenants who largely shared their sympathies.[7]

On the death of their half-brother Thomas in the fight with Thomas Langton at Lea in 1589, the Hoghton succession passed to his son Richard (1570–1630). Destined to become the first baronet and first of the Hoghton lords of Walton, it has been claimed that great efforts were made to raise Richard a devout Protestant in order to break the family's Catholic loyalties. Certainly his position was quite different from that of his uncle. In 1601 the bishop of London wrote of him, 'The High Sheriff of Lancashire and Sir Richard Hoghton, both heretofore and now of late, have done great service in apprehending of sundry priests, pestilent persuaders to rebellion, and are the ablest and fittest persons in regard of their state and their dwelling to the most corrupt places in Lancashire, to hunt out these seditious priests and to suppress the insolencies of the people & being encouraged therein, will be willing doubtless in such services to do their best'.[8]

The great mass of ordinary people were affected to a much lesser extent, so that when services at church were not to their liking they simply stayed away. During the last quarter of the sixteenth century the chapel at Walton seems to have been served by the Established Church rather infrequently. In 1590 the bishop of Chester complained that 'There maie be seen usualie

A mid-nineteenth-century artist's impression of what the completed church of St Mary's, Brownedge, might look like. As at All Saints, Higher Walton, the spire was added to the tower as funds allowed. By the 1870s the interior of the church was recognised as one of the architectural wonders of the region, and Brownedge was still a largely rural locality, quite distinct from the village of Bamber Bridge, and the hamlet of 'School Lane'. (*Print, R. Burns*)

The completed church, showing the reconstructed chancel and side transepts, c. 1910. Already the stonework had become blackened by the smoke from the adjacent foundry. (*R. Burns*)

The blessing of new church bells and the High Altar, St Mary's, Brownedge, 1928. The bells were re-hung and increased in number to eight in February 1928. The new peal was rung on Sunday 4 March. (*South Ribble Museum*)

every Sonday and holieday ... as many people repayre to places suspected in Religion as to the Parishe Churche ... The people in moast parts of the countie ... doe slide back from all duetyfull obedyance to the utter contempt and neglect of Religion and the religious service of God'.[9] In 1619 parishioners at Samlesbury were accused of 'Having piping music and dancing in their homes at divine service time upon the Sabbath day', and of 'burning candles over corpses, for crossing with towels and praying where crosses are and have been'.[10]

The tolerance of the magistrates, the efforts of the missionary priests, the remoteness of the district, and the attitude of the people, thus enabled Catholicism to survive in some strength into the seventeenth century in mid-Lancashire, and particularly in the parishes of Walton-le-Dale and Leyland. In the parish churches Puritanism gained ground in the years up to the restoration of Charles II in 1660. Accordingly in 1622 Walton had an unlicensed preacher who did not come to church on holy days, stand up for the Creed, wear a surplice, or bow at the Name of Jesus.[11] Loyalty in the Civil War was closely related to religious background, which thus became only one element of the political complexion of the time, with alternating periods of toleration and persecution for both nonconformists and Catholics alike. Lists of politically suspect Catholics were kept nationally during periods of high tension. The Recusancy Roll of 1595–96, for example, lists Thomas Cowpe 'husbandman', and John Cowpe 'linen webster', 'late of Walton-le-Dale', Ellen Dandy of Cuerden 'widow', and Rosamund Sothworthe of Samlesbury 'spinster', each of whom had been fined £40.[12]

The 'Protestation Return' of 1642 contains detailed listings by parish, of all males over 18 years of age who were required to take the Protestation Oath to defend 'ye true reformed Protestant Religion expressed in ye church of England, against all poperie and popish innovations', and also 'ye power and privileges of Parliament'. Although the wording linked politics and religion, the returns from the parishes around Preston are generally considered to provide a fairly accurate estimation of the extent of local Catholicism. In Walton and Cuerdale 196 took the oath (including the Hoghtons of Walton Hall), but over one third of the male population (112) refused. In Leyland the figures were 189 and 83, at Samlesbury 137 men took the oath and 32 refused (including John Southworth). Refusal to take the oath was concentrated in the countryside, for in the town of Preston only 23 refused, but in the rural parish over half refused.[13]

After the Restoration a more moderate Church of England made great progress, but a list of convicted recusants drawn up in 1674 recorded 93 prosecutions at Walton-le-Dale, including John Woodcock of Walton Moss 'Webster', Anna and Thomas Anderton 'Alehouse Keeper', and several members of the Coupe, Charnley, and Duddle families.[14] Although Catholicism had developed the attributes of a secretive nonconformist sect, revivalist tours by leading Catholic clerics could provide spectacular proof of its abiding hold. John Leyland visited Lancashire in 1687 and confirmed almost 1,200 people at Preston. When Bishop Smith confirmed a great crowd at Samlesbury in 1709, the vicar of Blackburn found that 'the neighbouring Protestants seemed to take little notice of the matter, it being no novelty with them'.[15] In 1714 there were reported to be 'Four or five conventicles of Papists, one of Presbyterians, and one of Anabaptists in the parish. The number of Catholics grew steadily, from the 499 'known' in 1717, to 823 in 1767. Bishop Gibson confirmed 165 people here in 1784, and a note in the parish register from c. 1780, gives a figure of 178 'popish families', or 875 people in the total population of 2,662 – again, as in 1642, around one third.[16]

Although details are rather sketchy, the Benedictines clearly had a mission established here from the late seventeenth century. In the early eighteenth century Mosney seems to have been their centre, moving to Brownedge – then the most remote part of the parish – in the 1760s. The first burial at Brownedge seems to date from 1764. The district has close links with a number of Catholic martyrs, most notably Edmund Arrowsmith (1585–1628), and John Woodcock (1603–46). Woodcock was executed with Thomas Whittaker and Edward Bamber at Lancaster in 1646, and the association with Bamber has often been seen as the source of the Bamber Bridge place-name. The latter, however, is of much older origin. Walton-le-Dale thus has an extremely interesting ecclesiastical history, with a size-able Catholic minority served by its own clergy throughout the penal times. The Civil War and the Jacobite risings were to give further political twists to these ancient loyalties.[17]

Mines and mortgages: The Hoghtons

In the rising hill country to the east of the manor, the de Hoghtons had been the principal family from the time of the Banastres, and their succession can be traced fairly accurately from the twelfth century. In the following three centuries they established themselves as one of the largest landowners in the region, acquiring lands in some forty parishes, largely through marriage and inheritance. As the political, social and economic centre of the district, their influence in Preston was particularly important, and was to last until the industrial revolution. In the early fourteenth century Sir Richard de Hoghton founded the Chantry of the Holy Rood in the parish church, and the family had long been established as leading out-burgesses of the Preston Guild Merchant. Not infrequently, they sought to interfere in those aspects of the townspeople's affairs not to their liking.

An inquest into the affairs of Sir Henry de Hoghton made in 1489 reveals the extent of the family possessions by this time: 'The manors of Hoghton and Lea, and half the manor of Ashton, with 200 messuages, 2,000 acres of land, 5,000 acres of meadow, 2,000 acres of pasture, 300 acres of woodland, 1,000 acres of turbary, and 500 acres of moor in Hoghton, Lea, Alston, Grimsargh, Goosnargh, Whittingham, Halghton, Cuerden, Ashton-juxta-Preston, Tulketh, Ravensmeles, Chipping, Dilworth and Goldborne'.[18]

Sir Richard Hoghton, who died in 1559, was a man very much of the age. Though married five times, the Herald reported of him that he 'Hath putt away his lady and wife, and keepeth a concubyne in his house, by whom he hath divers children'. The Boars Head public house takes its name from the badge of Alice Assheton, his first wife. Sir Richard broke up a meeting to elect the mayor of Preston 'with a heygh voice and angry cowtenence', and when ordered to desist 'In The King's Name', replied, 'Scornfully and in derysion "Commandest thou mee in the King's name ... Get thee hom to thy soper"'. Having lost a court case over property in 1524, he was ordered to pay £75 compensation in 'the Lawe Churche in the towne of Walton in the dale at the feast of St Martin in Wynter and Penthecost between x of the clock in the forenoon and ij of the clocke in the after noon of eider of the same days'.[19]

Ironically Sir Richard was succeeded by his son, the saintly Thomas Hoghton, the religious exile and founder of modern Hoghton Tower. With his death in 1580, and that of his brother Alexander the following year, the estate passed to a younger half-brother, Thomas. In 1589 a dispute between him and Thomazine Singleton, widow of John Singleton of Staining, over cattle, led to the celebrated affray at Lea. Thomas Langton lord of Walton was convinced of the justice of her case, and with others took part in an attempt to repossess the animals from the manor house at Lea. A force including Langton and Thomazine '... armed with long pickes, gunnes, long staves, welshe hooks upon long staves, swords and dagges, bows and arrows and bills, on 20th November at 11 at night assembled on Preston

Marsh ... and agreed to go and drive away the cattle'. Richard Hoghton
had got word of these warlike preparations, and mustered a force of about
30 armed with 'Staves, 1 pike, 1 gunne charged with haile shott, 2 pistols,
1 bow and arrowes and swords and dagges', which lay in ambush in one
of the outbuildings. When Langton's party appeared it 'offered resistance,
and a great affray began within 60 yards of the house, in which Thomas
Langton's company often used the watchword, 'The crow is white', and
Thomas Hoghton's people used the word 'Black, black'. Amidst the pro-
fusion of heads broken in the dark, Thomas Hoghton and another were
killed, whilst Thomas Langton 'Being sore wounded ... was presently
apprehended lying in his bed at Broughton tower'.[20]

Three years later the affair had not been settled between the families,
and the earl of Derby wrote to Lord Burghley warning him of the danger
of the dispute, and urging pardons for the estate people involved ('the
poorer sorte'). There was a real danger of the dispute escalating among
the gentry involved, for the 'Better sorte are great in kindred and affynitie,
and soe stoared with friendes, as yf they should be burnte in the hande, I
feare it will fall oute to be a ceasles and most dangerous quarrell betwixt
the gentlemen that any Countie of her Ma[jest]ties hathe theis many yeares
conteyned'.[21] Mrs Hoghton's troubles were not restricted to the loss of her
husband. In October 1592 it was reported to the government that 'Mrs
Hoghton of the Lea, hathe kepte sithence the deathe of her husband one
Richard Blundell ... who is an obstinate Papiste, well acquainted with a
number of Seminaries, and he teacheth her children to singe and plie upon
the virginalls'.[22]

The settlement ultimately agreed, saw the manor of Walton-le-dale pass
to Thomas Hoghton's son, Richard. Sir Richard (d. 1630), became the first
baronet in 1611, and entertained King James at Hoghton Tower in 1617.
Raised a Protestant, he effectively broke the line of Catholic loyalties in
the family which had been such a feature of local politics in the second
half of the sixteenth century. To the inhabitants of Walton the change of
manorial dynasty, and their religious affinity, must have appeared to be
something of a revolution. Nor was the transfer of the estate amicable. It
seems to have been in Langton hands at the death of Thomas Langton in
1605, but in April Walton Hall was attacked, and Richard Asheton (Langton's tenant) with other gentlemen including Sir Edward Stanley, were
forcibly driven out. The transfer and financial settlement of the affair is
still extremely confused.

Thomas Langton's financial difficulties are the key to these problems.
Thomas Langton 'being much in London and lying here at great expense'
had entered into a series of loans and advances from John Lacy 'Citizen
and clothworker of London'. A series of bonds, one for £3,500 and later
£14,000 were advanced as mortgages on the security of the Walton estate.
The advance of £3,500 came at the end of a number of earlier debts, and
was the subject of a court case between the men in 1601. The complaint

was given by Langton as 'Manor and lordship of Walton-le-Dale mortgaged to defendent who is charged with usury'.[23]

The manor which passed to the Hoghton's, probably on Langton's death, was thus heavily mortgaged, and the existing financial arrangements may have been transferred over. Although they seem to have possessed the title to the property, the series of mortgages, leases and bonds makes the actual ownership unclear for some years. The estate became something of a make-weight in the wider speculations and affairs of the more distant owners of the mortgage. In 1612 Sir Richard re-mortgaged the Walton estate to fund the exploitation of the alum mine at Pleasington, and obtained a licence to make and transport 500 tons of alum per year, probably via the quay by the Ribble bridge. This enterprise was described in 1672: 'Sir Richard Houghton sett up a very profitable mine of Allum nigh unto houghton Tower ... where store of very good alome is made and sold'. By 1617 the funds had been used up, and he was in great difficulty and facing the loss of both manor and mine. His entertainment of the king in that year was a gloss on his efforts to gain royal support for the venture. A greater measure of control over the Walton estate was gained by his son Gilbert in 1624, but in the previous year Sir William Cockayne 'Alderman of London', had sold property including Walton Mains. Such are the complexities of early seventeenth-century estate management. In 1673 a large part of the Hoghton estate, including Walton Hall, the park, the demesne, and the demesne of Lea was mortgaged to London cloth workers for £3,000, to be paid off in instalments totalling £3,540 by April 1677.[24]

A memorandum made after 1673 described these complicated affairs, 'Walton ... which being formerly mortgaged by Sir Ric. Hoghton the grandfather was redeemed by Sir Gilbert his son and settled by him to himselfe for life. (If dead to his wife Lady Margaret, then to his son the now Sir Richard.) In the 24th of Car II [1648] Sir Richard suffered a common recovery of Walton to the use of himself and his heirs ...'.[25]

Thus the old story of how the Hoghtons were ruined by King James's visit does contain a grain of the truth, though the hearty picture often presented of good and cheery 'Sir Dick' is well wide of the mark. A strident opponent of the local Catholic tendency, he was closely involved in the plantation of Ulster, and was beset at home by seemingly intractable financial difficulties. Nor was this to be the end of these problems for the family. His son Sir Gilbert (d. 1645), was one of the leading participants on the losing royalist side in the First Civil War, during which the 'tower' of Hoghton Tower was destroyed in 1643. His grandson, Sir Richard (d. 1678), supported the parliamentarian side, but saw the devastation of Walton during the battle there in 1648. Only in the early eighteenth century (George Miller suggests c. 1710) did Walton Hall again become the principal residence of the lord of its manor.

'Plundered to their skins': The Civil War and Cromwell

The remarkable strategic position of Walton-le-Dale placed it at the very centre of the Civil War in Lancashire. Irrespective of any loyalties the inhabitants may have had in the years 1642–51, it was to be frequently invaded by the forces of all the warring parties, who were consistent only in their enthusiasm to plunder the locals, with all the consequences of disrupted trade and agriculture which followed. In 1648 the inhabitants of Wigan were not alone in having been plundered to their skins, and when Charles II rode through the streets of Proud Preston in 1651 he was disappointed by the lack of public response.

The Hoghtons and Faringtons with the great majority of Prestonians were firmly in the royalist camp. Enthusiasm for the parliamentarian cause was strong only among the leading families who comprised much of the town council, and who consistently opposed the interference of the neighbouring gentry from south of the Ribble in their affairs. The king's cause was led in the county by James Stanley, the seventh Earl of Derby, and in mid-Lancashire by Sir Gilbert Hoghton. As lord of Walton, Hoghton looked to his tenantry for support. As tension grew in the summer of 1642, he grew increasingly nervous. The rumoured approach of a parliamentarian army of 20,000 men, led him to 'set a stronge watche about his house', and to order the locals, 'that they should be readie upon an howers warning'.[26]

The war began in Lancashire with the royalist attack on Manchester in September. In November Hoghton 'set his beacon on fire which stood upon the top of Houghton Tower and was the signall to the countrey for the papists and malignants to arise in the Fylede and in Lealand Hundred'.[27] Having disarmed Whalley, this force occupied parliamentarian Blackburn, but a counter-attack put them to flight. Sir Gilbert 'was pursued so hotly, that he quit his horse, leaped into a field and by coming on of the night managed to escape to Preston. And their makes great defence by chaining up the Ribble Bridge and getting what force he can into the town for his security'.[28]

A second attack on Blackburn, during Christmas Eve 1642, ended in farce, and was typical of much of the localised warfare of the period. A force of gentry with their retainers and clubmen (mostly estate tenants pressed into service), marched via Mellor and attacked the town from the north: 'And having a small piece of Ordnance plaied most of that night and the day folowing against the Towne, the greatest execution that it did, as was heard of, a bullet shot out of it entered into a house upon the South side of the church yard and burst out the bottom of a fryen pan'. Despite the warlike cries from both sides, each seems generally to have been adept at keeping out of the range of the other. On Christmas night Sir Gilbert broke off the engagement, 'His forces being weary of the siege and his Souldiers and Clubmen were glad of it that they might eat their Christmas pyes at home'. A parliamentarian tract rejoiced that, 'Taking advantage of the darknesse, they fled in fear ... trusting more to the night for protection than to ther courage or strength'.[29]

The fighting in the north continued throughout the winter, and climaxed in the capture of Preston by the parliamentarians in February 1643. A force from Blackburn led by Sir John Seaton was able to pass through Walton Cop and cross the Ribble bridge on the early evening of the seventh. Sir Gilbert again fled, this time, so it was said, leaving behind his hat. More seriously, his wife was captured and his brother was killed. With Preston captured, it was decided to attack Hoghton Tower. Three foot companies commanded by Captain Starkie were sent, and after a parley the defenders surrendered. While the buildings were being searched for arms a violent explosion destroyed the tower killing or injuring 'three score' men. Though treachery was suspected, a contemporary account blames 'Our Swearing, Cursing, Drunken, Tobacco-abusing Commanders and Souldiers', so that the powder store may have been ignited by some careless smoker. The truth will never be known.[30]

Exploiting the river crossings below Walton bridge, the Earl of Derby was able to recover the royalist position in March, capturing Lancaster and retaking Preston. At Easter all was lost, a royalist invasion of east Lancashire was routed between Whalley and Padiham, and the earl was forced to flee to Penwortham Hall. Amidst extensive plundering by both sides, all of Lancashire was in parliamentarian hands by June 1643, and the first civil war in the county was over. Only Lathom House and Greenhalgh Castle held out. The latter was a most remarkable affair. Strongly built, on a small hill half a mile south of Garstang, the defenders led by 'Mr Anderton' of Lostock Hall, were not only able to withstand a siege, but were able to dig a passageway out and capture five barrels of the enemies' powder! On Anderton's death the defenders were 'given their liberty' and surrendered.[31]

In March 1644 Prince Rupert's royalist army passed through Walton on

Hoghton Tower. Since Walton Hall was perhaps too conveniently located, Hoghton Tower played an important role in the efforts of the Hoghtons on behalf of the Royalist cause during the Civil War. A beacon lit here in November 1642 was 'The signall to the countrey for the papists and malignants to arise in the Fylede and in Lealand Hundred'. Early in 1643 the hall was captured by the Parliamentarians, and a perhaps accidental explosion in the 'tower' resulted in a heavy loss of life.

its way into Yorkshire. Notwithstanding the 'sumptious banquet' laid on for him by the mayor and council of Preston, he took members of the latter with him, and left them locked in the cells of Skipton castle. Only with difficulty were they later released. After his defeat at Marston Moor the district was again inundated with groups of desperate and plundering men. Col. Nicholas Shuttleworth's attempt to visit Preston fair in August 1644 is a good illustration of these troubled times: 'He with a part of his troop and some Countreymen being desirous to go to Preston if possible (it being the Fair there) when they came to the Coppe at Walton they meeting with some of the Kings part, scirmished with them and put them to flight ... And after that they met with more of that Companie about Ribble Bridge Hill and there had a sore disput with them ... it was with great difficulty that they cam off with honour and safetie – yet did'.[32]

The passage of Walton Cop and the two bridges, was central to the great, if misnamed, Battle of Preston of 1648. This ended the Second Civil War and resulted in the execution of Charles I. In July 1648 the Duke of Hamilton led a large and ramshackle army of perhaps 20,000 men into England, intent on restoring the imprisoned king. By 9 August this force had reached Hornby, and it was decided to pass through Lancashire. Cromwell with 8,500 men of the New Model Army had expected invasion through Yorkshire, and had to march quickly to intercept Hamilton in the west. Hamilton seems to have had no inkling that Cromwell was fast approaching through the Ribble valley, and his force was stretched out over a long distance. By the 16th as his cavalry was nearing Wigan, his foot was still north of Preston. Between them lay the narrow Ribble and Darwen bridges and the Cop. The Ribble was in flood, and that evening Cromwell's forces reached Stonyhurst.

Late the next morning Cromwell's advance guard attacked the English royalists under Marmaduke Langdale on Ribbleton Moor, near modern-day Gamull Lane. Hamilton did not reinforce his English troops who fought well. Eventually the parliamentarian force was able to enter Preston, and drive their way 'at push of pike' over the Ribble bridge and clear Walton of royalists. Edward Robinson of Buckshaw Hall near Leyland described the events around the village:

> At the bridge they had a great dispute for a long time, but at last Cromwell's Army did beat them off and they fled over Darwen Bridge and soe up that hill above Walton Toune. In the feilde upon the east of the way they made cabbins and lodge there that Night ... so night coming the Armies guarded both Bridges and General Cromwell returned to Preston ... And when morning was come with the Armie he followed the duke who fled before him ... The Duke's artillery and Carieges were all taken standing on Walton Coppe.[33]

Oliver Cromwell himself left an account of the battle in a letter to the Speaker of the House of Commons, Lenthall:

The Unicorn Inn, c.1912. Although much extended by this date, the central portion formed the ancient Unicorn Inn which was long home to the celebrated Mock Corporation of Walton-le-Dale, and this was one of the last buildings in the district to preserve its thatched roof. Despite traditional links with Oliver Cromwell and the great battle of Walton Bridge in 1648, and much local support, the frequently discussed schemes to establish this much-loved building as the district's museum have so far come to nothing. Adjacent to Darwen Bridge, Walton Green, the manor corn mill and Townfield, and the birthplace of Joseph Livesey, with links to some of the most important events in the histories of England and Scotland, it is both geographically and socially at the very core of the history of Walton-le-Dale. (R. Burns)

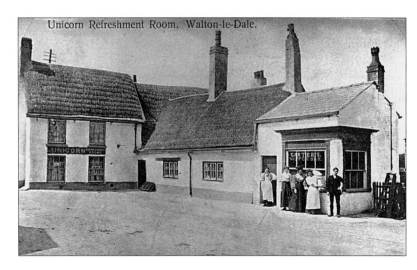

Unicorn Refreshment Room. Walton-le-Dale.

At the last the Enemie was put into disorder, many men were slain, many prisoners taken, the Duke with most of the Scots Horse and foot retreated over the Bridge, where after a very hot dispute betwixt the Lancashire Regiments, part of my Lord Generals, and then being at push of pike, they were beaten from the Bridge, and our horse and foot following them, killed many, and took divers prisoners, and we possessed the bridge over Darwent and a few houses there, the enemy being driven up within musket shot of us where we lay that night, we not being able to attempt further upon the enemy, the night preventing us.[34]

Transposed onto the modern Walton and Bamber Bridge landscape, these events are most interesting. The 'few houses' by Darwen bridge referred to by Cromwell could relate to the 'Unicorn Inn', and/or, to the original houses on Walton Green. That night the royalists controlled the heights of Cinnamon Hill and Hennel, whilst their forces 'camped' 'in the feilde upon the east of the way'. The latter would seem to indicate the vicinity of Holland Park, perhaps extending southwards along Chorley Road through Bamber Bridge. Hamilton's council of war, probably held above Hennel Lane, decided to retreat at once to Wigan. The disintegrating force was defeated near Winwick Church on 19 August.

With their defeat, the locals turned on the Scots. Having looted the district comprehensively on the march, small parties had fled into the Fylde, whilst others tried to make their way back north. 'The county will scarce suffer any of my men to passe, except they have my hand, telling them they are Scots. They bring in and kill divers of them as they light upon them'.[35] A careful watch was kept on the Ribble bridge, and Edward Robinson recalled that:

The cariag of Duke Hamilton's Army in their march was very evill, for they plundered extreamly, yea abundance of sutty vacabound women that folowed the Duke's camp vexed the poore country sore; yet in their Retreat without doubt it was well paied home into their Bosomes many getting by them, though against their wills. The better sort of them were well stored with money and when they saw themselves defeated and that there was noe way for them to escape but to be taken prisoners, some hid their money in the feildes about Preston and have, since times were more quiet, come and found their owne money and enjoyed it. And it was thought that Preston and the townes about it lost not, but gained much by their flight.[36]

In August 1651 the future Charles II led a Scottish force of 15,000 men south in a further attempt to recover his father's throne. Although this army was better disciplined and under orders not to plunder, he won little local support, crossing the Walton bridges and the Cop on Thursday the 14th. The army was defeated by Cromwell at Worcester on 3 September.

From 1643 those who had sided against Parliament were heavily fined and their property was seized. The Hoghtons were luckier than most, because Sir Gilbert's heir, Richard, had taken his stand for Parliament. On his father's death in 1648 he succeeded to the estates. Problems came when the monarchy was restored in 1660. On 8 March Sir Richard was declared an outlaw, and the Crown let Hoghton Tower, and much of the Hoghton estate to tenants. On 6 June, before the speaker of the House of Commons, he declared, 'I Richard Hoghton of Hoghton in the County of Lancaster baronet doe with humble and harty thankfulness declare yt I doe lay hold upon His Ma[jest]ties free and generall pardon ... and that I am and will continue his Maties loyall and obedient subject'. Only in May 1661 was he pardoned, 'For all acts of lese majeste committed since the death of Charles I, his share in the late insurrections, having accepted commissions etc. from the late Lord Protector etc.'.[37]

In 1648 Isaac Ambrose, vicar of Preston, described the local suffering which ensued from Hamilton's invasion: 'It would melt any good heart to see the numerous swarms of begging poore, and the many families that pine away at home not having faces to beg ... and often to hear of some found dead in their houses or highways, for want of bread'.[38]

The Jacobites and the Mock Corporation of Walton-le-Dale

By the mid-seventeenth century much of mid-Lancashire, with its old Catholic, High Church and royalist loyalties, had become a natural con-stituency for the Catholic Stuarts. The extent of these ancient ties is revealed in the lists of local people persecuted by Parliament at the end of the Civil War, the Lancashire Composition Papers. These included representatives from many of the old Walton yeoman families, including Thomas Baldwin, Thomas and Christopher Bannester, Ann and William Blackburne, William Osbaldeston, Ralph Shorrocke, Thomas Walton and John Woodcock.[39] By the end of the century these sympathies had developed a political aspect. The old Catholic and High Church interest 'For the king', formed a 'Tory' camp, whilst the dissenting and Low Church interest 'For the king and Parliament', favoured the Whigs. In Walton-le-Dale a majority of the lesser gentry and most of the tenantry probably supported the Tories, whilst Sir Henry Hoghton was a prominent Whig and religious dissenter. Walton Hall was duly registered as a place of worship for Dissenters in 1689.[40] Political tension in the district was thus closely related to the series of national crises in the years up to 1750, resulting from these conflicts at the national level.

In 1701 local Tories and Jacobites (supporters of the Stuart James II and his successors, exiled in 1689), formed themselves into club calling itself 'The Mock Corporation of Walton-le-Dale'. This came to hold its meetings in the Unicorn Inn, by the Darwen bridge, just a short walk from the Hoghtons' manor house at Walton hall. Meeting regularly for dinners and drink, clubs of this sort were extremely popular at the time, and Preston could boast a great array of them, dedicated to all sorts of activity. This group parodied the affectations and ceremonial of Preston corporation, which at this time was an unrepresentative clique of the town's leading families. The club provided itself with all the trappings of power, with staffs of office and swords of state. The corporation had the usual array of officials, such as a mayor and town clerk, together with a range of less conventional officials deemed essential for its proceedings. These included a 'Champion', Poet Laureate, Physician, 'House Groper', Jester and 'Slut Kisser'.[41]

The earliest account of this original and highly meritorious institution was given by Dr Whittaker in the early nineteenth century: 'At an obscure inn, in the neighbouring village of Walton, has been held from the beginning of the last century, a meeting of noblemen and gentlemen, styling themselves the mayor and corporation of the ancient borough of Walton. All their proceedings were conducted with ludicrous formality; and they had a register which still remains, together with a mace and sword of state, and three large staves'.[42] Through the timely interest of the curator of the Harris Museum and interested locals, these items were saved from sale to collectors in America in 1947.

Up to about 1740 the region's Catholic and Jacobite gentry are well represented in the list of officers, and there can be little doubt that it was a thinly veiled Jacobite fraternity. How closely members were involved in the insurrections of 1715 and 1745, however is uncertain. Probably the local members, such as the Faringtons, Fleetwoods, Rawstornes and Ashetons had no involvement at all. Alternatively the Earl of Derwentwater, appointed Mayor in 1711, led the invasion of 1715. Feelings of nostalgia for the days of the Stuarts, drinking to the health of the king 'over the water', and having a good laugh at the expense of political enemies in town, was a quite different matter from taking part in a military coup against the government. Certainly in the event, the alehouse Tories kept well away from the events in Preston in 1715. As Patten, chaplain to the Scots army at Preston complained, 'The High Church Tories were never right hearty for the cause till they were mellow and that they did not care for venturing their carcasses any further than the tavern'.[43]

By the 1720s this partisan assembly seems to have restricted its attentions to conviviality and food and drink. It became natural for visiting judges, senior soldiers and gentry to be enrolled as a matter of course. In 1723 even Sir Henry Hoghton, the most prominent local dissenter and opponent of Jacobitism, was enrolled as a freeman. No extravagance on the part of the corporation of Preston was missed, and duly mocked at the country inn. In 1724 John Clayton mayor of Preston was elevated to the office of custard eater, and Rigby Mollyneux became 'Grand Master of the Sellars [cellars]'. In 1727, Matthew Ashton was appointed the corporation's 'Principal Painter', and John Walmesly became 'Barber Surgeon and Tooth Drawer' in 1744.

The record book contains lists of officers, and brief details of business. Between the entries for 1705 and 1706, one scribe recorded that it was then '5,620 years since the creation'. James Scarisbrick, appointed Poet Laureate in 1723, found himself inspired to such an extent that he began to versify 'immediately after ye election':

> I've bought my freedom with a glass of ale.
> And am rewarded with the post of Laureat.
> And if my verses are not on record.
> The Devil take me if I speak a word.

Meeting seem to have formed a part of the local holiday, the 'Walton Wakes', when freemen could be enrolled for a fee of 2s. 6d., 'money to be spent at the next meeting'. The failure to attend meetings was 'severely' punished. In September 1744 a list of 11 members was duly fined 2s. 6d. each, 'These notorious Delinquents are to pay the whole fine or go to the stocks'. From the mid-1720s entrance money was used to build up a stock of civic paraphernalia. In 1740 'A list of the regalia belonging to the corporation of Walton' was drawn up, and found to comprise, 'Two Staffs covered with Silver Hoopes, One other Staff covered full half way, One Hunting Staff with a silver head, One Sword of State, One Mace, Two Bailiff's Wands, Two Halberds'. These were kept at the Unicorn, and put on display 'at the sessions'. By the 1750s the affair had become essentially a diners' club, open to a wide range of people. In 1789 Joseph Hilton became landlord of the inn, and in 1791 Robert Hilton was the mayor. The final meeting recorded in the record book took place in 1796.[44]

The 1715 and 1745

The accession of the German George the First in 1714 was marked by riots in Walton-le-Dale as elsewhere. In September 1715 a Scottish force led by Thomas Forster and the Earl of Derwentwater began the march into

Jacobite House, c.1905. According to Frank Coupe this old house at Walton Corner had traditional links with the Stuart cause in the area. The ground-floor windows suggest that it may at one time have housed a loomshop. (R. Burns)

England, hoping to raise the northern counties, and win back the throne for the 'British' Stuarts. In mid-Lancashire the resistance was organised by the energetic Sir Henry Hoghton, the local Colonel of Militia. Those locals 'well disposed to the government' were to defend the Ribble crossing, and the estate workers were mustered, 'The officers here design to march at break of day for Preston ... raise all the force you can, I mean lusty young fellows to draw up on Cuerden Green ... to bring what arms they have fitt for service, and cythes put in streight polls, and such as have not, to bring spades and Billhooks for pioneering with. Pray go immediately all amongst your neighbours and give this notice'.[45]

On 9–10 November the Scots army entered Preston, and the blue and white rosette made its first appearance in the market square. General Wills' force of government troops and the militia, were able to block its progress on the Ribble, allowing General Carpenter's force of 2,500 men to come up and surround the town. Once again the village was central to national events. The Scots made no effort to defend the Darwen or Ribble crossings, and this once more was to prove militarily decisive. After the firing of part of the town to force the Scots back from the baricades, and fierce fighting, heavy losses were inflicted on the government troops. Once general Carpenter's force arrived the issue was beyond doubt, and much to the disgust of their Scottish allies, on Monday the 14th the English officers decided to surrender. Over 1,500 prisoners were taken at Preston.[46]

Local people taken at Preston were treated particularly harshly, and were made an example of to deter others. In January 1716 a government Commission of Oyer and Terminer was held in Liverpool to try the local prisoners. Of the Walton contingent, Thomas Cowpe (Yeoman) was

executed at Preston on 28 January, James Finch (Labourer) at Wigan on
10 February with William Whalley (Whitster), and John Finch at Manchester on 11 February. The executions at Preston were the most
impressive, and by tradition took place by the site of English Martyrs'
Church on Garstang Road. The Sheriff's accounts record: 'JAN 27th. Erecting gallows and paid for materialls, hurdle, fire, cart, etc. in executing
Shuttleworth and 4 more at Preston [including Cowpe], and setting up his
head etc £12 os. 4d.'

The two executioners were paid £60 for their tour of the Lancashire
towns.[47] Such events, although cowering the people, clearly did little to
further the popularity of the government. At the Preston Assizes Mary
Livesey of Samlesbury was accused of saying in January 1716 'that the
king was a murderer and "God Damn king George for a cuckold, his hams
now begin to budd out. He may go sow turnips where they fecht him
from"'. In 1722 John Heaton and William Forshaw were accused of crying
'Down with the rump', and Thomas Waring of Brindle was accused of
'Swearing profane oaths'.[48]

As the army of the Young Pretender approached Preston 30 years later,
Sir Henry Hoghton was again at the head of the local militia. A large
proportion of his correspondence has survived amongst the Hoghton
deeds and papers, and it is possible to reconstruct the events in some
detail. Hoghton clearly felt that the sympathies of the local people were
questionable:

> I thank you for recommending it to me and other gentleman, to bee on our
> watch, but if nothing to depend on but our own zeal and courage we are
> in a bad case. We have some friends but few in comparison to those against
> us, and those few keep such company that they believe nothing, and I have
> not one gentleman I can discourse freely with on the subject but it would
> soon be as common as a newspaper, and telling of bad news can be of no
> service ... I can't end this without asking pardon for differing in opinion
> that the dispositions of the people and the strength of the enemy is farr
> different from what it was in the year 1715. As to our county, our enemys
> are as strong as then, and I know of no converts to be depended on.[49]

Bonnie Prince Charlie's army entered Preston on 27 November. To dispel
superstition that the force would not get across the Ribble, Lord George
Murray quartered a body of troops in Walton, probably on the Flatts.
Rumours that the Ribble bridge had been broken down proved to be
unfounded, and the force was able to pass through Walton Cop and Bamber
Bridge on the road south. Henry Hoghton's position at Walton Hall was
hopeless. On 22 November he wrote:

> We are in the greatest distress here upon the approach of the Rebells and
> that the king's army, both that commanded by Marshall Wade & General
> Ligonier at too great a distance to afford us any reliefe. Our militia have
> answered as to keeping the peace of the County, but can't be of any service

Jacobite House and the Queen's Arms, Walton Corner, c.1905. This site is now occupied by Coupe's garage. (R. Burns)

in stopping the progress of the Rebells … & the men must disperse if they have not their pay'.[50]

The baronet and his family fled to Yorkshire. Among the Hoghton Jacobite Papers are a series of *Copies of Orders from the officers of the Rebell Army to deliver forage and hay to them at Preston:*[51]

> Sir: Give the bearer instantly ten bushels of Oates for the use of the Cavalry quarter'd at the Bridge, under pain of Military Execution. By order of the Company of forage.
>
> David Hunter.
>
> To the principal Servant at Walton Hall.

On the return from Derby further demands were made.

> Preston, Decr 11th 1745.
>   These are ordering you Sir Henry Hutton to bring into Church Street here forthwith & immediately for the use of His Royal Highness the Prince Regent his army one thousand five hundred ston of Hay, with two hundred bushels of Oates and ten carts of Straw, and that under pain of Military Execution.
>
> Will. Comine. Commissr.
>
> To Sir Henry Hutton or any of his Doers.

The last Scottish occupiers of the district, up to the present time, left Preston on 13 December 1746 to the tune 'Hie thee Charlie Home again', closely followed by the advance troops of the Duke of Cumberland.

Local sympathies did not, however, disappear with it, and Sir Henry Hoghton's fears and distrust of the local Catholic population seem to have been intensified almost to the point of mania. Rumours of plots and invasions persisted for some years. A Jacobite letter claimed to have been found at Walton, was the source of much consternation in 1747. Almost certainly it was a government 'plant':[52]

A COPY OF A LETTER FOUND THE 18TH OF OCTOBER, 1747, UPON DARWENT-BRIDGE, IN WALTON, NEAR PRESTON, WHICH CONTAINED BESIDES A PAPIST BOOK AND TWO CROSSES.

To Mr James Ratcliffe, in Whittle-in-le-Woods, near Chorley in Lancashire.

Dear and loving friends ... So dear friends, be ready, for the Time is at Hand, that the Hereticks must have their Reward, you must go to Manchester ... and raise what forces you can ... and there was above three hundred men ready in an Hours Warning; get them to write a great many letters for you to drop at the Hereticks houses in Whittle, Brindle, and Walton ... and demand great sums of money from the damn'd Hereticks; and if they don't obey your commands, set fire to there houses at night time, and kill them in their beds ... There is a contrivance in acting to blow up G- and his Parliament, but the day is not fixed on yet, but as soon as we hear we will let you know ... Pray think of Rump Hoghton, of Walton, plague him and fire his house; Benjamin Waddington must have part of his Estate, and Thomas Wearden & William his brother, must have the rest. Pray now begin to drop letters and Hostilities upon the Rumps and Hereticks. Now we take our Leave of all. Be not afraid.

William Hargreaves

George Hartley

George Waring.

CHAPTER FIVE

A lost world: the sources of local history

ROM the middle of the sixteenth century the range and quality of surviving documents expand very markedly, and for the first time it becomes possible to see clearly into the lives of ordinary people. The systematic keeping of parish records was begun in 1538, and from the early seventeenth century large numbers of wills have been preserved. Alongside these developments the extension of local and state government reveals much of the public affairs and problems of the time. When these sources are combined a fairly clear picture of everyday life begins to emerge.

The parish records

The earliest Walton parish registers have been lost. Although copies of some of the earlier records (the Bishop's Transcripts) exist from 1609, the main series begins in 1653. They are the most important historical source before the Births, Marriages, and deaths Act of 1837 and the Census of 1841. From time to time the formula of recording church events changed. This is particularly interesting where secondary information such as a person's occupation or age at death are given. In very large families a more detailed place of residence was sometimes given in the early records to identify individual members more closely. The Coupe clan of the early seventeenth century are a good example of this:

9 June 1618 [Christening] Thomas Cowpe filius Willm Cowpe of ye heis [the hays or heys, sometimes given as heie, heige, the riverside meadows].
23 July 1620 [Burial] Wm. Cowpe of the Browage [Brownedge].
6 April 1641 [Burial] John Cowpe de Manybrooks.
7 October 1653 [Burial] George Cowpe of the Mille.[1]

The more distant areas of the manor are given fairly consistently, and by the early nineteenth century had begun to develop as settlements, and later parishes, in their own right. The following examples are burials:

3 September 1655   1 child of Richard Banester of Brige.
11 July 1658   John Poope [Pope] of Tardie Yate. [1664 Tardieyeat].
15 December 1659   Richard Poope of Mire Yate.

12 June 1662	One child of Henry Poope of Midlford.
18 April 1670	Will Tasker de Many Brooks.
20 June 1671	Child of John Woodcock de Walton Mosse.
29 June 1693	Widdow Charnley de Brown Hedge.
1 June 1694	Ellen Gregson de Gregson Lane.
21 January 1695	Widdow Shorrock de Bamber Bridge.
29 September 1701	John son of Will Serjeant of Watering Pool.

Occasionally the ages of very old people are given. Adam Balshaw reached 88 (1779), Wm Waring 84 (1782), and Mary Charnley 90 (1789). Robert Baldwick of Walton, who died in October 1697, claimed to have been born in 1594. The recording of people's occupations is not consistent, but they occur in the Walton registers for the following years: burials 1703–32, baptisms 1698–1732 (occupation of father), marriages 1703–25, 1754–55, 1763–1812 (occupation of groom).

Independent registers for the Catholic mission at Brownedge run from 1764. These are of great interest, and contain the familiar geographical information, mentioning Walton Poor House (1764), Back Lane (Brindle Road, 1764), Charnley Fold (1765), School Lane (1766), Moon's Mill (1773), Duddle Lane and Mosney (1785). They also contain information as to the age and cause of death. A sample from January 1790 to December 1805 included 125 burials. Children and infants under 10 were very rarely listed, so that the records can tell us nothing about infant mortality, and the age of a further 43 people were not given.[2]

With these important qualifications, two clusters occur in the age at death, from 10–30 years (31 people), and from 70–90 years (24 people). The largest age groups are 10–19 years (16 people), 20–29 (15), and 80–89 (14). Throughout middle age the numbers of deaths rises with each 10-year block up to the octogenarians. Three people died over 90 years of age. The causes of death are very mixed, but the largest categories are 'age' (38 people), consumption (28), dropsy (8), child birth (7), and 'change of life' (3). The consumption and 'age' categories correlate the older and younger clusters. Outbreaks of typhus fever and smallpox are recorded in 1818 and 1819. John Parkinson, who died in 1792 (42), was described as 'Consumptive thro cold and poverty'. 'Old Alice Markland', who died in 1810, had been '6 years confined to her bed'. Most poignant were the burials of a husband and wife, Thomas Goodeare (Consumptive) (44) was buried on 10 March 1789, followed by his wife Alice 10 days later. The cause of her death is given as 'Excess of grief for ye dead'. Surprisingly only one death through cancer is recorded, 'Mary Hoole, Cancer in the breast'. The most remarkable thing about these figures is the considerable age that a fair percentage of the population surviving childhood were able to reach in the years before the industrial revolution. In the subsequent period such longevity appears to have been less marked.

Parish records can also provide a guide to the population of the district;

Walton Corner, looking north along Victoria Road, c.1900. An amazing range of houses fronted the densely populated centre of Walton village which had grown up in the late eighteenth century. Many of the houses had loomshops or weaving cellars, and the growth of the local textile trade is a constantly recurring theme in the parish and manorial records from the early seventeenth century onwards. (*R. Burns*)

'This year [1781] an Account was taken of the Number of Inhabitants within this Chapelry – By this Account it appeared, that in Walton and Cuerdale there were 2,662 Inhabitants, of which the Village, including those families about the Church, contained 868'.[3] Frequent gaps in the church records make estimates of the population based on them very uncertain. Catholics and nonconformists might choose not to be married there or to have their children baptised there, but up to the 1760s most would have to be buried there. In the period 1654 to 1675, only 10 years are without serious gaps (defined as 3 months without entries). The total number of burials is 344, giving a yearly average of 34.4. Multiplying this by 30 (based on a supposed death rate of 30 per 1,000, per year) indicates a potential population of 1,032. Similarly the Protestation Return of 1642 lists 308 men over 18 years of age. Assuming a similar number of women would indicate an adult population of 616, to which the number of children must be added. From nineteenth-century estimates a number can be arrived at by multiplying the number of adults by 0.7555. This gives a figure of 465 children, and a total population of 1,081.[4]

The Hearth Tax or 'chimney tax' Returns of the 1660s provide another line of approach. The return of 1664 lists 136 dwellings in Walton and Cuerdale. Assuming 5 people per house would give a figure of 630 people. Yet the returns reveal marked inequalities in the distribution of wealth in this very small community. Of the 126 houses in Walton, the inhabitants of one third were reckoned to be exempted from the tax on the grounds of poverty. Only 14 houses claimed to have more than a single hearth. The homes of William Osbaldeston (Osbaldeston House), Edward Walmmesly (Bannister Hall) and Thomas Walton (Little Walton Hall, Bamber Bridge), had 5, and Sir Richard Hoghton had 9 (at Walton Hall). At Samlesbury 83 houses recorded 127 hearths, 13 of them belonging to John Southworth of Samlesbury Hall. In Cuerdale, 10 houses had 25 hearths, 12 of them belonging to Richard Asheton of Cuerdale Hall.[5]

None of these estimates of population based on the parish records is entirely satisfactory, but they suggest that the population of the district in the mid-seventeenth century may have been in the order of 1,200 people. Perhaps half of these would live in the village, with the rest spread out across a still rural landscape, in which the single farmstead was still the norm. Occasionally, beside a cross road or wayside inn, a sprawling hamlet of three or four houses or crofts, was the only evidence of urbanisation. The modern townships of Bamber Bridge, Lostock Hall, Higher Walton and Gregson Lane simply did not exist.

Man proposes and God disposes: wills and inventories

Perhaps the most interesting insight in to people's private lives can be glimpsed through the large collection of their wills which survives. In many cases these have an inventory of the deceased's moveable goods attached, and it is possible to ascertain their affairs in some detail. For the years 1545–1760, 373 Walton wills are listed at Chester, and most of them are held at the Lancashire Record Office (1545–1620, 32; 1621–50, 44; 1660–80, 100; 1681–1700, 60; 1701–20, 36; 1720–41, 65; 1741–60, 36). This form of will and inventory making began to change to a drier more legalistic form

The Hob Inn, Bamber Bridge, c.1890. With its quite low thatched roof and windows set high into the eaves, the inn was a good example of the local vernacular style of house building. Locally hand-made bricks enclosed an internal timber frame which supported a thatched roof composed of reeds. Though early seventeenth century in date, the Hob's place in History was not to come until the night of 24 June 1943. The strange structure in front of the building is a gentleman's urinal; at this time the Leyland Local Government Board considered the demolition of the ancient Leyland Cross to make way for a similar structure! (R. Burns)

Todd Hall, Todd Lane, Lostock Hall, c. 1980. A fine example of a local, very well-to-do yeoman farmer's residence of the seventeenth century, reflecting the locally available building materials – Hoghton or Whittle sandstone for the base and cornices, locally hand-made bricks around an internal oak frame, to support a stone or thatch roof. (*South Ribble Museum*)

Pickerings Farm, Brownedge Road, Lostock Hall, c. 1985. Now extensively restored, the original moss-land thatch was found beneath the corrugated iron roof. Though it had been extensively extended, the original structure of a small timber-framed thatched cottage with its large ingle-nook fireplace could still be seen. In the past the situation of the farm was very different from the bustling crossroads of the present day. For over a century the upstairs window looked out over the remote tracts of Walton Moss, largely empty of all but seasonal wildfowl, and the labour of the occasional peat cutter. (*South Ribble Museum*)

in the later eighteenth century, and it is the earlier documents which are the most interesting.

Seventeenth-century wills frequently contain three elements, a religious introduction, the statement of the deceased's intent or his 'will', and the inventory of his goods. Wills were made very close to death, and subtle variations in the wording can be very revealing. A good example of the first element is given in the will of Thomas Yates a tailor, made on 3 July 1663:[6]

I Thomas Yates of Walton-Le-Dale in the county of Lancaster, Taylor, sick in body but of good and perfect memory, praise and thanks be given unto God for the same, Doe constitute make and ordaine this my last will and testament in manner and forme following, first and principally I comit my Soule into the hands of Almightie God my maker and creator trusting through the mercy of Jesus Christ my alone Saviour and redeemer to bee one of those to bee saved, and my body to Christian buriall. My mind and will is that ...

John Banke (1669, linen webster) made his will 'Knowing the certainty of death', John Aynescough (1666, webster) was 'Penitent and sorry from the bottom of my heart for my sinns past', whilst James Martin (1666, fustian maker) called 'to mind the mortalty of my body ... knowinge it is appointed for all men to dye'. Many people looked upon their worldly goods as the direct gift of God. Hugh Dickinson (1688, husbandman) described his 'estate', 'which it shall please God to bless me with at the time of my death'. Valued at £16 9s. 0d., it is one of the smallest amounts among the Walton wills.

The second element, the disposal of the deceased's goods, is also usually divided into three parts, with portions to the deceased's wife, family and friends, and to the deceased himself. Richard Woodcock (1614, yeoman) divided his goods into three parts 'According to the custom of the county'. Again, the will of Thomas Yates is very clear in this respect:

> ... My mind and will is that my personal estate bee divided into three equall parts, one third part I give and bequeath unto Mary Yates my loving wife, one part whereof I give and bequeath unto my children equally divided amongst them, and for the last third part being the deads part, my will and mind is that all my debts and funerall expanses should bee paid out of my personal estate, or out of the whole part. Lastly I constitute make and ordain my brother Robert Yates and Richard Duddell my whole executors, and what debts (however) are due to me to be paid unto the above named RY and RD my whole executors, in testimony whereof I herunto set my hand and seal the day first above written.
>
> THOMAS YATES His mark
> Witnesses   KATHERINE POLLARD
>   JAMES MAWDESLEY

Gifts to grandchildren, godchildren, nieces and nephews, and servants were carefully proportioned. James Lemon (1665, yeoman) left 'all the children to whom I am Grandfather' 2s., and his godchildren 6d. The poor of Walton were to have 10s., and his best clothes were to go to his servant, 'If he be in my service at the daie of my death'. Thomas Banester (1663, gentleman) bequeathed a third to Millicant 'My welbeloved wyffe'), and a third to his two daughters Alice Livesey and Elizabeth Rishton. His grandchildren were to receive 5s. each, his godchildren 6s. 8d., and his brother Christopher's children 2s. Of his servants, Lawrence Thornley was to have 6s. 8d., John Whitley 3s. 4d., whilst Richard Whalley was to have 'My little birding piece ... and tenn shillings'. Euan Catterall (1678, yeoman) gave 25s. to the poor, 20s. to Elizabeth Wynnard 'My servant', and 10s. each to 'Robert and Richard Lucas that do dwell with me'.

Where the deceased was leaving a young family his will could be carefully stated. Richard Duddell (1717) took pains to ensure that his young son Richard would be looked after if his wife Anne also died, and James Baldwin (1733, shoemaker) left instructions to his wife Margaret as to how their young children were to be brought up. If the family was involved in a specific trade, this may already have been taken over by younger members, and gifts in respect of it would thus already have been made. Gifts of tools and goods could be used to provide a livelihood for the deceased's dependants. John Bankes (1669, linen webster) gave his son Richard's boy, 'Whom I am Grand ffather unto one paire of loom and geare. He shall have choice of them', and his clothes to his own brother Richard 'With hat bands, shoes, and hose'.

All this could clearly lead to bitter disputes. Elizabeth Anderton (1740, widow), 'Being infirm of body but of sound and disposing mind and memory', had to divide her goods worth £20 10s. 0d. (£17 of it debts), among her five sons and three married daughters. She took great pride in her small collection of books, and specifically recommending one, 'The Practice of Piety', to one of her daughters in law. A valuable piece of land along Ribbleton Lane, Preston, was to go to one son. She clearly envisaged trouble, and took care to guard against disputes, 'Now if any one be displeased at what I have ordered or given, that person or persons, shall have paid to them the sum of five shillings, and shall have no other part or share in my said estate'.

The inventories

The detailed inventories reach deep into all aspects of everyday life. They range from the simple lists of the goods of the poor tenantry, to the extensive surveys of the possessions of the rich. The fifty or so documents consulted in the course of the present study provide a reasonably valid sample of the seventeenth-century Walton wills. In terms of value, two clusters appear, in the £10–£40 and £100–£160 ranges. A great variety of occupations is indicated among the will makers, though agriculture and textiles predominate, and many people were engaged in both.

Among the larger inventories members of the old yeoman class of the agricultural interest predominated. Richard Woodcock's goods (1614, yeoman) came to £141 14s. 0d., of which his animals comprised just over £50, and 'corn growinge upon the ground £20'. Thomas Banester (1648, gentleman) had crops worth £30, and animals valued at £84 2s. 0d., in a grand total of £199 19s. 2d. Thomas Walton's goods (1619, gentleman) were worth £147 5s. 4d., and included a long list of furnishings, agricultural tools, and beer-making equipment. The largest list of the goods – £390 2s. 8d. – is that of Sir Richard Hoghton (1635, baronet). It is rather misleading, however, because it relates principally only to his household goods. The inventory lists furniture and other possessions, including, 'One paire of Virginall £21 8s. 0d. ... 26 fether beds, 24 bolsters, 4 pillows, one paire of sheets etc. £40 10s. 0d. ... 1 Champrepott 12d. ... 11 hogsheads 22s.'. A much more modest agricultural estate was that of Richard Baldwin (1661, yeoman) whose goods worth £92 2s. 1d. included, 'In corne on the ground £16, calves and 5 yonge beasts £20, 9 geese, 4 other hens and 2 doggs 7s. 6d., 1 steere and 4 weening calves £7 5s. 0d., 1 horse £3 10s. 0d.'

Alongside the long established families was a rising class of prosperous tradesmen, although many of the old landed families also had textile interests. Euan Catterall (1678, yeoman) for example, had 'Yarne, flax and tow' worth £13 12s. 0d., and 'weavers loomes and all other necessaries there unto £3 10s. 0d.'. The textile trade, based principally on flax and linen, was strongly established by the early seventeenth century. Alexander Osbaldeston (1639, linen webster) had goods worth £148 18s. 0d. and Thomas Shorrock (1708, fustian weaver) £227 4s. 4d. Though seventy years apart, both men had invested their profits in loans or 'bonds' to other people, a very common practice with ready money before the evolution of the banking system. Osbaldeston had £78 'Upon severall bonds', and Shorrock had £120 in 'Credits and money', and £70 in linen cloth and yarn. Even quite small debts were carefully listed. Euan Darwen (1669, linen webster) listed Henry Houghton of Preston £1 8s. 0d., Isabell Chaigley 4s. 0d., George Gregson 10s. 5d., and Richard Ridley 1s. 4d. Alternatively, and very significantly for his son, the preamble to Sir Thomas Langton's will (1569, Lord of the Manor) specifically states him to be 'Being indebted to divers and sundrie persons in greate summes of money'.

Euan Darwen had goods worth £106 12s. 2d., which included £27 in yarn and cloth, two pairs of looms £4, and flax and tow worth £1 5s. 0d. The valuation of Edmund Gregson's estate (1663 linen webster) at £73 15s. 0d. included 'Linen and canvas geare', 'Linen cloathe', and webster looms. Richard Duddell had a spinning wheel valued at 4s., two stones of flax 16s., yarn worth £6 10s. 0d., looms £1, and £20 in linen yarn. Linen cloth seems generally to have been valued at one shilling per yard. Roger Brewer (1694, fustian maker), had goods worth £130. His house had a 'workhouse' which contained his scales and weights worth 4s., a 'paire of looms, healds, reeds, one wheel, warping walls and bobbing picks' worth £19 0s. 3d. In stock he had 'gray yarn £2 10s. 0d., white yarn £1 1s. 6d. ... More in whit yarn and pack £14 14s. 0d.'.

James Baldwin (1733) was, by contrast, a prosperous shoemaker. He had leather worth £42 5s. 0d., animals worth £50 (including 'George an old cow worth £3 5s. 0d.'), and money 'att interest' £20. Cheese production was another line of his business; his cheese press and tools were worth 15s., and his stock of 118 great cheeses £13, in a total sum of £158 6s. 8d. The inventory of Thomas Talbot (1714), reveals something of the stock in trade of an innkeeper. He had malt worth £6, 15 barrels £1 10s. 0d., drinking glasses 1s., 3 dozen bottles 5s., and a great array of small cheap pictures, tables, chairs, pewter pints and quarts, and '1 brass clock and case

The inventory of the goods of Thomas Balshaw of Walton, drawn up by John Clayton, William Leyland and Thomas Hawkshead in April 1731. The contents of each room are carefully listed, with his looms and stocks of yarn. Of his fortune of over £300, £200 comprised 'bills, bonds and credits' (LRO, DDH 633, by courtesy of the County Archivist)

£1 5s. 0d.'. Significantly he also had two cows and a calf (£8), and a sow with seven pigs (£1 10s. 0d.), in a total sum of £57 19s. 1d.

By contrast, much poorer farmers, husbandmen and weavers abound. John Banke (1669, linen webster) had goods worth £37 17s. 0d. (animals £15 6s. 8d., looms and geare £1, yarn and cloth £2 2s. 0d.), and John Aynescough (1666, webster) goods valued at £30. The latter included 'a clok in the workhouse' £1, 27lbs of pewter items worth £1 7s. 0d., and his books 5s. 6d. 'The shop or workhouse' of Francis Dootson (1773, linen weaver) contained 'In weavers gears, two pair of looms, swifts and wheels and odd things' worth £2 10s. 0d. James Livesey (1727, weaver) had goods worth only £14 17s. 1d., mostly in furniture, divided between a house at Higher Shuttlingfields (beds £7 4s. 6d., 'cuphoard' and settee 13s. 7d.), and Bankhead (table and lumber £1 0s. 6d.). The goods of John Pope (1687) valued at just £4 15s. 6d., included his cow (£3), an old mare and pack-saddle 12s., '1 old bed with some old bed cloathes belonging to it 8s.', and his clothing – worth just 5s.

Detailed inventories, where goods are listed room by room, also reveal much about people's homes and their contents:

A catalogue of the goods and chattles of Roger Wooderofe of Walton in Lay dale (joiner). June 10th 1696.
The house chamber;
A bedsted and curtains, halfe a dozen chears, one table, one little box, one stool and one footer chest   £1 5s. 0d
The parlor chamber;
A chest of drawers and furniture   £1 10s. 0d.
The cellar chamber;
A bedsted and furniture   10s. 0d.
The parler;
Half a dozen chears, two tables and two buffet stools   18s. 0d.
The cellar;
The pewter   £1 0s. 0d.
The lead and bruine [brewing] vessels   £2 0s. 0d.
The house;
One clothes presse. Nine chears and a table, a settle, one iron grate and cubord   £2.
A griddle, ffryingpan, spittle, tosting iron   4s. 0d.
The brass   10s. 0d.
One carte and wheels broken timber and whole   £1 10s. 0d.
One more   £1 10s. 0d.
Working tools   5s. 0d.
Apparell and pictures   £1 10s. 0d.

In addition to listing the principal moveable assets, animals, crops, tools, stock in trade, and debts, the inventories provide details of personal possessions and the necessaries of everyday life. Very valuable objects are quite rare. Thomas Banester (Gent. 1648) had 'Pewter of all sorts 30lb £1 10s. 0d.', and a silver bowl and four silver spoons worth £4. Thomas Shorrock (fustian weaver, 1708) had a brass clock worth £1 3s. 4d., whilst Alexander Osbaldeston (linen weaver, 1639) had £1 in 'spoones and other broken silver'.

More mundane everyday vessels and treenware occur in most wills. Euan Catterall's goods included 'Brasse and pewter £4, in wooden and treen vessell £2'. Richard Baldwin (yeoman, 1661) had brass pans and ladles worth £1 12s. 0d., pewter 16s. 8d., and 'earthen vessel 3s. 9d. James Baldwin had a salt box, Robert Shorrocke (husbandman, 1676) had 13lb of pewter at 8*d*. per pound, and brasse items worth 18*s*. Richard Duddell's inventory differentiated between his 'pott brasse' £1 12*s*. 0*d*., and 'pann brasse 10*s*. Most inventories list a frying pan and fire irons, and the 'Iron ware and fire irons tongs' belonging to Roger Brewer (fustian maker, 1694) were valued at 15*s*. 9*d*. Elizabeth Anderton's 'Warming pan and frying pan' was worth 2*s*., and her 'Seven petty panns, seven dishes and ten plates' were valued at 8*s*. 0*d*. Thomas Talbot's inn (1714) contained a pair of bellows worth 6*d*.

Furniture of all kinds is recorded, but beds, bedding, and bed linen predominate. Sir Richard Hoghton's '26 fether beds' (1635) have been noted, whilst Edmund Gregson's (1663) 'Bebstedes, boulsters, cloaths belonging to them, sheets and linnen ware' were valued at £11 10*s*. 0*d*. Robert Shorrocke's house (husbandman, 1676) contained 'One pair of bedstockes from the chamber next the lane, with furniture to itt 10*s*. In the great chamber beneath a paire of bedstookes, with furniture thereto 10*s*.'. By contrast, 'One auld chaff bed' was worth just 1*s*.. William Balshaw (yeoman, 1711) had, 'A cupbord 10*s*., a settle 3*s*., A meat chist and meat in it 15*s*.'. Thomas Walton's inventory (1619) included a great stock of 'Bed ware', 11 lots of 'Quishons', 17 lots of bedding, 7 lots of linen, 'Fore dozen of table napkins' and 'foure pewter chamberpotte 10*s*. 0*d*.' Roger Woodroffe (1696) had 'Half a dozen chears, two tables two buffet stools 18*s*.'.

Stocks of fuel and food are also listed. In the seventeenth century coal was coming into wider use, but peat, presumably from Walton Moss, is described in the inventories as 'turffe', and turf carts are occasionally recorded. Richard Baldwin (1661, yeoman) had 'Turffe and coale worth 10*s*. Butter, cheese, ham and bacon are often recorded, sometimes in quite large amounts. Euan Darwen had 'Meale, wheate, beefe and bacon' worth £3, and cheese and butter worth 5*s*. Ellen Cowpe of Cuerden (widow of George Coupe, 1608) had 'Meale and groattes' worth 21*s*. and salt worth a guinea, in addition to her stock of ham and beef, butter, bacon and malt.

Thus the wills and inventories provide a graphic picture of the cares and possessions of Walton-le-Dale's hard-working, God-fearing, and frequently poor population. Outside of the manor house luxury items are rarely encountered. Of course, the dutiful legatees were quite capable of removing those items they felt to be theirs of right, long before the inventory makers could appear on the scene.

Death by unnatural causes: the Coroner's records

From 1624 to 1827 the Hoghtons held the office of hereditary coroner of Walton-le-Dale, and the manor records contain transcripts of many of the cases that came before them. Although in the early nineteenth century it became customary for the coroner to appoint a deputy, it is clear that in the earlier period the lord of the manor himself presided over the

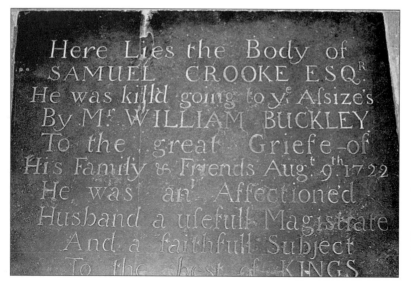

Here Lies the Body of
SAMUEL CROOKE ESQ[R]
He was kill'd going to y[e] Afsize's
By M[r] WILLIAM BUCKLEY
To the great Griefe of
His Family & Friends Aug[t] 9th 1722
He was an' Affectioned
Husband a ufefull Magistrate
And a faithfull Subject
To the best of KINGS

The grave of Samuel Crooke beside the altar in St Leonard's Church. The strange circumstances surrounding his death in a duel in Knot Lane are revealed by the Walton Coroner's records. Since his killer was a gentleman, he was accorded the due title of MR William Buckley. (*Author*)

proceedings personally. When death occurred suddenly due to other than natural causes, the coroner was informed at once, and he summoned a jury of 15 'Good and lawful men of Walton in le Dale' at a convenient house. Witnesses were interrogated before this court, and decided on the cause of death. It was the usual practice to have the body of the deceased before them 'then and there lying dead', and to hold the court on the day of the death. When suspicious circumstances were suspected, the case was passed on to the relevant authorities for further investigation and punishment. The circumstances of the deceased, and his or her family, would thus be well known to their neighbours who formed the court. Many of the witnesses were clearly still traumatised by the suddenness of the tragedy that had just overwhelmed them. Alternatively, the court records frequently reveal deep understanding and concern for the bereaved.[7]

A large proportion of these accidents occurred to children, and the main causes of death were drowning, fire, and miscellaneous accidents involving crushing, falls or blows to the head. By the late eighteenth century 'road accidents' began to be more commonplace. Deaths through murder or manslaughter are very rare, though suicide (a cause of death difficult to prove) was quite common. Only rarely do the records refer to the drunkenness of the deceased, though in many cases this must have been a contributory factor.

Many cases concern drowning. Robert Heath was swept off Walton Cop during the great flood of December 1737. In August 1783 George Charnley was making his way along the bank of the river Lostock when he stumbled. The inquest held at John Charnley's house found that he 'fell into the said river or brook which was then much raised by the Great Rains and the force of the stream was carry'd down the said river and remained therein until he was suffocated and drown'd. In July 1782 William Wilding finished work at the Mosney print works about midnight, and 'walked along the Darwen home along the mill pool'. When he failed to arrive, a search was made, and he was found 'under the water in the pool'.

Wayside ditches and fords were especially dangerous. In 1714 William Parkinson (62) a linen weaver from Farington, 'Going along the high lane in Walton near a place called the Headless Cross (probably the cross at the junction of Station Road and School Lane, adjacent to the 'Pear Tree' in Bamber Bridge) ... on Saturday 6th of February about 9 o'clock in the evening, accidentally and by a mischance fell down into the said ditch and was there drowned and by that means came to his death'. Henry Sharples was returning home from Preston along Walton Cop in March 1773 'and being intoxicated with liquor fell into the river Ribble and was thereby suffocated and drowned'. His money was still in his pockets and no suspicious circumstances were found.

A horrific accident befell Alice and James Turner and their six-month-old son George, from Samlesbury, in April 1708. James Turner was crossing a ford on the Darwen 'called Lemon fforth near Banaster Hall', on horseback, with his wife and child behind him on a pillion. In mid-current the strap on the pillion broke, and wife and child were swept into the river, 'the stream whereof carrying them with violence into a deep place whither he alighting of his horse imediatly swim after them did through God's assistence bring the said Alice living out of the water and also the child which was drowned before he could recover it out of the water'. John Chew of Banister hall described their frantic appearance at the hall the previous day, and both husband and wife were still deeply shocked.

During the summer months, swimming in the Darwen seems to have been a very popular recreation, and one that contributed to a steady toll of fatalities. Disaster befell a swimming party between 2 and 3 p.m. on a hot Sunday afternoon in June 1715. George Catterall (18) got into difficulties whilst 'trying to swim on his back'. Thomas Waterhouse (18) went to help him, and in front of half a dozen of their helpless mates both were drowned. In June 1766 John Carr, a whitener (bleacher)

> Yesterday ... stript himself naked and went into the River Darwen to Bath, and ... accidentally went into a part of the said river near a mill belonging to John Moore called Mill Dam in Walton ... which was too deep for him.

Away from the village, many houses had a nearby pit for drinking water, or perhaps sometimes for retting flax. Death of children in such pits were a very common occurrence. Mary Abbot, a girl of 12, was the servant of Anne and Robert Rigby, a linen weaver. One Thursday morning in February 1709, Anne got up between five and six and called to Mary to fetch a bucket of water from the pit by their house 'to wash her in'. When the girl did not return, Anne went to look for her, and her frantic screams woke her husband. Robert Rigby, William Coupe and John Brindle recovered the girl's body with a sickle fastened to the end of a long pole. Henry

Hoghton and the jury of 15 (including Coupe and Brindle), assembled the same Day in Coupe's house, and visited the pit which they reckoned was 'a yard and a half deep'. They found that Mary had accidentally slipped and drowned. The following year a similar fate befell Margrett Abbott (10). John Brindle was again a witness, having been called from his 'workhouse'. Being a long time fetching water, a search was made, and her wooden clogs were found floating on the surface of the water. Suicide was strongly suspected – it is not clear if she was related to Mary – but Thomas Calvert said that 'she was not melancholy but rather of a cheery disposition'. She had got on well with her mistress and 'carried well towards her', having 'a free merry disposition'.

The tendency of mothers to wrap up their infants in highly flammable clothing (particularly clean cotton) during the winter months resulted in a large number of deaths. In February 1803 Betty Farnworth left her two-year-old daughter sat in a chair by the fire, while she went to see a neighbour. Returning twenty minutes later she 'saw the child on fire sat in the same chair that it had been left in'. In March 1797 Miriam Bibby saw smoke coming from the house of her next-door neighbour James Markland. Rushing into the house, she was shocked to see his three-year-old son's clothes on fire. The jury found that the child's clothes 'caught on fire and burnt with great violence'. In such cases the witnesses, parents and members of the court reaching out to the whole community, were very clearly deeply shocked and overwhelmed by events.

Alternatively, where suspicious circumstances surrounded the deaths of infants every effort was made to detect the evil-doers. In June 1757 the body of an infant was found 'wrapped up in a black or brown woollen cloath' in a pit in a field called 'the Two Acres'. Since the child had been 'born alive' the jury's verdict was murder by 'a certain person to them unknown not having god before his eyes but being moved and seduced by the Investigation of the devil on a certain day and time unknown'. Infanticides were severely prosecuted. In 1741 an 'Inquisition' was 'taken upon the death of a bastard child found dead in the mill floam issuing out of and running from a certain River called Darwent'. The court found that 'The said male child was violently feloniously and of malice forethought by force of arms thrown into the said mill stream and was thus murdered by drowning ... by persons unknown'.

The deaths of babies born to unmarried mothers, in the absence of a known father, were carefully scrutinised. In January 1703 an enquiry was held into

> The death of a Bastard child born upon the body of Elizabeth Turner of Walton-le-Dale ... spinster ... We the jury doe find ... that a female childe was borne uppon ye body of Elizabeth Turner ... at about one o'clock on Thursday night on 28th day of January, and found dead in bed with Elizabeth Turner its mother and for much as noe evidence doth appear to

prove the said child to be dead at time of its birth, we doe find Elizabeth Turner was guilty of ye murder of a late child.

Evidence was brought in her defence: four days earlier she had fallen, and the midwife had 'found no bruises [on the baby] nor anything upon it which did occasion her to think it had received any harm'. However, her failure to prepare baby clothes for the child counted against her, and she was committed for trial at Lancaster.

Many deaths resulted simply from carelessness, lack of supervision, bad judgement, or ill luck. Three-year-old Alice Holland fell down a well '4 yards deep' in 1750, William Holderness fell through the ice on a pit near his father's house in January 1803 and Thomas Rothwell died when struck in the head by a farmer's fork which had been thrown by a fellow workman at a troublesome 'howndd' (1707: 'felony by miss-adventure'). George Coupe was helping to plaster the ridge of George Clayton's roof, a few days before Christmas in 1763. Carrying a 'board full of daub on his head', he had a fit of giddiness or vertigo, and fell 'six yards' from the ladder. James Hurst, a child of six, was watching Robert Worden build a timber cistern. Playing, or perhaps trying to help, the child dislodged a heavy balk which fell onto him. Despite Worden's desperate efforts the child had received 'a mortal bruise' and died a quarter of an hour later (1822). Marl pits were a common feature in the local landscape. Henry Dawson was helping Richard Clarkson 'Hacking up marle' in a deep old pit in the grounds of Walton Hall. Despite the latter's shout, the sides collapsed in on him and he was crushed before he could be dug out (1730).

Road accidents were quite common, usually involving young children, running playing alongside large or heavy loads. It seems to have been quite normal to allow children to ride along on such loads, and they not infrequently fell off them. In 1728 Sarah Berry was riding on a cart pulled by four horses belonging to John Fletcher, a whitster. The cart overturned and she was killed. Richard Pomfret was killed in May 1757, when a heavy 'cart chest' fell upon him. On such occasions the jury found that 'a chattel' (the vehicle or animals) had caused the death, which under very ancient law 'Being responsible for a persons death was given to God'. In Walton this church right had passed to the Hoghtons. Accordingly as late as the mid-eighteenth century such items became technically the property of the lord of the manor, but were usually restored for a nominal payment.

On 17 September 1723 a cart drawn by a horse and two mares was passing along Walton Cop. A child, Thomas Anderton, fell under the rear wheels. John Holden of Duxbury, the distraught driver, ordered that 'nothing be wanting in order to recover the child'. The boy died a fortnight later. The confiscated horses and cart were valued at £10. The subsequent doctor's bill, however, was thought by an officer of the court to be excessive:

To ye Apthcarie Bill is	4s. 5d.
and Dr Swansy demands for his pains	5s. 0d.

More charges he adds	5s. 0d.
Ale 3 gallons	3s. 9d.
Church dues	4s. 10d.
Coffin	2s. 6d.
los of time and candles	10s. 0d.
Paid to attend severall night calls	2s. 6d.
Total	£1 18s. 0d.

Suicide was also quite common. In 1706 Anne Taylor gave evidence of the circumstances surrounding her husband's death. The previous night, lying together in bed, she had told him that the landlords were pressing for the rent of the land that they farmed, and that if they did not get their money they would take their goods. She 'asked him how they might do in the matter, to which he said little'. He left the house at 4–5 a.m. and shot himself. On 30 September 1712 the court found that Ann Cowper 'Did voluntarily and of her free will drown herself in a certain pitt in a field called the New Close ... and by that means and not otherwise to their knowledge the said Anne Cowper came to her death'. A number of suicides were found to be 'a Lunatick and a person of unsound mind' at the time of their deaths. John Cowpe was found 'not of sound mind, memory, and understanding on the present day between the hours of five and eight of the clock', when he had hanged himself from a beam in his barn. In 1798 Joseph Hilton, prosperous innkeeper of the Unicorn Inn, cut his own throat. Robert Morrila hanged himself in 'Yatefield Wood', having been ill for some time. In May 1770 his son gave evidence that 'His father appeared to be dejected and low spirited, and refused to eat as usual and said he should never sleep again and continued in that state of mind'.

A number of cases are particularly interesting, and provide deep insights into contemporary life and behaviour. On 29 May 1708 an enquiry was held 'the Black Bull, Walton-le-Dale, on the death of John Royle there lying dead'. Royle had been sent with Nathaniel Knott to serve a warrant on John Taylor. The latter fled through his workhouse, and ran upstairs 'defending himself with a pike', whilst a general fight began in the house, during which his wife was much to the fore, and Royle was hit on the head several times. Taylor was eventually captured and taken to Preston. On the way Royle said that he felt sick and had been hit on the head. Elizabeth Baines at the Black Bull had given him some beer, but could see no wound. Growing pale, Royle became very ill; he lost the use of one side of his body, and was taken in to a nearby house where he died.

Personal disputes between gentlemen could be settled directly. Between 8 and 9 a.m. in August 1722, Samuel Crook and his servant Joseph Clough were making their way down the steep and narrow Knot Lane, as by chance 'Mr Buckley' and his man were coming up. The two were old enemies, having fallen out 26 years previously in 1696. After some words, during which it was claimed that Crook hit Buckley's servant, Crook hit Buckley with his whip. The two dismounted and moved to a more open space, and set to with swords. After six or seven minutes of fighting Buckley killed Crook, saluted him with his sword, kissed him and fled. Buckley was described as 'A blackish ruddy complexioned man, tall and bulky, and in black cloths and a cap on his head under his hett'. The following day he surrendered himself in Yorkshire. Samuel Crook was buried by the altar in the chancel of St Leonards. His fine black gravestone can still be seen, and is remarkable for its statement that his killer was 'Mr Buckley'. Even the fatal assailant of a prominent local was thus due his correct form of address – if he was a gentleman.

Family ties, and the economic interdependence they represented, were very strong, and the community provided a basis of parish relief for its members in the event of dire poverty or distress. Poor 'strangers' without family were not so fortunate, as the death of 'Staffordshire Dick' in the winter of 1749 illustrates. The case aroused much controversy at the time, for locals were strongly discouraged by the authorities from giving help to homeless people, who might thus become a burden on the local community. Cuthbert Holland said of the boy, 'He went by the name of Staffordshire Dick ... he has had an Ague upon him for these five weeks last ... he always was a Slothful Lazy Lad and very Lousy ... he has heard the deceased say he had a bite upon his leg which gave him much pain'. George Barns said, 'He came from Wharley Banks, that a woman brought him into this county and died ... that he was a Bastard'.

As to the circumstances of his death, John Harris, innkeeper, told how he had come to his house on Saturday night, and asked for help. He was given something to eat and drink, and came again the following evening. This time he was allowed to sleep in the stable. On Monday night he was not allowed into the barn because of the dirty mess he had made in the stable the previous evening, but was given a pot of hot ale. The boy left and went to the house of Thomas Noblett. Elizabeth Noblett testified that he had come to their house at 7 o'clock, 'and asked to warm him'. He stayed for two hours. 'He was so offensive and Lowsey but he refused to go saying his belly acked and was then shaking.' He left between 9 and 10 p.m. He then went to Edward Sharrock's house, complained of the cold, and asked to be allowed to warm himself. Mary Sharrock told how he, 'lay down before the fire and complained of his being griped in his Belly and said he was in a cold fitt ... after an hour I bade him go'. Reluctantly he left, but stayed sat by the house door. Some time later he asked to come back in, but was refused, and was found dead at 1 a.m.

These rather exceptional cases apart, the affairs of the inhabitants of Walton-le-Dale, revealed in these earliest detailed records of their type, are not so markedly removed from those of today. In death, as in life, the continuity of English social history once again asserts itself.

St Leonard's parish walking, *c.* 1930. The parish with its institutions and officers was a principal feature of English local government from very early times, and in the nineteenth century formed the basis of modern local democracy.
(*H. Hunt*)

CHAPTER SIX

Local administration: the manor and parish

HE ANCIENT INSTITUTIONS of manor and parish remained the principal units of the system of local administration well into the 'industrial revolution'. From the middle of the seventeenth century the Hoghton estate began to try to transform itself into a more recognisably commercial enterprise. The surviving Hoghton papers from this period are thus an important historical source, though records from before the eighteenth century often seem to have survived more completely than the later records. The collection preserved in the Lancashire Record Office can be broken down into rentals and accounts, the manor court and coroner's papers, and the Walton estate land deeds. Smaller collections relate to specific aspects of the estate, such as the roads and Walton Cop, Brownedge Common, and the Walton corn mills.

The surviving rentals and accounts are very mixed, only rarely provide any sort of systematic guide to events, and are very thinly spread over a long time span. Rent lists and related lease books are especially interesting, since they relate specific land holdings to the individual tenants, with details of the value of holdings and the rents paid. The rental of 1648 is in the form of a wonderfully clear book, providing such information for the entire Hoghton estate at that time (Hoghton, Withnell, Wheelton, Walton-le-Dale, Grimsargh, Lea, Ashton, Dilworth, Whittingham, Ribchester, and Haighton, with properties in Preston):[1]

> A true perticular of Sir Richard Hoghton Estate with the perticular view of every part thereof according to what hath beene maid of it in his fathers time, and Since he came to be Lord of it.

The estate produced a total annual income of £2,352 15s. 11d. The tenants at Walton are carefully listed, with any additional duties due from them. William Duddel paid 26s. 6d. rent for his holding, to be paid in halves due at Pentecost and Christmas. The ancient days of service due to the lord had been transferred into cash payments, and he paid 6d. for ploughing and harrowing, and 1s. for shearing. William Kellett paid just 6d. rent with 'a day at shering and a day at hay'.

The main elements of the estate had clearly changed little from the holdings of the earlier lords of Walton:

	Acres	Rods	Annual Income
The Townfield	22	o	£22 os. od.
The Flatt	17	1	£17 5s. od.
Whirlins	12	o	£12 os. od.
Little Whirlins	4	1	£4 5s. od.
Stony Rydinge	8	o	£8 os. od.
Barne Flatt and Foulde	8	o	£8 os. od.
The Connerey	7	o	£6 os. od.
The Intacke	6	o	£6 os. od.
The Redd Carr	12	o	£18 os. od.
The Wood Carr	20	o	£6 os. od.
The Greene Hayes	7	o	£6 os. od.
The Parke	40	o	£30 os. od.
The White Croft and part of the Copy	5	o	£5 5s. od.
The Mill called Walton Mill and the Kill [kiln]	o	o	£60 os. od.
Many Brookes Mill and Kill	o	o	£6 os. od.
Fishing in the Ribble	o	o	£10 os. od.
Boon Plowinge and Harrowinge due in money the 25 March Per Annum			£9 16s. od.
Boon Sheringe in Walton due in August Per Annum			£3 16s. od.
The Hous rents in Walton Per Annum			£47 12s. 3d.
The Cheife Rentes Per Annum			£9 17s. 11d.
Rent Charch due at Mikl Per Annum			£1 14s. 3d.

The records indicate the existence of a corn mill at Manybrooks, whilst the mill at Walton is by far the most important in the entire estate. The latter was traditionally reckoned to be worth £100 *per annum*, in comparison with the mills at Goosnargh £40, Moulding Water £30, Brinscal £30, and Lea £20. Similarly the Walton estate ('The Demesne lands in Walton') was worth £140, compared with the larger proportion of the family holdings in Hoghton £200, Lea £400, and Alston £300. Though by far the largest single landowners in Walton-le-Dale, their share of the total lands there was much more restricted.

In the rental of 1720, 96 tenants are listed at Walton, working an estate of 502 acres, in comparison with 446 acres at Hoghton (38 tenants), 1,124 acres at Withnell (70), and 437 acres (420) at Wheelton. Income from the entire estate had now risen slightly to £2,525 1s. 4d. The Walton estate was reckoned to be worth £564 15s. 8d. a year, with the Walton Hall estate accounting for £300, and the house rents £72 2s. 2d. The salmon fishery was worth £5, and 'A Water Corn Mill, the call when in repair makes Communibus Annis clear money £33'. Efforts were made to increase this income, and a footnote optimistically asserts that 'If all Walton leases be filled up could rais £1,067', and that from the entire estate might be hoisted to £3,643.[2]

The Rentals of 1648 and 1720 are exceptional, and the financial records are similarly restricted to occasional runs in the eighteenth and early nineteenth centuries.[3] Sadly the Hoghton Estate Rent Book of 1662 – George Miller's 'Hoghton Book' – contains little material relevant to Walton, and the Hoghton Estate Survey of 1802 was never completed.[4] A large, if largely uncatalogued collection of Walton land and property deeds has, however, survived from the period 1763–1853. This sheds much light on the early industrial period, and the very complicated affairs of the Hoghton estate at this time. A search through these records is an essential prelude to detailed research on any specific locality within the estate, since house and field names abound in the mass of mortgages and deeds.[5]

The following lease, for example, is fairly representative of this material. It was granted by Sir Henry Hoghton in 1790, to Thomas Moraley, for the lives of William Sherrington aged 11, Thomas Brierley 10, and George Holderness 5, at 5s. per annum:

> That piece of waste ground situate at the Many Brooks … lying on the south side of the turnpike road leading from Preston to Blackburn. In length out the side of the said road in a direct line with Parkinsons South Gate Stubb, to a Necessary adjoining to Mr Livesey's Barn about 56 yards or thereabouts, bounded by Mr Livesey's Meadow on the east, by the Many Brooks Carding Engine Dam on the South east, and leaving a road of 6 yards wide between and Parkinson's garden on the west, containing in the whole 32 perches of land or thereabouts.

The great Walton-le-Dale Tithe Map of 1839 is central to the later sources, which are further expanded by the availability of the first detailed census material from 1841.[6]

The court leet and baron

Many of the functions of the modern local authority can be traced to the officers of the court leet and the parish. The 'Court Leet and Baron of Walton-le-Dale' was presided over by the lord of the manor and had its own annually appointed officials, who served a court comprising the district's prominent residents. The 'Orders' of the court became in effect, a basis of case law for the administration of the manor. Agricultural matters loomed large in its affairs, with frequent orders for the cleaning of ditches and the like, but its remit also extended to areas of 'public health', 'trading standards', and general social behaviour. The court usually met twice a year, and such occasions were in no way 'trials' in the accepted sense. Wrongdoers were simply found and punished. Ominously many charges begin with the words 'For as much as information is given to us …'[7]

The court appointed a wide range of officers to carry out its duties. In August 1672 15 men were appointed jurors. So constituted, the court appointed its officers. John Dudley and George Room were appointed constables, and William Sergeant and Henry Hodgson became ale-testers (upholders of the statutory quality and price of drink). Four apprisers (appraisers) were appointed, whose job it was to value items and payments as required, with two pinders to control stray animals and grazing on Walton Moss and Brownedge Common. Euan Catterall and Richard Atkinson were to be houselookers, officials whose job it was to keep track of strangers, and any newcomers who might become a charge on the parish. The manor was divided into seven 'wards' and two barleymen were appointed for each ward. The wards extended: 'Betwixt Brindle Stoops and Many Brooks – from Tardy Yate to ye towne of Walton and from Lostock Bridge to ye Headless Cross and from there to ye town of Walton – Betwixt Burscough Bridge and Cuerdale Lane – for ye town of Walton – Betwixt Burscough's house and Osbaldeston Cross – betwixt Clayton Green and ye Towne Banke – Betwixt Tardie Meare Yate and Yate field stile'. 'Barleyman' is derived from the Scandinavian 'burlaw', meaning local law, so that a barleyman was an officer charged with upholding the local regulations.

This considerable number of officers were duly sworn in, and then threatened by the jury with fines of 40s. if they failed to carry out their duties to the jurors' liking. Over many years a body of local common law had accumulated from which the court drew its pronouncements. Since the institution had probably existed in some form since Saxon times, this was of great antiquity. In the 1630s efforts were made to codify these practices into the 'Walton Court Leet Orders':[8]

> We the Jury ... Doe Order that ...
>
> Any person ... suffer any woman to be brought in bed of a bastard child within the mannor aforesaid, except that they give good and sufficient bond that neither she nore the child shall be troublesome to the said town, that the owner of the house shall forfeit to the Lord of this Mannor the sum of 20/–. [1631]
>
> Any person ... harbour or Lodge any wandring person or persons, either suspitious Rogues or sturdy beggars, but that they be born in this Mannor (except some old blind impotent or Lame person or some little child) shall for every night so harbouring any forfeit to the Lord of the Mannor the sum of 10/–.
>
> Any person ... did delve or get any matter or soil from ye Lords waste or Common of Walton (except clods, sodds, clay and sands, such as shall be cast out of their ditch or ditches) without the special Lease and Lycense of the Lord of this Mannor upon paine of every one making default as aforesaid to the Lord of this Mannor the sume of 6/8d. [1638]
>
> Any person inhabitting within the said town of Walton or att the Lawe Church yard side do keep more swine but two a piece, or any piggs longer than such time as they shall be twenty weeks old, or do keep them or any of them unringed after they be 10 weeks old they and every of them so making default shall severally forfeit to the Lord of this Mannor the sume of 6/8d.

Any person ... shoote within ye said Mannor of Walton either in a gun or a Crosse bow at any quick marke except they be quallified by the statute or Licensed by the Lord of this Mannor, they and every of them shall severally forfeit to the Lord of this Mannor the sum of 10/–.

In 1672 ten people were detected and fined 'for not selling ye assize of bread and ale according to ye statute'. Thomas Darwin had failed to strengthen the sides of his ditch, he was fined 6s. 8d., and threatened with a fine of 13s. 4d. if the work was not done quickly. John Shawe had assembled a huge dunghill outside his door in Tardy Gate, 'Lying in ye high way'. It was to be removed promptly. Footpaths and rights of way were carefully preserved: 'Wee the jury doe order yt Roger Briers shall laye a sufficient plat or bridge in ye Brooke within his fields leadeing betwixt Houghton Lane and Gregson Lane at or before ye first of November next or forfeit to ye lord of the Manor ye sum of 3s. 4d.' When James Hodgson's animals strayed and were promptly corralled in the pound, he broke in and released them. For this heinous offence, and for defying the officers of the court, he was duly fined £20![9]

Complaints by neighbours could speedily be dealt with. John Barrowes planted a line of plum trees on James Duddell's side of their boundary, he was ordered to remove them. When Cuthbert Holland cleaned his ditch out onto the road, blocking it, he was ordered to remove the rubbish quickly. Some court business was directly related to the lord's interests. In October 1674 Thomas Balshaw was fined 'for not Gryndinge his oats that did grow on ye Lords Land at ye Lord's Mill'. Tenants whose homes became dilapidated were ordered to repair them, orders being made to Ellen Blaco (widow), and Widdow Linlay in 1676.

The court's own officers frequently found themselves threatened: 'We the jury order that the Constables now being shall well and sufficiently repaire or cause to be repaired the rampier at this end of Bamber Bridge (the approach to the bridge) at or before the 24th June next (1675) or forfeit to ye Lord of the Mannor the sume of 6s. 8d.' When the 'Highway leading along Darwin side from Darwin ford towards Walton Hall' was found to be 'Ruinous and in decay', all the people living along the road were ordered to mend it.

Great care was taken in the seventeenth century to exclude any poor outsiders who might become a burden on the parish. Local people who took in the homeless were consistently prosecuted by the court. In 1672 Thomas Johnson was fined 20s. 'For takeinge into his house Ann Toogood, Spinster, as an inmate or insitter contrary to a former order'. Isabell Tasker had taken in George Hall. In future any repetition was to be punished by a weekly fine of 6s. 8d.

The full sequence of manor court records must have contained a great deal of similarly interesting material. Lumly lists earlier rolls dating from 1586–89, and continuing to 1766, which were at that time stored in the de Hoghton estate office. However ,in the course of the present study only a single volume for the years 1672–94 has been located. This is doubly unfortunate as the surviving records of the parish council or vestry are restricted to a single volume, 1703–96. Very narrowly, the two sets of records fail to overlap. It may be that some form of reform of the local administrative system took place at this time, for both bodies seem to have fulfilled similar functions. Over the long term it was to be the parish administration which emerged as the forerunner of the local district council.

The parish

The 'parish church', through its officials, had the right to set parish rates, from which a very basic range of local services could be maintained. Annually two churchwardens were appointed to watch over parish business, two overseers looked after the parish poor, a modicum of law and order was preserved by two constables, and a pair of supervisors mended the roads. Each of these groups levied an annual rate, which was based on the extent, and later the value, of an individual's landholding. The total rates to be levied fluctuated with prices. For example, 1740 was described as 'A very dear year'. In 1777 the churchwarden's rate was 2d. in the pound, the overseer's 6s. 0d. (the 'poor rate'), constable's 6d., and the supervisor's 2d., making a total of 6s. 10d. in the pound. The officers from the various posts were drawn from the estates in the district; these included Gregson Lane (1777), 'George Hilton for his estate' (1782), Brownedge (1777), Shuttlingfields (1785), Toad House (1764, Todd Lane), 'Mr Farington's estate' (1764, Walton Mains), Cinnamon Hill (1779), and Bannister Hall (1784). Occasionally an individual was hired by the nominated estate. Robert Harrison hired himself out in this way as a constable in the 1760s, and in 1729–30 it was found that William Waring had been hired as both of the overseers, and was drawing a salary of £8 per year.[10]

St Saviour's Church, Bamber Bridge, c.1910. From the early nineteenth century the parish was steadily subdivided to take account of the growth of the former hamlets in distant parts of the manor. St Saviour's Church was built in 1836. (R. Burns)

The parish had a workhouse from at least the 1730s. A note in the overseer's accounts for 1731 states that 'The Popish Chappel in Brindle by ye mutuall charge and agreement of Walton [was] converted into a house to Employ ye poor'. In 1742 the overseers of the poor are styled 'Governors of the Poor House'. The workhouse was owned three parts by Walton, and one part by Brindle, and served some 30 townships, who contributed towards the upkeep. In 1740, for example, Samlesbury contributed £3 18s. 11d., Leyland £2 10s. 0d., and Chorley £2 10s. 0d., in order to be 'admitted to ye priveleges of the workhouse'.

By the 1820s the workhouse was located in Station Road, Bamber Bridge, alongside Withy Trees Mill. A solitary, but detailed 'Abstract of the Overseers Accounts' survives for the quarter 1 May to 1 August 1821. During this three-month period, the average number of inhabitants in the house comprised 29 men, 13 women, and 24 children, 66 people in all, and the 'Total expence for victualing each Person per Week, deducting the earnings is ten pence three farthings'. The food bill (£97 8s. 4d.) was dominated by meal (24 loads, £33 8s. 3d.), beef (543lbs, £7 18s. 4d.), milk (3252 quarts, £13 11s. 0d.), soap (178lbs, £4 18s. 7d.), and salt (365lbs, £5 10s. 8d.). Other expenses included coals (£8 9s. 3d.), clogs and shoes (£5 11s. 7d.), Shirts, sheets etc. (£2 14s. 3d.), 'For taking a Population' (the 1821 census) £8, 'coffins and carpenter's work £2 17s. 0d., and 'Doctors for medicines etc. £11 18s. 5d.

The largest elements of the overseers' income of £1,070 6s. 6d., comprised 'Poor Rate collected' £632 5s. 6d.', and 'Fathers of Illegitimate children' £68 1s. 5d. The employment of the house's inmates raised a further £58 19s. 6d. In addition to running the house, the overseers made payments to 'Mothers of Illegitimate Children', which totalled £84 2s. 3d. – almost £25

The old, narrow and high Darwen bridge looking downstream from the corn mill sluices, c.1895. The upkeep of the local roads was an important and expensive duty of the parish officers, but bridge repairs were the responsibility of the county magistrates. (*South Ribble Museum*)

less than they had received from the fathers in the same period. Payments of £200 in the form of 'out-door relief' were also made.[11]

Beyond these fragments, the known surviving parish records are little more than a list of officers, with only occasional additional notes. The constable's records for 1741 record 'There being a Trial at ye assizes of a woman who was supposed to have murdered her child'. References to any improvements made to the local roads proudly appear in the supervisor's entries. In 1740 Church Brow was repaired at a cost of £8, a 'great part of Clayton Brook Lane' was repaired in 1741, and in 1742 Hennell Lane was widened and gravelled. With great pride the entry for 1743 contains the words 'Remains in the purse £4 9s. 7d.'[12]

The Walton-le-Dale Free Grammar School

Bishop Gastrill's *Notitia of the Diocese of Chester* was unable to find any authentic evidence of the foundation of the school, but in his will of 1624, Peter Burscough left the annual interest on £100 towards the payment of the parish schoolmaster. It is generally assumed that the school was held in the church. The Walton-le-Dale Grammar School building was erected in 1672 on land donated by Sir Richard Hoghton, and the financial provision for the master was revised. The site of the new school is interesting, away from the parish church near the centre of the manor, in what subsequently became School Lane, Bamber Bridge. This may indicate that as early as the middle of the seventeenth century the village had begun to lose its demographic predominance.[13]

The *Notitia* found that the parish had the right to appoint six trustees and the schoolmaster. Henry Hoghton held the endowment funds of £181 11s. 0d., whose income was supplemented by smaller grants, and the fees paid by the children. The master 'takes all the children of the town of Walton who apply, and they are taught reading, pay only 4d. a week each ... but for writing and accounts, and for teaching other children to read, he is at liberty to make his own charge'. The school premises comprised 'a good dwelling-house, containing a school room, and a yard and garden adjoining thereto. The premises are occupied by the master rent free'. The Hoghton papers contain a series of receipts for the master's annual payments in the years 1753–90. In 1754, for example, four and a half per cent interest was paid on £285, £12 16s. 6d., to John Lawe.[14]

The master was an important factor in the smooth running of the institution, and problems frequently arose when he left or retired. In July 1810, the *Preston Journal* advertised for a new master. 'Interviews' were to be held in the Unicorn Inn, and it was boasted that an erstwhile candidate might earn up to £100 a year from his enterprise.[15] By this time the affairs of the school, like the workhouse, formed an important element of parish affairs. During the summer of 1834 preparations were made for the retirement of the Rev. J. Greenwood. In July it was agreed 'That the Free

Walton School,
c. 1870. The school
gave its name to
School Lane, which
was previously just
the north end of
Back Lane (Brindle
Road). The school's
location is an
interesting one, for
it is geographically
virtually central to
the manor, perhaps
indicating that as
early as the middle
of the seventeenth
century the
demographic centre
of the district had
shifted south
towards Bamber
Bridge, and away
from the former
population centre
in the shadow of
Walton Law.
(J. Scott)

School and premises in School Lane be forthwith put into repair'. Next the whole management of the school was brought into question, and meetings were held in October 'For the better Regulation of the Free Grammar School', and for the appointment of a committee 'To have power to dismiss the master if they wish'.[16] The retiring master was given a 'pension' of £10 per year, and at the end of the month the post was advertised:[17]

Walton-le-Dale Grammar School.

Wanted; A master for this school, at Christmas next. He will be expected to be well qualified to teach Writing and Accounts, Geography and English Grammar, and to initiate such as the scholars as wish to learn in the principles of the Greek and Latin languages ... The election to take place at Walton Hall, on Tuesday the 23rd of December, when proper persons will examine the candidates.

The following year the new terms of the establishment were announced:[18]

Walton Grammar School:

The Master, Mr Wm Houghton, would respectfully solicit the attention of the inhabitants of Preston and the neighbourhood, to this establishment for classical and commercial education. The terms are

For day boarders, £12 per annum.

The rest of the fees are per quarter;

For instruction in Reading, Writing and Arithmetic, 10s. 6d.

For instruction in Reading, Writing and Arithmetic and the Classics, 15s.
The school will re-open on January 18th.
A quarter's notice is required before the removal of a pupil.
School Lane, near Walton.

By 1857 a 'Girls Dept' had been established, and the master, Robert Bayley, was 'to appoint a mistress to assist him',[19] but the development of the National Schools heralded the end of the old schools at Leyland and Walton. The new National School for the village of Walton was built alongside the church: 'This school was erected by the Protestant Inhabitants of Walton-le-Dale, with help from the National Society, for instruction according to the principles of the Church of England, as now by Law established. Anno Domini MDCCCXXXV [1835]'.[20] The average attendance in 1853 was 163 boys and 84 girls. Both of these institutions survive, as St Aidan's and St Leonard's Junior Schools respectively, though clearly much reformed, and not on their original sites.[21]

With the reform of English local government in the 1830s, 1840s and 1850s, many of the functions of the parish became the basis of the modern system of local government, and only in 1974 with the formation of South Ribble Borough Council did the locality lose its ancient freedom to govern its own affairs.

CHAPTER SEVEN

Industrial revolutions: printers and bleachers

URING the Middle ages the woollen and linen trades became important staples of the economy of mid-Lancashire, with Preston as the natural market for local goods. By the seventeenth century the flax and linen trade came to predominate, and by the end of the eighteenth linens had largely given way to cotton manufacture. In April 1635 Sir Gilbert Hoghton and other local magistrates urged the protection of the local industry. Flax was 'so frequently used in the County of Lancaster, that if it be taken away all the poorer sort of people who live by spinning and weaving of linen clothes only, all yeare long (except in the time of harvest) will be forced to begge'.[1] In 1700 Preston town council petitioned Parliament that 'The making of linencloth hath for many ages been the settled trade of their neighbourhood and is the sole dependence of hundreds of families'.[2]

Walton and district were greatly influenced by developments in the Blackburn textile trade. During the Commonwealth the manufacture of cloths with a linen warp and cotton weft became established, so that the region was well placed to exploit the 'take-off' of cotton as a wonder product in the late eighteenth century. The Blackburn clothiers specialised in the manufacture of blue and white check cloths, or 'Blue bratting'.[3] These found a ready market in aprons, sheets etc., and in the 1670s were so successful that the Preston masters tried to exclude them from their market place. The diarist Ralph Thoresby, passing through the district in 1702, described Walton-le-Dale as 'Famous for the manufacture of linen cloth ... [and saw, probably around Bamber Bridge] ... vast quantities of yarn whiting (or bleaching) in the fields'.[4]

A trade directory of 1818 describes the broad developments in the Blackburn cloth trade; 'The former trade of this town was the manufacture of Blackburn Checks ... this article was afterwards superseded by the Blackburn Greys ... About 40 years ago [1780], another change took place in the manufacture of the town, and in its neighbourhood, when the greys were succeeded by Calicoes'.[5] Up to the mid-nineteenth century, Blackburn connections were fundamental to industrial development along the Darwen valley in Walton, and in the district generally. With the progress of the Preston-based industry, and particularly following the establishment of the Preston Masters Association, the balance passed to the near neighbour to the north of the Ribble.

The impression of a long-established, but steadily developing textile industry emerges clearly from the documentary sources. In 1556 the manor court at Samlesbury sought to regulate the movements of the district's hand spinners: 'We are agreed that no woman shall go abroad into their neighbours houses with the distaves neither by day or night, nor spin by the wayside. For every time, the spinner so doing shall forfeit and pay XII pence'.[6] The Walton coroners' records contain many references to linen weavers, whitsters and whiteners, and witnesses occasionally specifically refer to having been 'fetched from their workhouse'.

The fortunes to be made from the textiles business are well represented in local wills and their inventories. Richard Duddell, a yeoman clothier (1636), had goods worth £101 11s. 8d., with £20 in linen yarn, and Thomas Shorrock 'ffustian weaver' (1639) had goods worth £227 4s. 4d. (linen cloth and yarn £70). Euan Darwen (1669) left goods worth £106 12s. 2d., including yarn and cloth worth almost £30. Alexander Osbaldeston 'Linenwebster' (1639) and George Gregson 'linen weaver' (1682) had respectively £150 and £115. From the middle of the eighteenth century inventories become less common; James Haydock 'whitener' (1768) had goods worth £124. Peter Haydock, a linen weaver (1768) had goods worth almost £250, which included 'In bills, bonds, money ... £140'. John Nowel a chapman or cloth dealer, was able to leave £300 to his brother Alex in Leyland in 1762. Alternatively, Thomas Livesey, a poor linen weaver (1763), left his sons 'the loom they work on when they marry'.[7]

Where the parish registers list the occupations of fathers or bridegrooms the textile interest is all-pervading. Between 1698 and 1708, 14 of the fathers of christened children were 'husbandmen', 8 'yeomen', and 7 'tailors', and 38 described themselves as 'poor' or 'pauper'. Yet 47 were 'weavers', with a further 39 describing themselves specifically as 'linen weavers'. In addition there were 14 'whitsters', 3 'linen websters', and just a single 'woollen

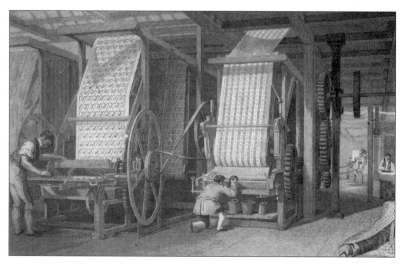

Cloth printing, c.1830. The development of the cloth printing trade was one of the most important developments in the textiles-based industrial revolution. Developments made at Mosney on the south bank of the river Darwen, near Higher Walton, were to be just as significant as the more celebrated spinning endeavours of Preston's Richard Arkwright. The cloth printing trade quickly became an important employer in the district, and was to survive here well into the post-war period.

weaver'. Of the 30 bridegrooms, for example, listed in 1789, 22 of them worked in the textile trade.[8]

The 'industrial revolution' of these years owed much to the intensified and efficient organisation of the industry. The mechanisation and rationalisation of the preparatory and finishing processes were particularly important. From the 1750s these trades begin to be strongly represented in the various sources, but particularly in the Catholic and Anglican parish registers, with significant numbers of 'callico printers', 'print cutters', muslin and calico manufacturers, and ultimately 'cotton manufacturers'. In the early years of the nineteenth century increased mechanisation saw the further development of new trades. Fardinand Kitchen described himself as a 'mekanic' in 1801, and James Melling as a 'macanick' the following year. Anthony Greaves was an early 'mule spinner' in 1806, and John Ditchfield described himself as an 'engenman' in 1811. The early consolidation of the ownership of the industry found local expression in the marriage of Miles Rodgett and Tibby Balshaw. From this date the registers also track the emergence of the pattern of small hamlets which came to form the nucleus of the manufacturing district – Moon's mill (Higher Walton), Bashall's factory (Lostock Hall), and Withy Trees mill (Bamber Bridge).

The lack of detailed census records introduces a great deal of uncertainty into any estimate of the growth of population in the eighteenth century. For example, a report to the Commissioners of Queen Anne's Bounty in 1714 estimated the population of the 'chapelry' to be, 'between 4,000 and 5,000 souls which daily increase by reason of the great manufacture of linen cloth in those parts'.[9] From the first census in 1801 the population of the district rose steadily and consistently from just under 4,000 to 12,000 in 1911. Between 1801 and 1820, the years of the expansion of the handloom weaving trade, the population grew at the rate of 20 per cent between each ten-year census. A period of stagnation in the rate of growth in the 1820s was followed by a renewed burst in the 1830s as powerloom weaving and large steam-powered mills were developed, and a fairly steady expansion up to the 1890s when the rate of growth began to fall markedly. Population trends thus accord very closely with the cycle of growth in the British cotton industry, which for 150 years was thus the engine of economic and social progress in the district.

Mosney

To the Blackburn clothiers, Walton-le-Dale in 'Lower Blackburnshire' offered the advantages of flat land with adjacent water power. The involvement of the Blackburn manufacturers in the development of the local trade is most clearly illustrated by the history of the Mosney print works. Although in operation only from 1780 to 1788 the works were on a considerable scale, and at the forefront of technical progress in the cloth printing

The site of the Mosney works today, left of centre. By the mid-nineteenth century Abram could find little trace of the print works, and the place-name today is applied to a farm which occupies the site. Yet in the 1780s it had been very different, and the great Mosney works was just one of a considerable series of enterprises which made the river Darwen among the most heavily industrialised waterways in the world. (*Author*)

trade. A number of economic historians have contended that the mechanis-ation of this finishing trade was as important as the inventions of Arkwright and his contemporaries in establishing British pre-eminence in the cotton trade. With the closure of the works, the machinery was taken away and the buildings demolished, so that some uncertainty surrounds the precise location of the individual buildings. The place-name 'Mosney' is today restricted to the farm and gardens of that name to the south of the river Darwen, midway between Knot Lane end and Higher Walton. These, it is said, overlie the site of the former works.[10] Up to the eighteenth century, however, 'Mosney' seems to have been applied to a wider area lying to the north of School Lane between the end of Brindle Road and the top of Kittlingbourne. The estate of John Charnley of Mosney, a prosperous yeoman who died in 1759 leaving goods worth £139 17s. 4d., included 'fields bought along the School Lane', and 'Charnley Fold' seems to have been the name applied to the higher part of Mosney on the plateau edge, whilst 'New Mosney' seems to have been the name applied to the valley floor along the Darwen. Here both the Mosney works, and the later farm of that name were located.[11]

The distinction between old and new Mosney is made in a deed of sale from 1791: 'William Charnley, Cotton Dealer and Chapman, a Bankrupt. Sale by his assignees (Robert Ainscough and Richard Mcaulay of Black-burn, cotton manufacturers)' to Henry Suddell 'All that messuage and tenement commonly called or known by the name of Old Mosney or Holland Fold otherwise Charnley Fold, consisting of a farm house, a barn, stable, shippon and other outhouses together with an orchard and 8½ acres of meadow and pasture lands ... and an acre of woodland, now or late in the possession of William Charnley and William Hunt ... also 10 cottages situated in the fold ... and also another farm or tenement called New Mosney adjoining to the first mentioned estate'. The estate had 'been part of that of John Livesey of Blackburn, John Hargreave of Manchester, Peter

Anstie and Joseph Smith both of the City of London, and William Hall of Mosney within Walton-le-Dale ... Merchants, Callico Printers and Partners (Bankrupts)'. A deed of 1796 draws a similar distinction.[12]

William Yates's map of 1786 clearly locates the works on a watermill alongside the river Darwen. A watermill shown by him at Manybrooks to the east is probably the 'carding engine dam' described in a deed of 1790, and subsequently became the site of the iron works.[13] Writing in the second half of the nineteenth century, Abram recorded that 'The only vestiges now to be seen of the once extensive arrangements for calico printing at this spot are a portion of an old wall, and remains of the brick culvert constructed for turning the water used into the river Darwen'.[14]

Thomas Livesey (1734–90) was a Blackburn merchant, and the cellar of his house in King Street was 'a warehouse for the reception of the calico pieces in which he traded'.[15] One of the senior partners in the Mosney enterprise, he inherited a very considerable landed fortune, which despite the eventual failure of the concern was passed on to his son Joseph (who is not to be confused with his contemporary, the great social reformer). Joseph Livesey's estate in the district was second only to that of the Hoghtons, and included the valuable Bannister Hall print works, and the site of Higher Walton mill. Thomas Livesey's cloth printing interests were centred on Mosney, and around 1780 a firm styling itself 'Livesey, Hargreave, Anstie, Smith and Hall' was established here. *Bailey's Northern Directory* of 1781 lists the firm as 'Livesey and Co, Calico Printers, Nr. Preston'. Mr Anstie lived for a time at Knott House, before the house was taken over by Thomas Livesey, and Mr Hall resided at Darwen Bank. Both properties long continued to have important textile connections: Knott House became the home of Edmund Calvert; and Darwen Bank that of Miles Rodgett.

John Graham's manuscript account of the printing industry written in the nineteenth century describes the scale of the premises: 'Mosney, near Preston, on the river Darwen, was a corn mill, began printing about 1776 by Mere and Croft who gave up soon afterwards. Smith, Hall and Co. built large and substantial buildings capable of doing a large trade. Continued to extend until they employed all the country – were large-scale manufacturers as well as printers, bought the estate as well as several others ... The Mosney company had about 150 tables – about 40 of their printers were females. The Printer's Union had scarcely commenced, they were under no restraint. They had the first surface machines, four in number, and had a great many female pencillers'.[16] The Walton parish register lists the burial of 'Wm son of Wm Croft, Callico Printer. 7 Oct. 1779'. Further detail is given by O'Brien in his *Treatise on Calico Printing* published in 1792: 'It is said this place was a means of giving bread to near 20,000 persons; cloth in whitstering has occupied ground 12 miles in length; near 300 tables have been employed, and near 40 coppers at work at one time; 600 or 700 cylinders have been cut or pinned; common prints etc., innumerable'.[17]

The firm was an early example of a vertically integrated concern: 'They had factories at Mosney and Bannister Hall near Preston, bleaching grounds at Hoghton Tower, a coalpit at Standish, and a house, offices, warehouse and factory at Manchester, a mill at Clitheroe and a London warehouse'.[18] Chapman revised the workforce figure down to about 800 (1784), though this would not include domestic workers, particularly handloom weavers, so that perhaps 200 were employed directly at Walton. The reference to Bannister Hall and Hoghton Tower (Hoghton Bottoms?) suggests that the firm had other sites locally which survived the crash of the firm. The company's London partners, Peter Anstie and Joseph Smith, were an important link, for it has been suggested that many of the firm's journeymen printers came up from London, 'holding the Lancashire men in great contempt'.[19] With the collapse these skilled men became spread throughout the developing industry in Lancashire. Some stayed on locally, probably at Bannister Hall, for the parish register lists the burials of 'Isaac Thomas Calico Printer from Hampshire, 12 July 1791' and 'James Wyatt Calico Printer from Hampshire, 28 November 1797'.

The technical innovations made at Mosney were crucial to the development of the entire industry, and established British pre-eminence in the printed cloth trade. Modern cylinder-machine printing was developed here, and to a large extent replaced hand printing by blocks in the bulk trade. Thomas Bell, an engraver, was brought by the firm from Scotland, patenting his process in November 1783: 'Thomas Bell, of Mosney, in the County of Lancaster, copper plate printer ... A new and peculiar art or method of Printing with one colour or with various colours at the same time, on linens ... cottons ... woollen cloths ... silks, and any other species or kind of linen cloth, or manufactured goods whatever'.[20] This was a six-colour cylinder printing machine, and Bell's invention was attested by William Waterhouse of Mosney, gentleman, and John Emmett of Preston, cabinet maker. A number of improvements were subsequently patented. In 1785 John Slater of Mosney, calico printer, patented a press 'For printing 1–2–3 or more colours on cotton etc.'. This document, bearing the Great Seal of Scotland can be seen in the Lancashire Record Office, Preston.[21]

The skilled printers, earning good wages of over a guinea a week, were very wary of damaging the London trade. The cost of labour, their control over the process, and the introduction of mechanical printing, were probably all at the root of the great 'Mosney Strike' of 1786. This lasted for 3 months, and though support from printers at other works did not last, the works was brought to a standstill.[22]

The company's collapse in 1788 closed the Mosney works for ever. A slump in the textile industry after the American War of Independence was followed by rapid expansion, and capital became fully extended. To fund expansion a number of firms began to issue bills or 'bearer notes', which were exchanged like modern bank notes. John Graham wrote that the Mosney firm 'were bankers, issued their own notes, made them to meet

The Mosney Works Bill of Exchange, 1787. The firm's failure was due in large part to the over-issue of its bills, which were used in a similar way to bank notes. The collapse of Livesey, Hargreaves & Co. was a major setback to the trade of the Preston area, throwing a large number of workpeople out of employment. The crash of John Watson & Co. in 1807 had similarly disastrous effects. *(Courtesy of C. Aspin)*

various purposes. If a weaver brought in a piece that was 2*s*. 6*d*. for weaving, he received a note for 2*s*. 6*d*. value and so on ... Their notes were received with great eagerness – they were the circulating medium of the country in and around Preston – men of all trades and calling had them in possession'. To raise capital, bills were drawn in non-existent persons, and the resulting collapse of the firm, which had been rumoured for some time, was a staggering blow to the area, akin to the collapse of Calverts in the 1930s, and the closure of A. S. Orrs in 1979.[23]

The failure of Livesey, Hargreave & Co. brought down many firms holding their worthless bills. Confidence in the banking system, and in paper money, was severely shaken. A 'Country Banker' wrote in 1793, 'The failures of 1788, and the losses the public sustained, by the rash and wicked proceedings of these banking Bankrupts will not soon be forgotten ... The amazing quantity of five guinea notes in circulation drawn by an infamous speculative house in Manchester, when this failed in 1788, together with paper of theirs payable to fictitious names, to an immense amount, and the attendant failures amongst these connections, was astonishing'.[24]

Despite this setback, the Livesey family fortune seems to have survived more or less intact, and calico printing continued to prosper at Bannister Hall.

The Bannister Hall Print Works

From the records of the Mosney concern the extent of the works upstream on the Darwen at Bannister Hall in the 1780s is unclear. Yet the site had many advantages over Mosney, where the fall on the river is only slight and the race shown by Yates on the Darwen is only a short one. By contrast, as early as 1786 the Bannister Hall works took water from the natural falls at Red Rocks, a considerable distance upstream, beyond Coupe Green. The potential water power available was thus much greater. The works was operated after 1788 by a bewildering variety of partners, which from the early 1800s came to be dominated by Charles Swainson. John Swainson (1746–1800) was a putter-out, and one of the pioneer Preston mill owners, establishing a factory there in 1790. He also had an interest in the early cotton factory at Kittlingbourne. Of his sons, Charles (1780–1866), Anthony (1782–1865) and John (1784–1867) followed him in the trade, and became partners of the Birleys of Kirkham. His daughters, Mary (1778–1819) and Elizabeth (1786–1836), married William and Edmund Birley respectively.

The Higher Walton concern was thus only one element of Charles Swainson's business activities, which culminated in the construction of the 'Big Factory' at Fishwick in the 1830s by the great firm of Swainson, Birley and Co. By 1818 Charles Swainson was resident at Cooper Hill, one of the township's most exclusive addresses. Alone of the Preston Cotton Lords, Swainson stood for Parliament in 1841, but failed to win election. The Harris Museum preserves one of the election banners, 'Parker and Swainson for ever. Down with the Whigs and Justice to the Poor'. A weak heart forced him to retire from the business at the age of 66 in 1846. His obituary in the *Preston Chronicle* described him as 'A friend and benefactor of the poor' (28 April 1866). He was a firm supporter of the Temperance movement, and presented all Walton's total-abstainers with a silk handkerchief in 1834. He was known by his family as 'Old Blowaway', and a descendant recalled an occasion when on entering the children's nursery at Cooper Hill he found one child eating porridge, one fish, one eggs, and so on. Finding this unacceptable, he proceeded to empty all the food into a single bowl, and made the children eat the mixture. Thus were habits of thrift inculcated among the rising generation of factory masters and their wives.[25]

A collection of Swainson partnership papers in the Lancashire Record Office traces Charles Swainson's involvement in the Bannister Hall works from the start of his career. In 1803, described as 'Charles Swainson of Walton, Calico Printer', he obtained a lease, in partnership with his brother John 'of Preston Cotton Manufacturer', and Richard Jackson, of a warehouse 'lately erected' at the foot of Church Brow. In 1809 his partnership with Jackson 'of Sloane Street, Chelsea' and John Stephenson of Walton, all calico printers, was dissolved, and he bought out their shares for £12,000.[26]

In January 1811 a new partnership was drawn up which was to be the basis of the long-term prosperity of the works: 'Deed of co-partnership for 5 years (1) Charles Swainson of Walton, calico printer, (2) Joseph Baxendale of Walton, calico printer, (3) Anthony Swainson of Liverpool, merchant, and (4) John Stephenson of Walton, calico printer … the trades of cotton spinner, cotton manufacturer and machine maker to be carried on by CS at Preston, and the trade of merchant and broker to be carried on by AS at Liverpool, the business to be carried on at their present works at Walton-le-Dale'. This was subsequently renewed, Richard Geill joining the partnership in 1815. The enterprise closely mirrors the structure of the old Mosney concern, and by the 1820s it was trading as 'Charles Swainson and Co., Calico Printers, Bannister Hall'.[27]

Occasional references to the works occur in the early Preston news-papers. In January 1808 the *Preston Journal* reported that the watchman's arm had been blown off by the explosion of his blunderbuss 'as he fired it off at the usual hour', and in February the company offered a dozen apprenticeships 'For the calico print business, apply Jackson, Stephenson and Swainson, Bannister Hall – None will be taken under 14 years of age'.[28] Thefts from the extensive bleaching grounds along the Darwen were fre-quently reported. Remarkably, the Victoria and Albert Museum possesses a collection of Bannister Hall printed fabrics from the early years of the century. This includes a set of block prints of exotic birds, which were clearly intended for use as luxurious and fashionable house furnishings. The quality of the firm's output was thus extremely high.[29]

A number of surveys and rentals list the land holdings which comprised the print works estate. In 1821 the Swainson holding comprised 'Bannister Hall farm £63 3s. 6d., Carver Bridge £74 6s. 2d., late Cooper £22 14s. 5d., the Works (with power) £125 15s. 0d., and 'Miss Cooper's 4 cottages'.[30] The Tithe Map contains a detailed plan and inventory of the works. This reveals the complex series of waterways and reservoirs along the Darwen which fed the works, and passed on to power the cotton factory at Higher Walton. The most spectacular of the reservoirs, within the bend of the Darwen, can still be seen from the higher ground to the south of the river upstream of the works, and the old waterway (later replaced by a pipe) can still be followed down from Red Rocks. Of particular interest is the 'Bleaching Ground' downstream of the works, which survive as pasture land attached to Bannister Hall Farm. Here the great lengths of cloth – the pieces – were laid out in lines to bleach naturally in the sunlight. The estate covered nearly 85 acres. A survey of 1848 valued the crofts, bleaching

F. A. Gatty's Bannister Hall print works, 1925. The works at Bannister Hall were begun by Livesey, Hargreaves & Co. Surviving the crash of that firm, they were operated very successfully by John Swainson & Co. and subsequently by Gattys. The patent for khaki dyes served the firm well through the Boer War and the two world wars, and the works operated into the 1960s. The nineteenth-century census returns list a large number of print workers and dyers as resident in the Higher Walton area.

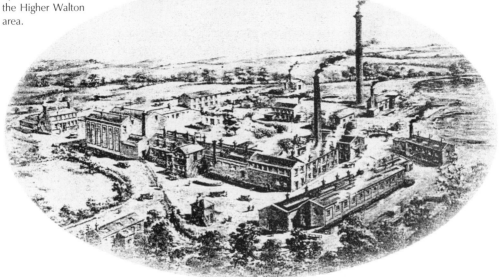

grounds, and printing works, at £427 6s. od. a year, of which the works alone accounted for £250.[31]

By the late 1860s, following Swainson's death, the works were taken over by Thomas Clarkson, and 'Thomas Clarkson and Co., Bannister Hall Printworks', are listed in the 1882 trade directory. By 1910 the concern had been acquired by F. A. Gatty and Co., of Church, near Accrington, whose long-term success well into the twentieth century was based on their patent khaki dye and the two world wars.

The Claytons of Bamber Bridge and Lostock Hall

Nineteenth-century writers firmly placed the establishment of the Lancashire bleaching and printing trade at Bamber Bridge. 'The trade was established in Lancashire in 1764 by Messrs Clayton of Bamber Bridge, near Preston; the cloth that was printed being made with linen warp and cotton weft, and produced locally at Bamber Bridge'. However, an entry in the parish register records a baptism on '1 July 1753. Frances d. of Edmund Cleaton printer and Frances his wife'. The works were actually located along the bank of the river Lostock in Cuerden. The Cuerden Tithe Map provides a clear illustration of both their size and complexity. Water was drawn off the river upstream of 'Bamber' bridge opposite the Hob Inn, and was directed into a series of reservoirs and tanks. According to Abram, Edward Clayton's sons John and George developed the art of calico printing (linens and calicoes) and 'For some years had no rivals'.[32] The use of acids in the industrial process gradually began to replace natural bleaching through sunlight, and it seems likely that the family pioneered the new technology. Walton was thus clearly at the forefront of the finishing trades in the first phase of the industrial revolution, with the works at Bamber Bridge, Mosney and Bannister Hall – though only the latter prospered into the twentieth century.

Edward Clayton is described as living at Lostock Hall, which seems to have been the family home for the following half century. George Clayton's first wife died in 1782; he married his second wife Dolly at the parish church in 1784; and he died in 1829, aged 85. Dolly Clayton kept diaries for many years (1777–1833), and most of these can be seen in the Lancashire Record Office, Small and written in a very cramped hand, they mostly relate to her social activities and letters. Only rarely did George's activities 'at the works' merit her attention. As a bleacher, cotton spinner and backer of the Bamber Bridge Tramway, these however were considerable.[33]

In 1792 John, George, and William Clayton took out fire insurance for their premises in the very large sum of £6,800.[34] The partnership was changed to accommodate Ralph Clayton, and to allow George to specialise in cotton spinning at Lostock Hall. In 1816 the firm was styled 'R. J. and E. Clayton, Calico Printers, Bamber Bridge', becoming 'Ralph Clayton, Bleacher, Cuerden', by 1825. Theft of cloth from their print grounds was a constant problem. In July 1802 the *Manchester Mercury* reported 'croft breaking at Bamber Bridge', and listed the thefts from the partners' premises. In May 1811 the *Preston Journal* reported that James Dagger, John and Richard Forest were 'charged with having stolen 44 pieces of calico in the bleaching grounds of R. Clayton and Co. at Cuerden'.[35]

The works continued to be operated by the family until the death of Ralph Clayton. They were sold in 1836; 'Extensive and Valuable Bleach Works ... All those valuable bleach works, buildings, and premises, lately occupied by Mr Ralph Clayton, deceased, and situate at Cuerden, in the Co. of Lancaster, 4 miles from Preston, 6 from Chorley, and only half a mile from the line of the North Union railway, comprising an excellent steam engine of 50 hp, water wheels, reservoirs, drying cylinders, hydraulic presses, beetles, callenders, cisterns, mangles and other machinery suitable for carrying on the business of a bleacher on a considerable scale, together with 14 foot fall of the River Lostock, 3 cottages, stable, garden and orchard, and 23ac. 3r. 12p. of land, statute measure. The reservoirs are capacious, and capable of supplying abundance of pure and clear water at all seasons'.[36]

Turnpikes and the tramroad

The development of industry placed heavy strains on the local transport system. A new Ribble bridge, 90 yards upstream from the ancient crossing, was completed in 1781. The incised inscription can still be seen in the wall at the south-east end: 'Built by John, Samuel and Robert Laws in 1779–80–81 under the inspection of Mr Richard Threlfall. Cost £4,200'. Work to widen this bridge began in 1939 and was completed in 1950. This in effect added a second structure to the downstream side of the eighteenth-century bridge. The remains of the timber supports used in its construction can still be seen in the river at low water. The Darwen bridge was rebuilt

Church Brow, on the former Preston and Blackburn turnpike road, c. 1904. The greatly increased volume of road traffic between the towns led to the construction of the 'New Road' between Walton Corner and the foot of Knot Lane. This removed the need to ascend and descend Church Brow. Accidental collisions between fully laden wagons of cotton bales were a not infrequent event here, and in addition traffic had to negotiate Burscough Bridge, and pass through the toll gate which had been located in the foreground of this view. The new toll gate was located at the bottom of Knot Lane. (R. Burns)

in 1752. This rather eccentric, high-arched, humped structure, was in turn rebuilt and widened in 1901.[37]

The main roads were turnpiked in the eighteenth century. The Blackburn and Burscough Bridge Turnpike Trust (later renamed the 'Blackburn and Walton Cop'), operated from Burscough Bridge at the foot of Church Brow, to Blackburn, and the Preston and Wigan Turnpike Trust operated along the route of the present day A6/A49 through the district. Changes to the line of the former were to have important implications for the evolving plan of Walton village.

At the first meeting of the Blackburn Road trust in Preston town hall on 14 June 1755, it was ordered 'that two gates or turnpikes shall be erected, one betwixt Burscough Bridge ... and the place near Walton church where the roads leading to Blackburn and Mellor ... do divide [at the top of Knot Lane] – as near as may be to Burscough Bridge – and the other betwixt Moulding Water Smithy and the finger post leading to Chorley'. A further turnpike was to be constructed 'on the Cuerdale–Fishwick ford'. John Calvert was to be treasurer, and Thomas Garlick the surveyor on wages of £20 per year. They had to lodge sureties of £1,000 and £500 respectively. Richard Simpson was appointed toll collector at Burscough bridge with a wage of £20, and sureties of £100.[38]

In 1767 it was decreed that no wagon with wheels less than nine inches wide was to use the road. Loads of crops *en route* to Walton corn mill were to pass free of toll at this gate, which was located just below the Red Lion on the Church Brow. The gate was so narrow that wagons could not pass. 'Several injuries haveing been done to peoples property especially to Cotton Baggs being very much torn', the gate was moved in 1775. In 1783 the

Nos 43–45–47 Chorley Road, the new Darwen bridge, and the Unicorn Inn, c. 1910. The improvement of the road system was to have a tremendous impact on the geography of the district in the twentieth century. Both the Ribble and Darwen bridges were extensively remodelled, and a number of the buildings which literally protruded into the road were demolished. The Unicorn Inn narrowly escaped this fate on a number of occasions, though a section of the building was removed in the 1960s. (R. Burns)

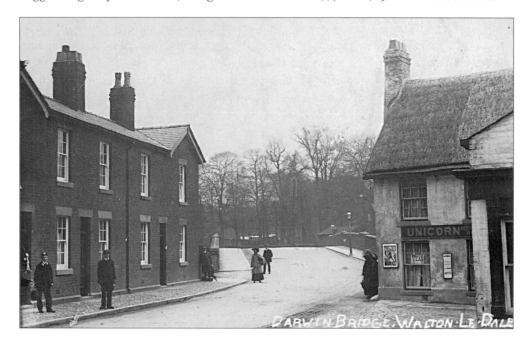

steep and narrow road was ordered to be widened by cutting down the hedges. In 1792 it was decided to divert the road, since the existing route was 'narrow and cannot conveniently be enlarged and made commodious for travellors without diverting and turning the same'. In 1809 consent to construct the direct route from Walton corner to the foot of Knot Lane was obtained – over the town field, the old mill stream, and through the pleasure grounds of Cooper Hill – and the toll house was subsquently moved to Knot Lane end.[39]

The company's servants were frequently accused of misappropriating its funds, and it became the practice to contract out their collection. In 1764 Henry Livesey of Hoghton was allowed this 'franchise' for £262 per year. By 1771 this figure had risen satisfactorily to £361. The road users often tried to avoid paying the tolls, and in 1756 William Grove was accused of claiming exemption on the grounds that he was taking his corn to the mill, when in fact he was on his way to market. In July 1778 Richard Ratcliffe succumbed to road rage at the Moulding Water toll, and smashed the gate to pieces.[40] The gate at School Lane End in Bamber Bridge, on the Preston and Wigan road, was moved to Hennel Lane End in 1856, and the Knot Lane gate was finally removed about 1870.[41]

With the extensive growth of the textile industry in the 1780s it was felt to be essential that Lancaster and Preston be linked to the canal network. Plans for the canal had been drawn up as early as 1760, but the Lancaster Canal Act was not obtained until 1792. The main engineering problems concerned the Lune and Ribble crossings. By 1797 the 'North End' from Tewitfield to Preston had been completed, but John Rennie's wonderful Lune viaduct – 600 feet long over five semi-circular arches – had cost £48,321. Rennie proposed a similarly spectacular crossing of the Ribble. The canal was to descend 222 feet from Clayton Green through 32 locks, to an embankment across the valley floor at Walton, and on to a viaduct over three arches of 116' each. The towpath was to be 57 feet above the low water mark. Work on the 14-mile 'South End' from Walton Summit to Wigan was slowed by the difficulties with the 259' long Whittle Hills tunnel, and Rennie's estimate of £95,000 for the Ribble crossing led the company to opt for a temporary tram plateway.[42]

A double line of tram plates, each one yard long, was laid over stones $24 \times 12 \times 8''$, obtained at a cost of 5d. each. The line was five miles long, and ran north from the canal terminus at Walton Summit to the embankment over the valley floor, onto the wooden tram bridge, up the Avenham incline and along to the canal wharves behind the Corn Exchange in Preston. The way had three stationary steam engines to assist the lines of $6 \times 4 \times 2$ 'trams', by 'endless chains' up the steep inclines, particularly at Avenham and the Summit. A 'Machine House' was built at Lime Kiln Cottage on Todd Lane; goods sidings were located where the line crossed Station Road in Bamber Bridge, and small-scale port facilities were developed at the Summit.

On 1 June 1803 a boat loaded with coal navigated the Whittle Hills tunnel and discharged its cargo at the Summit. Thereafter the fuel's progress was a triumphant one matched only by the arrival of cotton at the end of the 'Cotton Famine' sixty years later:[43]

> 27 wagons were loaded, each containing about one ton, and were drawn by one horse a mile and a half along the rail road, to the works of Messrs Clayton at Bamber Bridge. The wagons extended nearly 100 yards in length ... George Clayton Esq. of Lostock Hall, rode upon the first wagon, and the tops of the others were fully occupied ... news spread quickly ... Old and young left their habitations and employments to witness a sight so novel, and before the boat reached her discharging place she was completely crowded with passengers, who anxiously rushed into her at every bridge. Whilst the wagons were loading, the crowd kept increasing, and the report of the day brought an adjoining 'village band', who with their music and colour preceded the wagons along the road, amidst the acclamations of hundreds. The workmen were regaled with ale at Bamber Bridge, and amongst the toasts of the party were given; 'The Glorious First of June', The Memory of Lord Howe', and 'The Health of the Surviving Heroes of that Memorable day.

Old barges at Walton Summit, c.1900. With the development of the railway system, the Bamber Bridge tramway passed out of use. The terminus at the summit, located in the beautiful countryside between Bamber Bridge and Brindle survived into the 1970s, when it was swept away during the development of the Walton Summit industrial estate. (*South Ribble Museum*)

The effect on the company's revenues was instantly marked, income rising from £4,332 in 1803, to £12,467 in 1807, and £15,550 in 1811.[44] The 'South End' was particularly important in serving the Preston and Walton mills, in reducing their fuel costs, and so offsetting the disadvantage of their non-coalfield location. The coal yards at Bamber Bridge were quite extensive,

Sailing boats on the river Ribble, c.1912. Beyond the bridge of the East Lancashire railway can be seen the old timber tram bridge. A key link in a tramway system which linked the ends of the Lancaster Canal at the Preston basin with the Leeds and Liverpool Canal at Walton Summit, the rebuilt bridge and a good length of the line survive as one of the most interesting relics of the industrial archaeology of the district. Although conceived as a temporary expedient, it proved extremely profitable, and the Preston & Lancaster Canal was able to buy out its rail rival. The name of one of its early and most successful entrepreneurs, Mr Mackenzie, survives in the name of a Bamber Bridge public house. (R. Burns)

and their operator Mr McKenzie (whose inn alongside the line still survives under his name) was an important supplier of coal to Horrockses mills in Preston. Sales worth £137 were made in March 1803, rising to £314 in June, and £296 in September after completion of the link. In the years 1805–8 his sales to the firm averaged around £700 a year.[45] In November 1810, the *Preston Journal* advertised: 'To be let by ticket; New erected building for a smithy (4 hearths) and wheelwrights shop adjoining. By the tramway and the Preston–Chorley road, where the rail road crosses. Apply to Cuthbert Mc Kenzie, Timber Merchant, Bamber Bridge'.

The 1821–22 poor rate valuation lists:[46]

Mr McKenzies house £20 13s. 4d.
Lime kilns [on Todd Lane?] £17 0s. 4d.
Wheelwrights shop and ten cottages £27 13s. 4d.
Coal Yard and Machine [for weighing?] £10 13s. 4d.
Land £1 10s. 11d.

After 1837 the line was owned by railway companies, who worked it until 1859. In 1868 the iron plates were taken up north of Bamber Bridge, and the Avenham engine house was demolished. The link from the Summit to Bamber Bridge continued to be used for coal deliveries until 1879. The last driver on the line, still alive in 1882, recalled riding twice a day from Preston to the Summit, and needing to have his clogs resoled every week! In his career it was estimated that he had travelled 199,000 miles on the line. The failure to preserve the line as a public footpath and heritage trail is much to be regretted. Up to the 1960s most of the line could still be easily followed, and many of the stone sleepers were still in place. The timber bridge was replaced by a structure of similar design in concrete in the mid-1960s, but the terminus at the Summit was completely emasculated by the development of the Clayton Brook industrial park by the Central Lancashire New Town Corporation. A section of the track, found to be largely intact alongside the McKenzies Inn on Station Road, is preserved in Worden Park, Leyland, and plates and stone sleepers can be seen in Leyland Museum. The Harris Museum, Preston, has the remains of a tram recovered from the bed of the Ribble, where it had long lain following a failure of the endless chain on the Avenham incline.

CHAPTER EIGHT

The first cotton mills

HE COMMERCIAL EXPLOITATION of the mechanisation of the spinning process, achieved by 1780, required a constant supply of cheap labour and cheap power. This was most optimally met by the employment of orphan labour, and the development of water mill sites. The extent of child employment in the local mills is revealed in evidence given to the Select Committee on the State of Children Employed in the Manufactories of the United Kingdom, 1816:[1]

	Weekly wage	Children's ages				Total
		−8	8−10	10−18	18+	
Penwortham Factory	2s. 8d.	3	10	44	59	144
Moon Mill	2s. 7d.	5	10	44	26	85
Cuerden Mill	2s. 6d.	16	69	60	153	
Lostock Factory	3s. 1d.	15	72	38	127	
Roach Factory	3s. 3d.	7	36	56	100	

Water mill sites were developed along the rivers Darwen and Lostock, close-by the north and south boundaries of the manor. The first Walton mills thus conform closely to the classical model of early cotton mill location and operation, and provide an informative case study.

'Wat's Apprentices': Roach Mill and Penwortham Factory

In the Walton district John Watson, pioneer of the factory movement in Preston, was able to develop two sites successfully, at Roach on the River Darwen, and at Penwortham Factory, in Factory Lane, near Middleforth Green (now Vernons and Co.). Both mills exploited orphan labour. The Roach site tapped the fall of the Darwen, as it cuts deeply into the rock strata, from around the back of Hoghton Tower down to Higher Walton. The river's incision into the soft underlying rock strata is best seen downstream of the mill at Samlesbury Bottoms.

The mill at Roach was started in 1784, and was insured eight years later by 'John Watson jnr. of Preston, Cotton Manufacturer'. The Sun policy covered the building for £1,000, and the machinery for a further £1,000. Two years later insurance for the 'Cotton water mill at Roach in Samlesbury' was increased to £1,200, with cover for the machinery at £1,000, stock £500, and houses £300. A further policy was taken out with the Phoenix company for £5,000. In November 1801 the factory was destroyed

Roach Bridge Paper Mill, Samlesbury, 1997. Established by John Watson in the 1780s, Roach Mill was one of the earliest factories in the region. Historian Chris Aspin has suggested that Richard Arkwright's machinery was installed here at an early date.
(R. Burns)

by fire.[2] In 1790 John Watson applied for permission to build a gallery at Samlesbury Church to accommodate the large number of 'workhouse orphans' he employed; 'Faculty – Wm Bishop of Chester to John Watson, the younger of Preston, cotton manufacturer – to erect a gallery, eighteen and a half feet by eleven feet, with forms and a staircase to lead between the two pillars at the west end of the chapel of Samlesbury'.[3] The apprentices seem to have been housed together in the growing community around the mill, for in 1805 the *Blackburn Mail* advertised, 'Roach Mill; Middle aged man and wife wanted to manage apprentices. Also a steady man of good character to take management of a shop for groceries and who understands the markets'.[4]

In 1807 the Watson empire collapsed. The apprentices were turned out at Penwortham and probably also at Roach. The mills and Watson's house and possessions were sold. The following year John Watson was a debtor in Lancaster Castle. He died in London in 1813, 'formerly a very eminent manufacturer in Preston'. His estate was valued at less than £20.[5] The sale of the Roach factory was advertised in 1808. The premises comprised a six storey mill with twist rooms at the north end of the factory five storeys high, and a number of cottages. This was clearly quite a large country mill, much larger than the paper works on the site today, though the very impressive waterfall survives. Significantly, the operators of the mill are described as 'Watson & Sharrock', and William Sharrock continued to run the mill well into the 1830s.[6]

In 1833 Sharrock gave evidence to the Factory Commission. He described himself as a Mule Spinner 'of Roach Mill in Samlesbury'. The works was powered by a waterwheel of 25hp, and manufacturing depended on the steady flow of the river. Most of the workpeople lived within 100 yards of the mill, in his 22 houses, 'and if not cleanly are discharged'. Sharrock claimed that no children under nine were employed, and that the mill worked 12 hours per day, and just nine on a Saturday, except when time 'had to be made up' due to 'accidents to our water wheels … and when we have lost time through a deficiency of water'. In the twelve months of 1832 the factory had worked for 310 days, 7 hours. A half hour was allowed for breakfast and an hour for dinner, during which the entire workforce left the factory. He opposed the shortening of the hours of work, which could not be achieved 'without incurring great loss to myself in respect of capital rendered unproductive, and to the workpeople in a deduction of their wages by reason of their having performed less work'. No corporal punishment was inflicted on the children, who, he claimed, were reprimanded and then dismissed. The mill had no long serving hands, 'owing to a turnout some time ago'.[7] The extreme violence associated with this turn-out is described in a subsequent section.

A cotton mill run by 'Smith, Slater and Co. Cotton Twisters' existed upstream at Samlesbury Bottoms as early as 1784. This mill was destroyed by fire in 1819, and the following year John H. Dall took over the small water-driven spinning factory. In 1834 Dall moved on to Roach. Samlesbury

Penwortham Factory or 'The White Factory' (subsequently 'Vernons'), Factory Lane, 1997. Greatly extended and still in production, the site was originally operated by Watson in conjunction with Roach Mill and his Preston interests. He employed large numbers of orphaned children who were housed in the nearby workhouse. The Royal Commission investigating the employment of children in the mills later reported that with the collapse of his business empire in 1807 they, along with their fellows at Samlesbury, were literally turned out into the fields and hedgerows to find their way home as best they could. The early development of the factory system in the district thus owed as much to child labour and the workhouse system, as it did to the great inventions. (Author)

Bottoms Mill was destroyed again by fires in 1856 and 1857, rebuilt and run by James Parker, until a fire in 1861 threw 120 hands out of work and caused £20,000 of damage. By 1869 the mill was running again, and by the end of cotton spinning here in 1873, was operating 16,000 spindles. The site was then redeveloped as a paper mill.[8]

John Watson's second local mill south of the Ribble, 'Penwortham factory', lies just within the Walton boundary near Middleforth Green. Whilst John Horrocks's first mill in Dale Street, Preston, was known as the Yellow Factory on account of its faded whitewash, Penwortham factory was always the White Factory. It was located on a small stream which later fed an enormous reservoir – 'Vernons Lodge'. Many of the workforce came from Penwortham workhouse, a short distance along factory Lane. A datestone here states that 'This workhouse was erected by permission of William ffarington Esq. Lord of the Manor, in the year 1796'. Whether this building replaced earlier accommodation is uncertain, for the factory may have existed before 1791. Watson obtained children from workhouses and from local parishes, and these are stated to have been 'housed in a building at Penwortham'.[9]

Joseph Livesey later recalled with some horror the appearance of these poor children: 'Every Sunday, 'Watson's Apprentices' as they were called, attended Walton Church. They were workers in the cotton mill known as Penwortham factory, and came in order, under suitable superintendence, wearing a uniform of brown coats, with cuffs and collars of yellow. It was said they were obtained from a foundling hospital in London. Many of them were crooked-legged, becoming deformed with having to stop the machinery by placing their knees next to it'.[10]

The 1816 Select Committee explored the conditions in the rural mills more remote from Preston in particular detail. Joseph Dutton's evidence drew heavily on the testimony given to him by Mr Tomlinson, a Preston surgeon. Tomlinson had attended the Penwortham mill 'four or five times a week when in the possession of Mr Watson'. He found 'That the children were in a wretched condition from being overworked; a great number of them had crooked legs; that they used to work night and day; that he had seen children sleeping over their supper, who were to go to work in about ten minutes for the whole night, owing to their having got up so early in the day, and tired themselves'. Most specifically and shockingly, Tomlinson 'recollected very well the circumstance of the parish apprentices from Mr Watson's factory ... when he failed, having been turned out upon the common to find their way home as they could'. Dutton claimed to have been 'motivated by feelings of humanity to look into the mills', and to have found 'a system of oppression incompatible with the principles of our constitution'. Conditions at Roach, Moons Mill and Hoghton Bottoms may have been no better.[11]

Well located by the Bamber Bridge tramway, the mill had five different tenants between 1807 and 1851. It was put to be let in May 1811: 'To be

Let: The capital and extensive cotton factories with the appropriate machinery therein, situate in Walton, near Preston, formerly in the possession of Mr Watson and late of Messrs Cooper and Sherrington … A number of cottages will be let with the mills … the machinery is ready for immediate use'.[12] By 1825 the mill was being run by 'Thomas German and Co. Penwortham Mills', becoming German and Petty by 1828. A small but distinct community grew up around the mill, and by the 1841 census 250 people occupied the 44 houses. About 1860 Edmund Cockshutt built a new factory. By 1910 the site had been occupied by 'Vernon and Co. Ltd, Cotton Spinners and Manufacturers of Surgical Dressings, Cotton Wools etc: Penwortham Mills. Telegrams "Lint"'. Enlarged in 1920, the mill remains in the same ownership today, the sole survivor of the cotton mills of Preston and district. The works, with the cluster of factory houses around it, still preserves something of the aura of a mill community.

Moons Mill, Manybrooks and Higher Walton

Below Bannister Hall the water sources in the area around the confluence of the river Darwen and the Manybrooks system, have probably been exploited from very early times. The development of these resources in the early nineteenth century led to important changes to the geography of the area, a process completed by the construction of the enormous factory by the Rodgetts in the 1860s. The principal change was in the course of the river Darwen, which formerly ran due north in a large ox-bow enclosing most of the Higher Walton sports field, before arching due south into the present course west of the Farmers Arms. Thus before the new 1860s factory was erected, the area formed a broad and open vale along the Darwen, extending all the way down to the Walton townfields. The steeply rising land to the south of the river here is further cut through by the Manybrooks, which with a large catchment area in the east of the district, has steeply eroded the foot of Kittlingbourne brow. Today the enormous embankment and bridge of the M6 motorway dominates the district and obscures the breadth of the vale of the Darwen at this point, but the very pronounced locational features must have been very apparent to the early promoters of water-powered sites. The remarkable geography of the area can be seen very clearly from 'The Drive', off Cuerdale Lane.

Yates's map indicates that both of the water systems were exploited by 1780, and one of the 'lost' medieval watermills may have been located here. A watermill was located on the Manybrooks at the bottom of Kittlingbourne within the modern foundry estate, whilst 'Moon's Mill' stood on the south bank of the Darwen at the base of the ox-bow, within the present-day Higher Walton Mill–Mill Tavern site.

A deed of 1790 mentions a 'Carding engine dam' at 'Many Brooks', and a notice in the *Blackburn Mail* (12 October 1796) advertises a 'Cotton weft factory to let, at Kitlin Burn, Walton-le-Dale … details from Mr (John)

Manybrooks Bridge, Higher Walton, 1997. By the early nineteenth century the long-exploited and plentiful water resources around 'Higher Walton' supported a developing industrial base. Cotton spinning, cloth printing and dyeing, and the iron foundry trade became important employers in the area, surviving well into the second half of the present century. (S. Cook)

Swainson of Preston'.[13] The Tithe Map clearly shows a small regular building abreast of the Manybrook at the centre of the ironworks which had subsequently been established on the site, and this may have been the location of the earlier factory.

The marriage of John Whitaker ('Mill Wright'), and Elizabeth Pomfret took place at St Leonard's in November 1781, and their son Robert was born in May 1784. Robert was a witness at the wedding of James Whitaker ('Mill Wright') in 1806. The poor rate valuation of 1832 lists property here belonging to Robert Whitaker worth £53 16s. 4d. a year, including blacksmith's and wheelwright's shops, and 'a throwing shop and water wheel' worth £8 10s. 0d.[14] By 1841 John and James Whitaker, both millwrights, had become influential members of the parish vestry. Robert Whitaker was the head of the business, which by the 1860s employed over a hundred workers, and had established a colony of foundry workers along Kittlingbourne. After his death in 1856 members of the family continued to live in the family home at 'Prospect Hill'. Thomas Whitaker, who was resident here in 1885, is listed as the owner of the foundry and 28 houses on Kittlingbourne. By the 1890s the works had closed, but was restarted around the turn of the century by William Coupe, whose son purchased the foundry in 1920. The foundry was operated by the Coupe family until its sale in 1988.[15]

On the Darwen, 'Moon's Mill' originated as a corn mill. Moon is locally an extremely rare surname. The property was owned by Thomas Livesey, who granted a 42-year lease in 1790. The mill may have been rebuilt at this time. In 1792 'Robert Hilton of Preston, grocer and corn factor', held the lease, and insured the mill for £1,600.[16] He had extensive milling interests which included a windmill in Preston, and a share in Brindle Mill. Moons Mill was a large corn mill 'adjoining the Turnpike road ... Plentifully and Constantly supplied with water, and capable of grinding more

Higher Walton seen from the top of Kittlingbourne, c.1930. This superb view of industrial Lancashire remains little changed, though the cottages on the right have long been removed. During the 1850s and 1860s the Rodgett family virtually rebuilt the village, forming what was in many respects a model community. In the late eighteenth century Robert Hilton had begun the mechanised spinning of yarn here in his small corn mill on the Darwen. (*R. Burns*)

than eight sacks of wheat in one hour, each sack containing 240 pound'. Part of the mill, and some adjacent buildings had been converted for the manufacture of textiles, perhaps with unfortunate consequences:[17]

> Preston June 10, 1799.
> To Be Peremptorily
> Sold By Auction
> By The Assignees of Robert Hilton (A Bankrupt)
> All that *substantially newly-erected* building called Moon's Mill ... Part whereof is now occupied as a water corn mill and contains a variety of suitable stones, machinery, water wheel (etc) ... for shelling, grinding and dressing corn and grain ...
> And *the other part has been used for the spinning of cotton*; also the dam or mound, sluice and stream of water ... Also the carding-room, stove-room ... And also other outbuildings ... *together with two Factories near to*, and on the contrary side of the lane to which the mill stands, one 18 yards long and 8 yards wide, and the other 18 yards long and 7 yards wide.

The 'factories' may have been used for preparatory purposes, for 'Several Carding Engines, Roving Billies, Stoves, Roving Frames, and other Machinery and Utensils of Manufacture', were included in the sale.

A brief history of the district printed in 1862 states that Moons Mill originated as a corn mill occupied by Mr Hilton, and was subsequently converted into a cotton mill by 'Messrs Salisbury and Co.' in the early 1800s. The mill was destroyed by fire in February 1811. 'On Tuesday morning, about 2 o'clock, a large cotton factory at Moon-Mill, near this town, belonging to Messrs Salisbury, was discovered to be on fire, and in the course of a few hours was burnt to the ground, not withstanding every effort to save it'. In 1814 the estate of Richard and David Salisbury, 'formerly of Walton, Cotton Spinners and co-partners', was sold to James Livesey and James Bailey of Walton and Thomas Livesey of Hoghton Lane for £1,200, including 'the site of a mill or factory some time since destroyed by fire'.[18]

A party of Blackburn magistrates visited the factory in 1823, during enquiries into the employment of children:[19]

> Mr James Livesey's cotton factory, at Moons Mill, in Walton-le-Dale: There are about 130 persons employed here, and several under 9 years of age. One boy stated to us that his mother told him to say that he was nine years old, though he admitted to us that he was not so much. Half an hour is allowed for breakfast, and an hour for dinner. This factory is worked by water, and in case of a loss of time is made up for by working an hour per day extra. The interior walls are whitewashed twice a year. There is a Sunday School attached to the factory at which the children are taught gratuitously.

The local valuation of 1832 lists property in the tenancy of James Livesey (but owned by Joseph Livesey) worth £109 3s. 4d. per year, including reservoirs, crofts etc., a factory (with power £30), two warehouses and three cottages. In March 1834 the mill was advertised to let: 'Eligible Cotton Factory to be Let. All that convenient and valuable cotton factory called 'Moons Mill', being in Walton-le-Dale, situate on the old turnpike road leading from Preston to Blackburn ... Also two warehouses and counting houses, a manager's house and cottages. The mill is regularly supplied with water by the river Darwen, having two extensive lodges, with a powerful fall. The situation is most excellent for carrying on the cotton business in a most extensive way, and such as is very rare to be met with being in a populous part of the county, the occupier will always be sure to be plentifully supplied with workpeople of all descriptions. The premises are at present occupied by Mr James Livesey, whose time expires in May next'.[20]

Miles Rodgett (1782–1872), 'Master cotton spinner', acquired the Darwen Bank estate before 1841, and a second mill was built alongside the existing one in 1850, when the company was styled 'Rodgett Brothers'. By 1851 'Moons Mill' was described in the local directory as 'Another populous village, with two large cotton mills, one of which is very extensive and was erected in 1850 by Miles Rodgett'.[21] Modern Higher Walton owes much to the Rodgetts, and the name 'Moons Mill' seems to have been dropped around 1859: 'Since the property came into the possession of the Rodgetts, they have made wonderful improvements at Higher Walton. They appear to be completely remodelling and modernising the village. Old cottages are being pulled down, and dilapidated houses are being removed, to make way for good substantial habitations. Two immense cotton mills have been erected by the firm of Messrs Rodgett Brothers'.[22] A new church, school and reading room for the workpeople followed. The new mills were a curiosity. Seen from the back they constituted two factories, each with an enormous chimney, but from the front they appeared to be a single building. Separate concerns, yet they were run collectively as Rodgett Brothers. By 1882 the concern had been taken over by G. and R. Dewhurst, forming part of a very large combine which included Cuerden and Farington Mill. The series of later extensions, culminating in the superb engine house, can be traced by the dates on the boxes at the top of the mill's drainpipes.

On the bank of the river Darwen in Cuerdale, between Bannister Hall printworks and Roach Mill, was the site of Cowp mill – a water-driven corn mill. All trace of this structure appears to have disappeared. In 1631 James Bronthwaite, husbandman, was charged with the theft of groats from 'George Cowpe's mille, Cuerdale'. George Cowpe died in 1653. By the final years of the eighteenth century this site had been developed as a bleaching works. The premises were advertised for sale in 1795, and comprised 'Two large stone buildings, lately erected by John Coupe, Whitster, and now occupied by him as a Cloth-House, a Drying-House, a Bowk-House, and a Souring-House, along with three waterwheels, and an exceedingly good stream of water, in the River Darwen', and 'Bleaching Utensils'.[23]

Walton Factory: the mills along the river Lostock

Industrial development along the river Darwen in the north of the district was matched by that along the Lostock to the south. Water from the Clayton's print works (itself later converted into an enormous cotton mill – Cuerden Mill) powered two mills further downstream. At the side of Lostock Hall, a watermill was established by the 1780s, and is shown as such on Yates's map. A directory of 1816 lists George Clayton, 'of Lostock

G. and R. Dewhurst's Cuerden Mill ('Down Below') c.1925. Developments along the river Lostock mirrored those on the Darwen, and by 1820 a sizeable workforce found employment in the Cuerden and Lostock Hall mills. At this time the operatives at Cuerden Green mill enjoyed a great reputation for upholding trades union rights, and for political radicalism. Overdependence on a single industry was to prove disastrous in the long term, and the closure of this enormous spinning mill in 1936, which had once claimed to have the largest spinning floor in the world, brought to the number of job losses in Walton and Bamber Bridge alone, since 1925, to 2,500. (R. Burns)

Hall, Cotton Spinner'. By 1825 Jonathan Haworth was established there, and 'Howarth and Sons' were running the factory by the time of the Tithe Map. The property included 16 cottages.[24]

The third enterprise on the river was William Bashall's 'Walton factory', in the fields to the west of Watkin Lane, later better known as Cuerden Green Mill. Like Penwortham factory, Moons Mill, and Withy Trees Factory, this also became a distinct community in its own right. William Winstanley of Cuerden died in 1791, and his widow (a Woodcock), sold a part of their property in 1799, including 'a newly erected cotton mill in Walton-le-Dale, occupied by Wm. Bashall'.[25] The site of the mill with its mill race fed by the Lostock, to the north of Woodcock Hall, was rather a remote one on the edges of Walton and Farington mosses. Yet the second William Bashall (1795–1871), 'Cotton Spinner and Manufacturer', was one of the most successful of the local millowners. In the township valuation of 1821–22 the factory was valued at £219 per year, the mill estate had 50 cottages worth £140, a warehouse, a sizehouse, and Lostock House – a gentleman's residence.[26]

In the 1830s the Bashalls, with their partner William Boardman, established the enormous factory at Farington, and built the elegant residences of Farington House (William Boardman), and Farington Lodge (William Bashall).[27] Located in a similar area of rural underemployment, beside the North Union Railway, this was to be an enormously profitable concern, enabling Bashall to become a noted art collector. As with most of the early Walton mills, the lack of alternative employment gave the masters considerable leeway over their Preston competitors in holding down wages. Cuerden Mill in particular was a stronghold of unionism; and 'Mr Bashall's factory at Cuerden' gave much practical support to the Chartist movement. By 1869 both the Farington and Cuerden Green mills, which had been run by separate members of the Bashall family and their partners, were styled 'William Bashall and Co.', but by 1877 the mill at Cuerden Green had been sold, and was being run by Henry Ward.[28]

Withy Trees Mill and Calverts

The origins of Withy Trees mill (subsequently William Eccles and Co., Ingham & Tipping's corn mill; 'Old Billys') are particularly obscure. Thomas Clayton is described as 'Cotton Manufacturer, Withy Trees', in 1816 and 1818, and James Clayton in 1825. The term 'manufacturer' was used to describe anyone who employed home-based handloom weavers, either directly or indirectly. With the advent of mechanised weaving the term was applied to cloth manufacturers, distinguishing them from the 'spinners'. Where the premises were located at Withy Trees is uncertain, but significantly one of the old buildings close by the mill had been a manufacturer's warehouse. The mill is not listed in the 1821 valuation, but was probably established by 1828 when 'Thomas Eccles, Withen Trees',

Thomas Eccles & Sons, Stone Mill ('New Side'), School Lane, Bamber Bridge, c.1890. The construction of this mill, and the later development of School Lane Mill by the Orr family, led to the development of a distinct community in School Lane, which was only swept up with Brownedge into 'Bamber Bridge' in the 1870s, when they were linked by housing along Station Road. The sense of this lost independence and vanished separatism perhaps still lingers in the nicknames 'Up the Brig' and 'Down the Brig'. (R. Burns)

is recorded, becoming Thomas and William Eccles & Co. by 1834. In 1854 the firm was trading as William Eccles & Co., and long continued in the Eccles family. William Eccles was succeeded by his son William II (1830–92), and this is perhaps the origin of the mill's nickname 'Old Billy's'.

The mill formed a part of the Withy Trees estate, dominated by the fine house, Withy Grove. The Walton-le-Dale workhouse adjoined the mill, and in the early years may have provided a source of labour. William Eccles was a prominent member of the vestry which ran the house in 1826.[29] The mill stood on the edge of the gathering grounds of Cockshot Brook, which was diverted a few yards from its course to run underneath the buildings. When these were finally demolished in the early 1980s it was noted that the brook had been run through a series of stone channels in a regular pattern, under the oldest sandstone-built block of the mill fronting Station Road.

A good description of the mill and the estate is provided by a sale notice of the 1840s:[30]

All that substantially built cotton mill, called Withy Trees Mill. With the engine-house and boiler-house, mechanics shop, sow-house, and warehouse adjoining to the said mill, together with the steam engine of 50 horse power, four boilers, and the mill gearing therein and belonging thereto; and also the watch-house, counting-house, gas-house, and cotton warehouse, and twenty four cottages near to the said mill. And also the several closes of land, formerly called Workhouse Field and lane, Further Meadow, Second Field and First Field (all now in one close) and Nearer Meadow; with the farm-house, garden, outbuilding, and fold belonging thereto ... The two

large reservoirs are in the close formerly called Workhouse Field. All that capital newly erected mansion house.

Thomas Eccles & Sons, School Lane, Bamber Bridge. An illustration from an advertisement of 1925, shortly before the mill closed.

In Walton village the best waterpower sites had long been taken by the valuable manor corn mills. Indeed, access to water power must be considered as a significant factor in the development of the settlement from very early times. The potential resources of the Ribble could only be developed at ruinous expense, and the flood threat loomed over any potential investment. The district's largest concentration of handloom weavers was located here, many of them in purpose-built houses with cellar workshops beneath. From the mid-eighteenth century a number of specific warehouses are listed in the manor accounts. The line of these developments slowly began to extend westwards across the Cop on to the frequently flooded land. This became more attractive for building following the raising of the Cop in the 1820s. With increasing housing congestion in the centre of the village, Calvert's first factory was pushed onto a site then at the extreme edge of development along Victoria Road, on a particularly low-lying length of the Cop.

Yates's map of 1786 shows the site of a watermill close by Burscough Bridge. This may have been powered by the old mill race, though this seems to have passed out of use by about 1810. In 1799 the *Blackburn Mail* advertised a 'Cotton Weft factory at Burscough Bridge, Walton-le-Dale', describing a new brick building of four storeys, 'Well calculated to be turned into a weaving factory'.[31] In 1803 Sir H. P. Hoghton confirmed the rental of the plot of land and the warehouse 'lately erected on the north side of the turnpike road from Preston to Blackburn, adjoining the the east end of the yard occupied by the turnpike house near Burscough Bridge, bounded on the north by the river Ribble', for £7 3s. 9d. per year to Richard Jackson and Charles and John Swainson, 'Calico Printers and Cotton Manufacturers'.[32]

In the Hoghton estate rentals two important warehouses can be identified along Walton Cop from at least 1785 – Flats warehouse, and Cop warehouse.[33] The Flats warehouse was located on the river Ribble below Ribble bridge. It was rented by Richard Cooper in 1785 for £20 per year, along with the Flats themselves, for which he paid £130. A 'John Cooper of the Copp within Walton, Merchant', is recorded in 1786.[34] By 1793 Roger Haworth was tenant of the warehouse, and also of 'Smithy warehouse', for which he paid £3 3s. 0d. The Cop warehouse may be the structure shown on Porter's map of 1765, as 'The New Warehouse'. In 1785 Mr Richard Martin was the tenant paying a rent of £3 3s. 0d., being replaced in 1790 by William Fisher, who is described in a deed of 1789 as 'Cotton Manu-facturer'. He went bankrupt, and was in turn replaced by Mr Suddell. In 1796 the warehouse was occupied by Messrs Sharples and Livesey, and in 1798 John Livesey alone was tenant.[35] The latter was almost certainly the father of Joseph Livesey, the temperance reformer, whose reminiscences of this period are described in a subsequent section. The district's home-grown mill-owning families, such as the Eccles, Bashalls and the Calverts, emerged from out of this class of fairly small-scale manufacturers. Many others, such as Richard and Peter Fletcher, whose spinning mill was ap-parently powered by a windmill, have left little trace.

William Calvert (1787–1861) 'Cotton manufacturer, Walton-le-Dale', is listed in a trade directory of 1825. Calvert's Flats mill is unlikely to have

William Eccles' Withy Trees Mill ('Old Billys', subsequently Ingham and Tipping's corn mill), seen looking north along Station road, c. 1905. The factory was located next to the site of the Walton-le-Dale parish workhouse, and the older stone block, which can clearly be seen on the extreme left of the photograph, was the site of a battle between a Chartist mob and the mill workers in August 1842. When the buildings were eventually removed in the 1980s, a carefully constructed series of waterways was found to have been laid out within the foundations, carrying the waters of the Cockshutt Brook to all departments of the original mill. The ancient brook still emerges to the west of Aspden Street. (R. Burns)

The Yew Tree Inn, and William Calvert's enormous Flats Mill, seen from Walton Cop (Victoria Road), c. 1935. Apart from the inn, all this great block of buildings has now been removed. From modest beginnings, Calverts Mill came to dominate Walton village, and by 1860 it employed over 800 people. The Calverts continued to live relatively modestly alongside their works, and their former home can be seen in the middle distance. Mr Calvert seems to have been extremely proud of his garden at the back of this property, albeit overlooked by his roaring spinning mills and their enormous chimneys. As the late George Fletcher recalled, the failure of the firm in the early 1930s was believed at the time to herald 'the End of Walton'. Many of the photographs of this period give a wholly false impression, being taken in summer, since they do not include the clouds of household and factory smoke. (R. Burns)

developed much before this time, and for some years the premises were very small, and extended only a short distance on to the Flats. William Calvert is not mentioned in the valuation survey of 1821. Alternatively the potential for development here was vast. As at Withy Trees, the expansion of the scale of production here must have been related to the development of steam power. Calvert's mill was to be the largest in the district by the middle of the century, and came to form a group of spinning mills and weaving sheds, each with their own power houses and steam plant. By the 1860s over 800 people were employed here, and the mills came to dominate the village completely – to such an extent that when the company failed in 1931 many people thought it heralded 'the end of Walton'.[36] By 1854 the firm was styled 'Wm. Calvert and Sons, Spinners and Manufacturers', becoming 'Calvert and Sons' by 1882, when their Preston and Walton mills employed over 2,200 people.

In the census of 1841, William Calvert is described as a 'Master Cotton Spinner', living in a modest house – Walton House – next to the works on Walton Cop. He was regarded as 'one of the most capable men involved in the cotton trade of North Lancashire'. He was born in Balderstone, but his wife was born in Walton. They had sons Edmund, William, Richard and Henry, and daughters Mary and Alice. The sons took a prominent part in the life of the village. Richard Calvert built the Working Men's Institution in 1881, providing it with a library in 1891, and gave large sums to local charities, including £5,000 towards the renovation of St Leonard's Church. 'He was of a somewhat retiring disposition, but was highly esteemed by all who came into contact with him, and by the workpeople, and by his death Walton has lost a good friend'. Although flags were flown at half mast, the press announcement of the 'Death of a senior member of a great cotton firm' was at pains to point out that 'it is not intended to stop the works during the funeral, as was the case with the late Mr Henry Calvert, although the works will stop at 11 o'clock, the ordinary time on Saturday'.[37] Alice Calvert married Robert Parker, and their son Harold Parker was a leading figure in the Lancashire cotton trade, and the final managing director of the firm. In his youth he was a noted amateur footballer, playing for Blackburn Etrurians, and making guest appearances with the great Deepdale club, with which he was long associated.

In 1903 Muriel Parker compiled her *Memories* – a brief history of the concern written for the family, drawing out the links between the Calvert, Bashall and Parker families: 'At first the business was one of handloom weaving, then the old mill was built, afterwards what is called the new one and now again in 1902, and 1903, extensive alterations have been made. 1871 brought Aquaduct mill which previously belonged to Mr Dawson. One great reason for the prosperity of the firm has been their sterling integrity. It is a well-known fact that their word is as good as their bond, and they are incapable of meanness. The fact that so many of their workpeople grow old in their service shows they are good masters and can be relied upon'.[38]

In the space of a generation, from 1820 to 1850, both the landscape and the society of Walton village had been changed for ever by the development of the enormous Flats mills. Early photographs of the village clearly reveal the extent to which the mill buildings dominated the village skyline. Across the ancient manor, the factory-based textile industry was well established, and around the scattered mills entirely new communities had begun to emerge, completely transforming the settlement pattern, and calling into being an entirely new industrial society in the process. With the development of the railway network the local economy became fully integrated into the broader pattern of world economic relationships.

The coming of the railway

The construction of the North Union Railway Company's Preston–Wigan line was greeted with much local apprehension. In the event this was to prove not to have been misplaced. Work began in the spring of 1835, and the line was completed in October 1838 at a cost of £500,000, or £21,000 per mile; 2,202,030 cubic yards of earth were excavated from the cuttings, and 2,118,498 cubic yards deposited as embankments, in the largest single investment the Preston region had ever seen.[39] Harsh weather during the winter of 1837–38 delayed completion of the line, and the race to make up time led to a number of accidents. The build-up of thick ice on the Ribble led to fears for the safety of the immense Ribble viaduct. During an apparent thaw the *Preston Chronicle* tried to reassure nervous readers: 'We trust there is no further ground for apprehending danger. Every precaution has been adopted to prevent the occurrence of any disaster'. Both the thaw and the confidence proved to have been misplaced, and when the ice finally broke up on 3 March a great deal of damage had been done.[40]

The contractors stood to lose 'a large premium' if the work was not completed on time, and by the early summer of 1838 over 3,000 men were said to be at work. This was in fact something of an Irish army of occupation for the residents of Farington, Cuerden Green and lower Penwortham. During the last week in May a dispute between two navvies, Owen and Peter Deans, and a local shopkeeper provided the spark for widespread rioting. Local spinners from 'Mr Bashall's factory' were driven from the Blue Anchor alehouse, and William Miller of Walton and Richard Livesey of Farington were 'inhumanly beat' on the road to Tardy Gate. The Irish seemed to be making good their threat to 'Kill all Englishmen'.[41]

The remainder of the night and the following Tuesday were spent by both sides in preparing for battle. At half-past seven that evening most of the workforce of Mr Bashall's factory set off for the Sumpter Horse in Penwortham, the headquarters of the navigators. Contemporary accounts do not make clear which was the 'Mr Bashall's factory' alluded to, Cuerden Green Mill or Farington Mill. In fact, probably both sent contingents to the fray. Estimates of the force varied between 300 and 800. The two forces met in the vicinity of Bee Lane. The locals were armed with a small number of firearms, scythes, hedging stakes and sticks, and about 40 of the navvies had blackthorn sticks, and the rest armed themselves with cudgels and iron bars. When asked to disperse, George Robinson was reported to have said 'No, we are not willing, we have received so much injury from the Irish, that we are determined to have revenge'. One man was shot dead and at least 40 people were wounded. Peace was restored by soldiers from Burnley.

Work on the line was pushed on. 'The operations on this line are now proceeding with extraordinary activity. The fine weather appears to have given a stimulus to the more rapid progress of the work, and an immense number of workmen are engaged in them'.[42] The opening was delayed just three months. Work on the viaduct began on 1 September 1835, it was 872′ long, 28′ wide, and the distance from the bed of the river to the parapet was 68′. During the excavation of the pier foundations in the river gravels, traces of prehistoric materials were found similar to those later discovered in the excavation of the Preston Dock diversion. Built at a cost of £40,000, the bridge contained 675,000 cubic feet of rusticated ashlar from quarries at Whittle, Longridge and Lancaster. The Southern Embankment was 40′ high and three-quarters of a mile long, and contained 464,431 cubic yards of earth. From here Penwortham Cutting was one and a half miles long, 38′ deep, and had four bridges, the largest of them being on Bee Lane. Half a million cubic yards of marl and clay had been excavated from here alone. The Lostock Embankment then carried the line 1,200 yards to Farington station.

On Wednesday 1 November 1838 the line was opened, amidst great celebrations: 'Not the least interruption, difficulty or accident took place in the arrangements made for starting ... twenty miles per hour was the rate of her course, but on reaching the Ribble viaduct, which is not yet completely finished, the speed was slackened ... The velocity with which the trains rolled along, so surprised the multitudes that crowded the different bridges over the railway, that they were actually held mute with astonishment, and confined the demonstrations of their joy to the waving of their hands, their hats, or their handkerchiefs'. The expected railway calamity did not occur, beyond 'Some slight but easily remediable derangement in its machinery'.[43]

In 1844 the Act of Parliament was obtained for the Blackburn and Preston railway. Work commenced in September 1844, and the line was completed in May 1846 at a cost of £160,000. The line linked Blackburn with Farington, a distance of nine and three-quarter miles, from where trains ran a further two and a half miles along the North Union's track into Preston. Although the line was 'thrown open unexpectedly by the directors on Saturday last', large crowds 'speedily gathered at Blackburn station'. Intermediate stations had also been built at Cherry Tree, Pleasington Chapel, 'Hoghton Turnpike Road', and 'Bamber Bridge Turnpike Road'.

The local press did their best to convey something of the continental pioneering spirit in their descriptions of the enterprise. The line's engineering marvel was the 'stupendous' Hoghton viaduct, which crossed the Darwen, 'a little rushing mountain stream', on three arches, 108′ high, and built at a cost of £10,000. From this vantage point could be seen 'the vale of the Darwen, on the left of which stands the ruins of Messrs Livesey's Mill, ravaged by fire a few years ago, and the little colony of Hoghton Bottoms', and Hoghton Tower, 'now long deserted'. At Bamber Bridge, so the *Preston Guardian* informed its readers, 'On either hand a magnificent landscape tempts the eye of the traveller – to the right a fertile and well wooded expanse, backed by the colossal heights of Rivington Pike and

Winter, or Edgar-Hill, and on the left the beautiful vale of the Ribble, together with the eminent and commanding town of Preston'. From here 'Mr William Eccles's new factory', and Mr Bashall's factory were the prominent landmarks, before the blue and black liveried trains ran onto the seemingly hazardous Farington curve to join the main line.[44] The press could report with evident satisfaction that 'the pleasure of the day was much enhanced by the fact that no accident or mischance occurred to cast a gloom over any part of the proceedings'.[45]

Although these lines were important improvements to the transport system, it was to be the close proximity of their junction which was to be the critical factor in the development of Lostock Hall as an important railway service centre. By the 1870s extensive goods marshalling yards, sidings, engine and carriage sheds had been constructed at Bamber Bridge, Brownedge and Lostock Hall, where the main Glasgow to London west-coast line crossed the Liverpool and the East Lancashire lines. The Lancashire and Yorkshire Railway Company emerged as an important employer in these districts, and its operations could be heard through day and night across much Bamber Bridge and Tardy Gate.[46]

Hospital Crossing, between Bamber Bridge and Gregson Lane, c.1920. Signal boxes such as this one became an interesting feature of the local landscape, and the district could boast a good variety. The coming of the Blackburn & Preston railway led to the development of 'Gregson Lane' as a rural mill community, with a quite distinct sense of its own identity and independence. (R. Burns)

CHAPTER NINE

The handloom weavers and the new society

 T IS ONE of the greatest ironies of the industrial revolution, that well into the 1830s the domestic handloom weavers formed the largest single group in the industrial workforce. With cheap machine-spun yarn readily available, British production of cloth could expand enormously. For a short time towards the end of the eighteenth century the trade enjoyed a golden age. Yet within a few years the oversupply of labour, the simplicity and cheapness of the technology, and the comparative ease of entry into the trade, began to exert a strong downward pressure on wages. Weavers at the coarse end of the trade found themselves working longer hours for less money per piece. The very cheapness of labour, and the flexibility of the workforce, ironically became a disincentive to manufacturers to invest in expensive power looms.

In and around Walton powerloom weaving seems to have been introduced during the 1830s. In the country districts, along Hoghton Lane and in Samlesbury, many hand weavers progressed to the manufacture of more expensive fabrics beyond the capacity of the early powerlooms, and here the trade survived well into the second half of the nineteenth century. The district's increasing demand for factory workers meant that the worst effects of the industrial dislocation attendant on the introduction of power weaving seems to have been avoided.

In 1843 Lawrence Rawstorne recalled the impact of the weaving boom on the local community fifty years earlier: 'At the time when weaving was at its tip top price, it was introduced into the different farm houses, when all other considerations gave way to it. A good handloom weaver would then earn his 30s. a week or even more: he would perhaps work half the week and drink the remainder. Farms by these means became subdivided: cottages were built; a large shop was attached to every building. The houses both of the farmers and the cottages were occupied by as large families as could be procured and these paid an enormous rent from the profits of the loom'.[1] Joseph Livesey's memoirs also noted the spread of weaving among the rural population: 'In those days, all the small farms at Walton, Penwortham, and the adjoining country places, were "weaving farms", having a "shop" attached to hold a certain number of looms'.[2]

A boom in land values resulted: 'The great range of fine land between the Ribble and the Mersey, is in general let off at a higher rent than any other, in consequence of its population, markets and other causes. In the parishes of Walton-le-Dale, Chorley and Leyland, the rents run from 40s., 50s. to £3 10s. 0d. (per acre, per year), some a little higher nearer the towns and adjoining manufactures. Around Penwortham, Croston etc., from 35s. to 50s., but little higher than that rate. In the neighbourhood of Preston from £2 to £3 10s. 0d. as farms; but for the convenience of trade, at £6 or £7 and sometimes more the customary acre for grassland'.[3] This process can be traced in the Hoghton's estate rentals in the period 1785 to 1800. At Hoghton rent income from the estate hovered at around £400–£500 per year up to 1794, and then began to rise above £600, reaching £700 in 1800. In Walton the rise in rents was spectacular. Rents fluctuated only slightly in a narrow band between £300–£400 from 1785 to 1795 (£400), then rose rapidly, to £550 in 1796, £750 in 1798, £1,150 in 1799, and £1,350 in 1800.[4]

In the centres of manufacturing, such as Walton and Bamber Bridge, a sellers' market for labour came into existence. Middle-class commentators deplored what they saw as its consequences. It was said of the Preston weavers of 'New Preston' in New Hall Lane, that 'they could earn good wages after playing 2 or 3 days a week. In their leisure time, or in the time in which they did not care to work, they used to swagger about in top boots, and extract what, to their minds was enjoyment, from badger baiting, dog-worrying, cockfighting, poaching and drinking'. They were in short 'an exceedingly rough lot'![5]

Joseph Livesey: the Walton weaver

Joseph Livesey, social reformer and temperance advocate, was born at a house on Walton Cop in March 1794. In his memoirs he left a graphic description of village life during his childhood. Both of his grandfathers were small farmers, Joseph Livesey living in Toad House Lane (subsequently Todd Lane), and William Ainsworth at Watering Pool near Tardy Gate. His father, John Livesey, was a rising manufacturer, and a friend of William Bashall of Walton Factory. The row of weavers' step houses where the family lived survives, and Livesey resided in at least three of them before his marriage and move to Preston in 1816. John Livesey had a warehouse and warping mill in the village, and put work out to the local weavers.[6] The raising of Walton Cop has obscured the lower stories of the stephouses – the workshops – but occasionally the lintel of a submerged cellar window can be seen above the footpath. The backs of these houses clearly show them to be of three storeys. The similar building by the newsagents at Walton corner (at the time of writing a chip shop), may be one of the warehouses listed in the Hoghton estate accounts.

Joseph Livesey (1794–1884). Educationalist, social reformer, political radical and Primitive Christian, the career of Joseph Livesey mirrored many of the currents discernible in the intellectual life of the local handloom weavers of the early nineteenth century. (*South Ribble Museum*)

Following the deaths of both of Joseph Livesey's parents, the family concern eventually failed, and young Joseph's status fell from that of the rising manufacturer's son, to that of a jobbing weaver: 'The cellar where my grandfather and uncle worked held three looms, and so soon as I was able I was put to weaving; and for seven years I worked in a corner of that damp cellar, really unfit for any human being to work in – the fact that from the day it was plastered to the day I left the mortar was soft – water remaining in the walls – was proof of this. And to make it worse, the Ribble and the Darwen sometimes overflowed their banks, and inundated this and other cellars adjoining. It has to me often been a subject of perfect surprise how I bore up and escaped with my life, sitting all the long day close to a damp wall ... I remember taking our pieces to Messrs Horrocks and Jacson's warehouse, and I never wove for any firm but this, and the late Mr Timothy France of Mount Street'.[7]

Livesey married, and the young couple rented a small cottage in the village and struggled to make a living in the trade: 'On the loom I was most industrious, working from early in the morning often till ten and sometimes later at night, and ... my wife ... not only did all the house work, but wound the bobbins for three weavers, myself, uncle, and grandfather, and yet, with all this apparently hard lot, these were happy days'.[8] A move to Preston was not a success, and with a young family to support Livesey's health broke down in 1816. Advised by a doctor to 'eat a little cheese', Livesey by chance discovered the considerable profits to be made from the cheese trade. Quite quickly he became established as a cheese factor, and the basis of his very considerable fortune was laid,

Houses at Walton Corner, c.1905. The core of the old weaving community, most of this property was linked in some way to the great trade. The remains of loomshops can still be discerned in the surviving houses. The property centre left, today a fish-and-chip shop, is a former manufacturer's warehouse. The crowded rows of weavers' houses behind this frontage were removed in the early 1930s. (R. Burns)

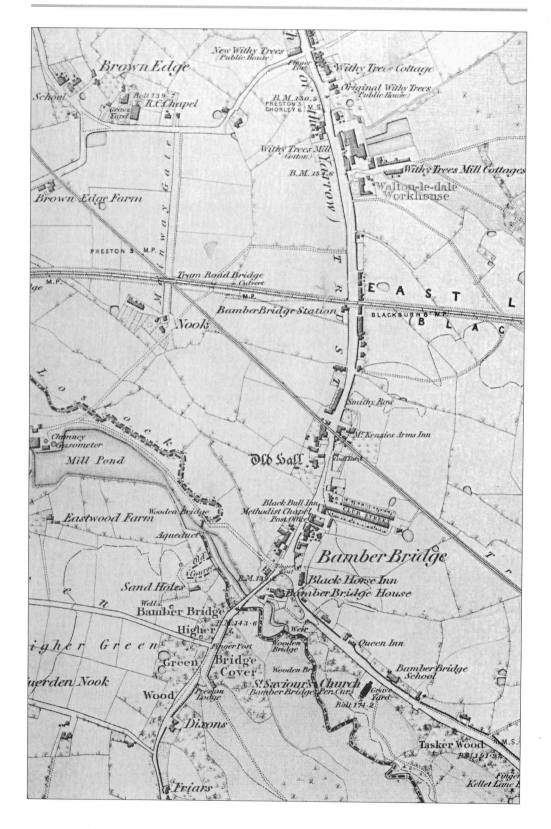

'Bamber Bridge' and Withy Trees, a detail of the first edition 6" OS map, 1848. The factory and the parish workhouse can be seen at Withy Trees, to the east of the former moss at Brownedge. To the south, 'Bamber Bridge' is dominated by the Commercial Building Society Houses in Club Street. Much of 'Station Road' was undeveloped at this time, and virtually all the individual houses shown were weavers' houses. This property can easily be identified today because of the use of stone as the predominant local building material in the handloom weaving period (c. 1780–1830).

enabling him to concentrate on his philanthropic career. He presented his loom 'to a poor man in Queen Street', but later bought it back, and had it made into a table, which can still be seen in the Livesey Collection at the University of Central Lancashire.[9]

The young reformer witnessed at first-hand the acute social problems of the day. In these drunkenness played a major part. 'The weavers crowded the public houses, and they regularly kept 'St Monday'. The villagers all thought well of drink ... We had a sad wet lot connected with the church. The grave digger and his father were both drunkards: ringers and singers, were both hard drinkers ... The parish clerk was no exception. When the church clock was standing for want of winding up in a morning, as was often the case, the remark was "The clerk was drunk again last night" ... I was surrounded by mental darkness and vice'. When the old bell ringers were replaced, Livesey joined the new group on the second bell. Fines were paid for lateness, and collected for Christmas. 'We had no-one to teach us better, so we decided to spend the money in a jollification at the White Bull ... I need not say what was the effect'.[10]

The golden age of the handloom weavers

With the industrialisation and increasing commercial integration in the years before 1800, the weaving communities came fully into the arena of world trade, and under the influence of the trade cycle. Events in distant countries now had formidable consequences at home. The Seven Years War and the American War of Independence disrupted the trade, particularly cloth exports to the West Indies, and imports of flax from northern Europe. Local merchants had a very brief flirtation with the slave trade, which seems to have ended when the *Blossom*, described as 'every way complete for the slave trade' and 'at Lytham in the river Ribble', was sold in 1756, but the records of Rawlinson Brothers of Liverpool record continued involvement in the colonial trade. In 1785, for example, goods from Walton, Clayton Green and Leyland were dispatched to the West Indies, and William Pollard and Henry Critchely of Leyland exported consignments of 'German linen', used for the manufacture of slave clothing, in 1787, 1789, and 1790.[11]

The fluctuating international situation during the Napoleonic wars was particularly critical, and the decade 1800–10 which saw such remarkable growth in the handloom weaving trade, also saw some of the most depressed years. Horrockses of Preston made losses in 1800, 1804, 1807, and 1811, but was to make losses in only four years of the next hundred (1826, 1842, 1843, 1847).[12] 1807 was a very bad year, and in the early summer of 1812 weaving wages in the Preston district were said to have fallen to 7s. per week. The bankruptcy of employers through unsound finance was a further problem. Of the three large employers in the district Livesey and Co. and John Watson and Co. failed, whilst Horrockses narrowly avoided failure

Club Street, Bamber Bridge, c.1895. This twin row of two-storey cottages built over loomshops is perhaps the most interesting of all the weaver building society colonies. Houses were added as funds allowed, as can be seen from the inconsistent roof lines. In Bamber Bridge this type of house was known as a step-house. Club Street won a fiercesome reputation for preserving the independence of its inhabitants, when in 1849 a force of fifty policemen 'armed with cutlasses' was required to support the bailiffs 'making distress'. The houses were demolished in 1973, but similar properties can still be seen in 'Union Street', Leyland. (R. Burns)

following speculation in cotton futures. Even boom conditions were thus marked by profound commercial uncertainty.

At the domestic weaving trade reached its peak in the years around 1820, few homes in the district lacked a loom. In Hoghton, Cuerdale and Bamber Bridge most of the stone-built property from this period originated as weaving houses. Fine examples of stone-built loomshops with houses above them can still be seen in Bamber Bridge, along Brown Lane, and on Station Road between Mounsey Road and Wesley Street. A short row of step houses – Lilac Houses – was demolished in the early 1960s on the site now occupied by Charleston Court, but two very fine pairs of houses survive along the east side of Chorley Road between Duddle Lane and Renshaw Drive ends.

Most of the surviving buildings on the west side of Victoria Road, from

Surviving weavers' houses, between Mounsey Road and Wesley Street on Station Road, 1997. Here a later, larger building has been inserted between two short rows of weavers' houses. An extremely fine short row of weavers' houses, 'The Stephouses', which stood in Station Road on the site of Charleston Court, was demolished in the early 1960s. (Author)

Surviving weavers' houses, opposite St Saviour's Church, Bamber Bridge, 1997. These examples reveal the key elements which identify weavers' houses: generally large windows, a semi-subterranean cellar or workroom sometimes with its own entrance, with steps leading to the first floor. The cellar windows may be extremely wide, and divided by lintels into three lights, as is the case here. External plastering (for example in the case of the houses just north of the 'Milk Marketing Board' on Station Road), or changes to the level of the road (as in the case of the Victoria Road houses at Walton) may mask some or all of these features. (*Author*)

the Conservative Club to the Yew Tree, are former weavers' houses, including the celebrated early home of Joseph Livesey. The level of the road here, in fact the eastern end of Walton Cop, has been raised, obscuring the distinctive loomshop windows. Demolition of the once extensive houses behind the frontage (Gray Horse Yard, Gillibrand Court, Fallowfield Brow, Johns Row, 'The Barracks'; Marginsons Row, Chapel Yard and Tongues Yard) must have removed much related property. The 1841 census records the remnants of what a few years before was a weavers' colony. To the south of Mill Lane, on Chorley Road, a superb row of weavers' houses was demolished in the late 1970s, though 'Hunts Houses', a row of four properties, have survived over the Darwen bridge. A row of rural, stone-built, handloom weavers' houses can be seen in Potter Lane. The careful scrutiny of architectural detail, deeds, and the census returns, is likely to reveal many more examples in the district. Many have been identified by Geoffrey Timmins, and very fine rows, of regional if not national importance, can be seen at 'Top o' th' Lane' in Brindle, in Fox Lane, Leyland, and in Preston Road, Clayton-le-Woods. Yet Club Street, Bamber Bridge, perhaps the most celebrated of all the local weaving colonies, was demolished in the summer of 1973.[13]

At the very height of the trade, terminating building societies were formed to construct weavers' houses for their members. The latter were a good, safe, and profitable investment. 'Club Row' in Longridge dates from 1793, and Union Street in Fox Lane, Leyland, dates from 1802. Members paid regularly into the society funds, and elected a committee to oversee their affairs. When the houses were built they were allotted by ballot. The building society then terminated. A second wave of enthusiasm saw the completion of Bradshaw Street in Leyland, and Club Street in Bamber Bridge. The following notice was placed in the *Preston Journal* of August

1811: 'To be sold by Private Treaty, at the house of Mr Collinson, Bamber Bridge, two shares in the Club Houses, called Commercial Buildings, on the 2nd day of September, at six o'clock in the evening'.[14]

A deed of August 1813 describes Charles Swainson of Walton, calico printer, and James Pennington of Preston, brazier, as trustees of the Bamber Bridge Commercial Building Society. The committee comprised Henry Clarkson, Kenneth McKenzie, James Lumming, William Rosbottom and William Clayton. Land on which to build 50 houses in two rows seems to have been acquired in 1807, and a society was subsequently established 'For the purpose of building by contribution certain dwelling houses to be allotted to the individual members of the society in severalty'. By 1813 all the houses had been completed, and were available at rents of 15s. 10d. a week.[15] Brick-built, with stone lintels and sills, the houses were simple two-storey cottages built over semi-subterreanean (or underground) cellars. The latter may have held up to four looms, giving a potential of 200 looms in the project. Occasionally non-weaving tenants would sub-let the cellars, and houses could be utilised as warehouses. The district valuation of 1848 shows Heys Hunt (a former master of the Leyland Workhouse – then essentially a weaving shop exploiting a captive workforce), and Kenneth McKenzie (whose name lives on in the name of a public house on his former property along the Walton tramway), to have been the owners of a number of houses. The property was demolished in 1973, though the public house at the head of the street – the Black Bull – where much of the weavers' business must have been conducted, has to date survived Chartist riots, battles between the locals and an army of police armed with cutlasses sent to quell them, a murder, internecine fighting among the American forces in 1944, and ultimately the Lancashire cotton industry itself.

The tradition of dissent

Though it had only a small number of adherents, religious nonconformity provided an important strand in the history of the district following the Civil War, and particularly after the ministry of Isaac Ambrose, vicar of Preston, 1646–60.[16] From this period the Hoghtons were leading nonconformists, and gave important support to local Presbyterians in the early eighteenth century. In the second half of the century the Methodist tradition became a key contributor to the new social order. The 1864 ecclesiastical census of St Leonard's parish recorded 4,545 people, composed of 1,548 Catholics and 2,997 Protestants. The latter comprised 2,737 Anglicans, with just 69 Wesleyans, 15 Baptists, 39 Independents and 137 Presbyterians.[17] The dissenting tradition encouraged independence of thought, and what was for the time a more radical political outlook, in which all individuals were seen to have valid rights which the constitution of the state ought to reflect.

Though few in number, dissenters came to the fore in most of the

The Methodist Walking Day, Station Road, Bamber Bridge, 1907. The old stone-built property, which survives adjacent to the top of Greenwood Street, can clearly be seen. (R. Burns)

reforming movements of the nineteenth century, and formed the backbone of Gladstone's Liberal Party. Many of their aspirations found expression in the reforms of Lloyd George in the years 1906–1914. Each member of a Methodist society, for example, was responsible for his or her own destiny, and accordingly lay people took the lead in organising discussion classes and running chapel affairs. Officers were elected at the church meetings and the stewards were answerable to their congregations for their actions and behaviour. Each member had a duty to assist fellow members, and when necessary had to be prepared to provide leadership, through example, practical organisation or preaching. The individual's responsibilities thus extended beyond their own life, and reached out to the advancement of society as a whole.

John Wesley visited Walton on a number of occasions, and 'Methodist' meetings were being held in the district as early as 1763. The following year services were being held at 'Cockshutt House', later Cockshot Farm which stood near the end of Duddle Lane. The class had 16 members, including four spinners and four weavers, and was led by William Livesey, himself a weaver. Bamber Bridge was listed on a circuit plan of 1791, and Moons Mill on one dated 1809.[18] In Bamber Bridge early meetings were held in a cellar or loom shop, leading one writer to reflect that, 'The Lord soon brought them out of this dark dismal cellar, and gave them a position of comfort, respect, and influence'.[19] During these years 'Mr Walmesly of Cooper Hill', the steward of the Hoghton estate, was class leader. A circuit plan of 1814 lists the small weaving and factory communities of Moons Mill, Clayton Green, Bamber Bridge and Cuerden. A room in Old Hall

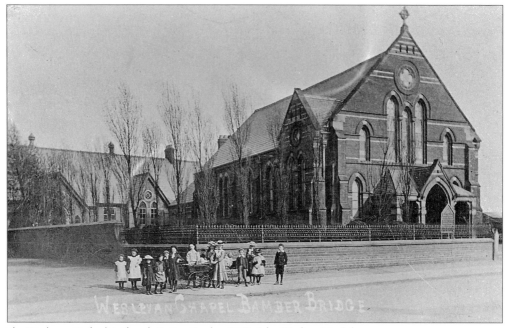

The Wesleyan Methodist Chapel, Station Road, c. 1900. John Wesley visited the
district on a number of occasions. In 1764 meetings were held at Cockshutt House, a
farm on Duddle Lane, and local Methodists subsequently met in members' houses
and loomshops. Despite humble origins, the local missions made great progress, so
that by 1890 a local writer could say of Bamber Bridge, 'The Methodists of this village
have accomplished noble things, and the workers are animated by great cheerfulness
and hope with respect to the future'. This photograph clearly pre-dates the
construction of the Bamber Bridge Spinning Company's enormous mill. (R. Burns)

was subsequently used until the first chapel in Bamber Bridge was built in
1821. A new church was opened in 1878 at a cost of £2,660, and work on
a new school commenced in 1885: 'Bamber Bridge has developed rapidly
during the last 15 years, and the growth still continues. The Methodists of
this village have accomplished noble things, and the workers are animated
by great cheerfulness and hope with respect to the future'.[20]

Higher Walton was established as a preaching place, and had a Sunday
school by 1804. Meetings were held in a part of the factory. In 1813 a room
was rented at the top of Higher Walton Brow near the site of the present
chapel: 'That old room for 57 years has been consecrated by the labour of
godly men who have trained hundreds of children to fear God. Many of
them are now prosperous men, holding responsible positions in society'.
In 1870 a new chapel was opened at a cost of £897 7s. 9d.[21] A Methodist
group at Cuerden Green (Lostock Hall) existed by about 1810, meeting in
'Old Pea Sally's cottage'. In 1840 Bashall's factory school began to be used
as a chapel and Sunday school. Bashall's successor Mr Ward also encouraged the Methodist society here, and provided cottages for conversion into
a new school/chapel, opened in 1876. This building could hold up to 400
worshippers and cost £730. Fund raising in the 1890s enabled an entirely

new chapel to be opened in June 1905. Only a short distance from Pea
Sally's cottage, it was hailed as 'one of the most beautiful in Methodism'.
The foundation stone for a new school was laid in 1910.[22]

Notwithstanding the claim that John Wesley himself stayed at Cooper
Hill on his visit of 1784, Methodism made only slow progress in Walton
village. Joseph King, a clogger, held early meetings in his house (probably
attended by the young Joseph Livesey), but it was not until 1867 that a
school/chapel was acquired, in Kings Croft. As at Cuerden Green the
interior walls of a number of cottages were taken out to effect a house
conversion. This location was very prone to flooding, and land was acquired at the bottom of Church Brow for the new chapel opened in 1882.
In 1925 a new school was built behind the chapel, which was itself converted
into flats in the early 1990s.[23]

Adult education and the Temperance Reformation

Only through education, reformers believed, could an individual be em-
powered to achieve his or her full potential as a citizen, and thus make
their full contribution to society. In the early years of the nineteenth century
a Walton Adult School Society was established, and was so successful that
it became a model for similar ventures all over the country. By 1817 it
could claim, 'there are now eight schools within the precincts of the Union,
most of which are taught in private houses ... The schools contain nearly
400 Learners'. James Whittaker (a local wheelwright) and James Dilworth
(a Quaker?) were the secretaries, and the society was able to publish a
Reading Book, which ran to a second edition in 1817: 'Lessons for the
Instruction of Adults, or An Introduction to the Reading of the Holy
Scriptures'. This was in fact an advanced system for the teaching of reading.
Meetings were held on Sunday evenings, and the society's aim seems to
have been 'to teach adult persons to read the Holy Scriptures; all poor
persons of both sexes and of any religious persuasion, of sixteen years of
age and upwards shall be considered eligible for admission into the school
as learners'. Such institutions were run by committee, and were democratic
in outlook. Learners, however, had to 'Testify their love to God and man
by regular attendance ... manifest their desire to improve ... manifest their
kindness and forbearance which are essential to the well being of society'.[24]

Joseph Livesey was strongly influenced by both the local dissenting
groups and the Walton education movement. A strong religious and political dissenter from his youth, though committed to reform through
constitutional means, he was nevertheless strongly opposed to all manifest-
ations of 'the establishment', and took a leading part in the radical cause
of Preston politics in the 1820s and 1830s. On the eve of the passing of the
Great Reform Act he proclaimed (rather prematurely as it was to turn out),
'The Sun of Toryism is set for ever!' Livesey's dissenting ideals and
educationalism led him into a life of reform agitation, supporting the

Reform Bill, the Factory Acts, and Free Trade, whilst opposing church privileges and the New Poor Law. These elements were particularly important in the shaping of the temperance movement, and many of his fellow pioneers shared a similar background. The temperance movement of the 1830s and 1840s thus became the first national mass reform movement led by working people.[25]

On his move to Preston, Livesey and his wife established a series of adult education classes in the town, and he advocated the formation of 'The Institute for the Diffusion of Knowledge'. This establishment later became the much respected Harris Technical College, and ultimately the University of Central Lancashire. That establishment can thus trace its origins to the pioneers of the Walton Adult School. Members of the classes and friends from Walton provided the core of activists within the Preston Temperance Society, which pioneered the Teetotal revolution. Among the 'Preston Pioneers' were Henry Anderton (the temperance poet), and John King (who formulated the first total abstinence pledge with Livesey and was an early temperance 'missionary'). Both of these men came from Walton, and shared Livesey's background. Indeed the 'Seven Men of Preston' who signed the celebrated pledge, included two Walton men, Joseph Livesey and John King. The combination of religious dissent, belief in education and personal and constitutional reform as tools of social progress, with personal experience of the realities of everyday life in the weaving and factory communities of the district, were thus the catalysts of a world-wide mass movement.

Local temperance societies were established throughout the district, and their progress was duly monitored in the temperance press:[26]

WALTON FACTORY

Dear Sir.

We, the spinners and rovers of Walton Factory, called Penwortham Factory, have signed the tee-total pledge this 20th day of July, 18 out of 26 men, for 3 months, and we have posted our names on the factory door for all to see.

Signed: Richard Lord

(*Preston Temperance Advocate*, August 1835)

PROGRESS AT MR BASHALL'S FACTORY

The spinners and other hands at Bashall's factory (Cuerden Green mill) having resolved to become sober persons, went in a body to the Walton-le-Dale temperance meeting last Monday night, when 34 of them signed the tee-total pledge. They are all enthusiastic in the cause, and have agreed among themselves to drag through the River Lostock any one of their comrades who violates his pledge.

(*Preston Temperance Advocate*, January 1837)

WORTHY OF IMITATION

At Roach Mill, near Preston, there is a Temperance Society, headed by the masters, which numbers about 100 members. A library is in the course of being formed in connection with it, for the use of the young men, and suitable periodicals will be provided. Those who can read are teaching those who cannot.

(*The Youthful Teetotaller*, January 1836)

A LANDLADY'S WISH

'What is to do yonder?' said a landlady at Clayton, as the people were returning from a temperance meeting. 'There has been a temperance meeting' said one of the party. 'The Devil temperance them!' was her reply. So much for the good wishes of the landladies.

(*Preston Temperance Advocate*, April 1835)

Radical politics: 'Sell thy garment & buy a sword'

By the end of the Napoleonic wars the golden age of the hand weavers had passed. Thereafter wages were steadily eaten away by the weavers' inability to control entry to the trade, and the advance of the powerloom. Richard Marsden, a Manchester weaver, moved to Bamber Bridge with his family in 1829. He became a leader of the Chartist movement, and his letters and speeches (preserved in the radical press of the time) shed much light on the conditions and politics of the period.[27] He later contrasted the 30s. he had earned in 1814, with the 7s. he was obtaining for the same work in the 1830s. Marsden's account of his family's poverty, 'which appeared in the newspapers, and which caused a sensation of horror whenever it was read', related how 'His wife and children had been utterly destitute of the means of existence with an infant at the breast, his wife was without food, and became so reduced in consequence of her privations that when her babe sought the natural nourishment which its mother should have afforded, instead of that nourishment, it drew from her nothing but blood'. His description of similar examples of poverty from 'his street', strongly suggests that he was resident in Club Street.[28]

Both the local weavers and the factory operatives, played their parts in the radical politics of the time. Their aims were improved wages and working conditions, parliamentary reform and representation, and the repeal of the New Poor Law. Although Preston became the natural centre of these struggles, local people were well represented, most conspicuously by Richard Marsden and Joseph Livesey. Bamber Bridge and Cuerden emerged as strongholds of this rising labour movement, and a letter from the former, published in the *Poor Man's Guardian* of December 1833, was signed 'A Few White Slaves'.[29]

From the 1770s the introduction of machinery progressively to replace long-established handicrafts, and devalue hard-learned skills, was violently opposed. In October 1779 'A Constant Reader', wrote to the editor of the *General Evening Post* in London, informing him of the anti-machinery disturbances in Lancashire: 'On Thursday October 7th the rioters made

an attempt to reach Preston, in order to destroy the factory belonging to Messrs Watson and Co., of this town, when the party of dragoons (who were then in number two serjeants and five privates) was again called upon, as also a party of invalids [retired soldiers], and other recruiting parties of foot, who were marched out of the town by the mayor and Capt. Culliford of the 10th. The mob were then assembled on Walton-hill and seemed very desperate, where the serjeant was ordered to give them a charge, which he and his party did, and totally dispersed them, after taking 10 prisoners, who are now lodged in the county gaol'.[30]

Brandiforth Street, off School Lane, c.1905. A good example of the purpose-built factory worker's houses of the later nineteenth century, which came to typify much of Bamber Bridge, and the mill communities at Higher Walton, Lostock Hall and Tardy Gate. They were frequently built by the factory masters, who regarded them, in J. K. Galbraith's words, as 'a place to shelter the work stock'. (R. Burns)

The strike and lock-out became the principal weapons in this rising class war between capital and labour, and wages became the battleground. Large-scale demonstrations attended the major disputes of 1808 and 1818. Strikes were frequently followed by the locking out of the workforce, as masters refused to take their former hands back. To maintain the solidarity of the Preston masters it was essential that their Walton counterparts co-operated in concerted action, and it is clear that from an early date they were part of an informal and probably illegal cartel of Preston masters to restrict wage levels, and to refuse future work to strikers. Accordingly, in May 1810 the following unusually generous offer appeared in the *Preston Journal*:

Wanted: A quantity of sober, steady men, to learn the business of Mule Spinning. Who will receive during the time of learning, or until they find themselves competant work by the piece, One Guinea Weekly, clear to themselves. Constant employment will also be given to any number of children above 9 years of age. NB A tolerable good spinner, can with ease, earn from 30 to 40 shillings per week, clear.

The list of ten signatories included Bashall & Pearson (Cuerden Green), James Wright (Penwortham), Wm. Sharrock (Roach Bridge Mill), George Clayton (Lostock), and R & D Salisbury (Higher Walton).[31]

The bitterness and extreme violence which came to be associated with employment disputes are revealed in the events at Roach Bridge mill in 1830, 'where in the course of last year there happened to be a turn-out of spinners and others in the employ of Mr Sharrock. The men chose to quit their employ, and they had a right to do so, having given their notice ... The mill was soon supplied with other persons. This excited a feeling of rancour among the turnouts'. Once established in their new jobs and 'the mill filled', Mr Sharrock stood his new workforce a 'Footing or jollification', held at the nearby New Hall Inn on the evening of Saturday 11th of December.[32]

As the merrymakers made their way home down the narrow lane, the first couple James Wells and Martha Wilding, 'perceived 4 men, but the night being dark, they had no opportunity of seeing their faces'. One of the men asked the time, to identify them, as another poured a jug of vitriol (sulphuric acid) over them, which 'falling on their clothes, hands and faces did them much harm'. Wilding's hair was burnt off, but the injuries suffered by Wells caused great shock when he appeared at the subsequent trial: 'His face was so much burnt that every feature was nearly destroyed. He had totally lost the sight of an eye, and nearly so the other'. Disturbances had continued well into the new year. A weaver, James Shorrock, was apparently mistaken for the owner and shot, and on 7 January 1831 a bomb was placed before Mr Sharrock's front door. Such events were not rare. Joseph

A group of local working men, probably from Bamber Bridge, c. 1910. In the space of half a century much of the district had been transformed from a pattern of dispersed rural hamlets into a series of industrial communities. A socially and politically distinct working class had come into being. (R. Burns)

Baxendale later recalled how he was shot at during the cloth printers strike at Bannister Hall in 1815.

The great Preston spinners' strike of 1836 and the Preston lockout of 1853–54 dominate the nineteenth-century labour history of the district. The Walton mills and the owners were fully involved, and although the specific dispute in each case concerned an advance of 10 per cent, the real point at issue was one of mastery. The response of the Masters' Association to the strike of 1853 was characteristic and straightforward: 'To this spirit of Tyranny and Dictation the Masters can no longer submit … and hence they are reluctantly compelled to accept the only alternative left – to close their mills, until … a better understanding is established between the Employer and the Employed'. Among the mills closed were those of the Walton owners, Miles Rodgett, William Bashall, William Calvert and Richard Eccles. Both disputes failed, the latter ending with a mass meeting along the bank of the Ribble by the bridge, on May-day 1854, which ratified the return to work.[33]

The early years of the nineteenth century thus witnessed the emergence of a distinct working-class culture, whose roots lay in religious nonconformity, self help, and the shared experience of the industrial revolution. During the harsh years of the 1830s and 1840s this found political expression locally in the Chartist movement. J. E. King has provided a detailed account of the career and ideas of Richard Marsden, and indirectly, reveals the aspirations of his fellow weavers and operatives. Chartism was a constitutional and democratic movement which sought social progress through political reform. Of the six points of the charter, only annual parliaments have not been attained. On 5 November 1838 local activists organised a great Chartist demonstration at Preston. Many trade unions were represented in the procession from the Orchard to Preston Moor, with 40 banners, eight bands and thousands of people. Among the speakers were Feargus O'Connor and Richard Marsden, who was described as 'A weaver from Bamber Bridge'. In the report of the 'Great Preston Radical Meeting' carried in *The Northern Star*, the workpeople from Cuerden Green factory were singled out for particular praise. Their banner bore the words 'No Bastilles For Me – I Intend To Be Free', on one side, and on the other more ominously, 'Sell Thy Garment And Buy A Sword'. William Bashall's employees had been offered the previous day off work to watch the opening of the North Union Railway. They had asked that they might be allowed to take off the fifth, in order for them to participate in the demonstration. This was refused, and the spinners were threatened with fines 'if they were not in their places'. Notwithstanding this, *The Northern Star* stated, 'To the people of this factory the Committee of the Radical Association are indebted for their generous aid'. Local radicalism thus drew on all sections of the textiles workforce.[34]

Yet Chartism also contained more direct 'physical force' elements. In May 1842 the second Chartist petition was thrown out of Parliament, and

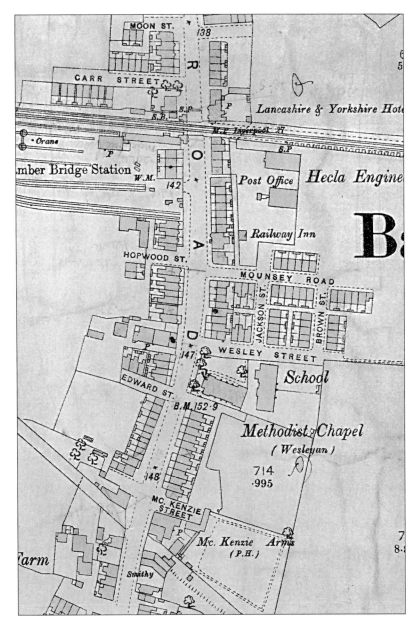

The progressive in-building along Station Road, south of the railway, Bamber Bridge, can be seen in this extract from the Ordnance Survey map, which pre-dates the construction of the 'New Mill' in 1907.

from July the celebrated 'Plug' strikes began. On Friday 12 August 1842 a general strike was declared in Preston. The next day became Preston's 'Black Saturday', and saw troops 'firing on the people' in Lune Street, killing four and seriously wounding three, as the authorities lost control of the district. Although local Chartists were at pains to distance themselves from the lawless elements, the whole district was in a state of turmoil. 'Quietness has been restored, but of course there is a great ferment in people's minds.'[35] On the following Wednesday word reached the town that a 'relief force' was on the way from Wigan and Chorley to avenge

the fallen. The inquisitive climbed the parish church tower to scan the
Bamber Bridge road, and troops were deployed on the tram bridge and
Penwortham bridge, with their main force on Walton bridge.

The mob, having started from Chorley, 'Made to the factory of Messrs
Bashall & Co., at Leyland [Farington Mill], where they obliged the hands
to turn out, pulled out the plug of the boiler, and extinguished the fire.
Bent however, upon further mischief they ... levied contributions on some
of the inhabitants of Leyland and the farmers in the neighbourhood'.
Whether this force visited Bashall's mill at Cuerden Green is unclear, but
the ragged force of perhaps 400–500 men, women, and children entered
Bamber Bridge unopposed, probably along Brownedge, and drew up
opposite William Eccles's Withy Trees.[36]

At the next Quarter Sessions a large number of local people gave
accounts of what happened next:[37]

> Thomas Seed being sworn in says ... I am a roller carrier and the day watch
> at the mill ... About noon ... I saw a mob approach the mill consisting as
> nearly as I can guess from 200 to 300 of men, women and children – the
> mill gates were then open for our workpeople to go to dinner. Mr Eccles
> ordered me to close them and I did – John Wood one of the leaders of the
> mob then came to Mr Eccles and said to him -'You had better not close the
> gates – we only want to pull the plugs out of the boiler so that we can help
> stop your mill from working'. Another of the mob came up and asked Mr
> Eccles if he would give him something. Mr Eccles said 'No I shan't give
> you any thing'. The same men and some others of the mob then said if the
> gates are not opened we will break them down. I then received directions
> from Mr Ashworth our manager to open them and I did. The mob then
> entered and filled the yard. Mr Eccles went with them a short distance and
> then said 'Now my men', addressing his own workpeople, 'let us give them
> a good thrashing'. We then made a show of resistance and the mob fled out
> of the yard one of them first having struck Mr Eccles. I then observed the
> defendant Walsh in the rear and saw Mr Eccles knock him down. When
> they were out again I closed the gates, and being much frightened as well
> as Mr Eccles we both left the mill. After hearing that the mob had left the
> mill, I returned to the mill and found that the gates had been broken down
> – the plugs of the boilers pulled out and from 1,300 to 1,400 squares of glass
> broken in the mill windows.

John Walsh, after being cautioned, claimed that 'he had been on his way
from Chorley to see his relatives in Preston', he had not been the first to
enter the yard, but had been pushed in by the crowd.

The crowd also visited the adjacent Walton-le-Dale workhouse, as
James Wilding the governor attested:

> I was near to Mr Eccles mill at Bamber Bridge ... After leaving the mill
> they came to the workhouse and filled it by 40 and 50 at a time, four or
> five times. The only person I knew amongst them was the defendant James

Bamber who had a bludgeon in his hand … he demanded drink, which he got. He was very violent in his language and terrified me whilst he remained. The conduct of the mob generally was such as to excite the fears of the neighbourhood.

Passing down Cinnamon Hill and over the Darwen, the mob: 'A large body of navigators, as they are called, that is excavators employed in making the railway, colliers, weavers and others … armed with … bludgeons and other deadly weapons, such as large iron bolts, iron bars, knives and scythes', visited and stopped Mr Calvert's factory. Their further progress into Preston was halted on Walton bridge. As troops stood by, 'rural constables' armed with swords, charged and dispersed the crowd. The routed host fled in panic'. Some got into the fields, others slunk behind hedges, others hid in water-closets, the yards and the gardens of Walton. One man secreted himself for two hours up a chimney, and three others crouched in a privy'.

Women were well to the fore in the violence, and one woman was taken in the River Darwen, into which she had waded up to her waist; 'The mob when it came on at first instance was headed by women, who had their caps full of the broken granite used for macadamising the road … we are informed that no less than a cart load of stone has thus been imported into Walton'. Richard Marsden was among those arrested at Walton bridge, though he was quickly released without being charged. The *Preston Chronicle* rejoiced that, 'the mob having been thus soundly thrashed dispersed, the constables and soldiers returned to headquarters, and so terminated the apprehended sacking of Preston by the Battle of Walton Bridge'.[38]

Station Road, Bamber Bridge, c. 1900. Much of Station Road was built up in the 1870s, and from this date the quality of life for the majority of working-class people began to improve. Notice the paved road and the flagged thoroughfare. Much of this well-built property survives today, most notably the former Bamber Bridge Police Station, the fourth building from the left. (*R. Burns*)

The reputation parts of the district enjoyed for violence and lawlessness was thus not without some grounds in fact. In 1848 a force of 50 policemen armed with cutlasses was required to assist debt-collectors about their work in Club Street,[39] but by 1890 reformers could look back on the enormous progress the century had brought: 'This village [Bamber Bridge] has undergone great changes during the last 50 years, politically, socially and religiously. For the first three decades of the present century, it was not very safe to be about alone after dark. Though the people of this district were comparatively poor, and lived by working the treadles, and throwing the shuttle across the handloom, yet they excelled in drunkenness, fighting and profanity: BUT ALL THAT HAS GONE BY, and it shows distinct traces of modern advancement'.[40]

The extremely severe times of the industrial revolution and its long aftermath, thus generated a strong working class culture in what had previously been a predominantly rural farming district. It is perhaps noteworthy that the two particularly famous people born and brought up in the area, Joseph Livesey and the trades unionist leader George Woodcock, were pre-eminently social reformers whose formative years had been spent in the district's cotton industry.

CHAPTER TEN

The nineteenth century: Cottonopolis

HROUGHOUT the nineteenth century and up to the Great War, the population of the district steadily advanced, as the primary industries continued to expand to meet the world's demand for cotton goods. Having approached nearly 6,000 in 1821, the population figure then reached a plateau, until renewed growth in the late 1850s pushed it to above 7,000 in 1861. Each census thereafter added around a thousand people, or 10 per cent to the number, until a second plateau was reached in 1911–31 (1861–67, 363; 1871–78, 187; 1881–89, 286; 1891–1910, 556; 1901–11, 271; 1911–12, 352). A fall in the population number was recorded for the first time in 1921. The demographic trend from the Napoleonic wars to the Second World War is thus very closely correlated to developments within the cotton industry, particularly the decline of the hand weaving trade in the period 1820–40, and the onset of severe foreign competition after 1921. Absolute growth, however, masks important changes in the distribution of the population within the district.

After 1840 a wide range of new sources of information becomes available to the historian. These include the detailed census returns (1841–1891), the Walton-le-Dale Tithe Map (1839), and the series of Ordnance Survey maps beginning in 1848.[1] They reveal a process of cumulative urbanism, as the first industrial communities developed into distinct settlements in their own right. The district which for almost a thousand years had been dominated by the single settlement at Walton steadily developed a mosaic of small villages, each clustered about a mill or railway access point. The ancient predominance of the river valley alluvials along the Ribble and particularly the Darwen, was overturned by the rise of Bamber Bridge in the central belt of the district. Through the stimulus of the mill and the railway, 'Gregson Lane' developed from a scatter of farm and weavers cottages around the 'Four Lane Ends', and the Tardy Gate–Brownedge Road–Lostock Hall district developed with the growth of the railway yards at Lostock Hall Junction.

These developments can clearly be seen from the 6″ OS map series, produced in 1847–48 (surveyed 1844–46), 1895 (revised 1891–92), and 1914 (revised 1909). By the edition of 1938 (revised 1929) extensive suburban and ribbon development (housing built along the sides of the main through roads) was well advanced. Tracing these developments through the enormous mass of census returns is fraught with difficulty. The enumeration

districts were often changed from one census to another. For example the 1851 census used just five districts, whilst that of 1891 used 11. The names of streets change, and house numbers have been re-ordered repeatedly. Important local landmarks, such as 'Wise Mary's' or 'New Side' have disappeared, and the inhabitants of 'School Lane' or 'Withy Trees' listed in the census of 1841 would have had little notion that they lived in 'Bamber Bridge' – then a cluster of houses nearly a mile away! 'Higher Walton' (noted in a deed of 1805) replaced Moons Mill, Kitting Burn and Many-brooks, but 'Lower Walton' never established itself as the name of the original settlement. Alternatively, 'Little Walton' (a name in use in the early seventeenth century) became Bamber Bridge.

From 1861 the difficulties produced by the variations in the census districts become more manageable, and the broad pattern of population changes becomes clearer. The proportion of the population living in Walton village (with Church Brow, and the property north of the Darwen, but excluding Cuerdale) fell steadily from 27 per cent in 1861 (2,020 people) to 18 per cent in 1891 (1,877 people). By contrast, the population of Higher Walton grew steadily from the 1850s, when the Rodgett family began their enormous investment in the district. From 1,094 people in 1861, the figures were 1871–1,173, 1881–1,359, and 1891–1,548, an increase of over 40 per cent in 30 years. Thus although the combined actual population of Walton and Higher Walton increased from 3,114 to 3,420 in this period, its actual share of the population of the district fell from 42 per cent (1861) to 32 per cent (1891).

The growth of the central district (Bamber Bridge including School Lane–Brownedge–Withy Trees, and Tardy Gate–Lostock Hall) was

St Mary's Road, seen from the corner of Brownedge Lane, 1890. The design of nineteenth-century houses closely reflected the means of their proposed inhabitants. The houses in St Mary's Road, with their well-kept front gardens, were clearly intended for those able to pay a higher rent, in an era when very few people owned their own house.
(R. Burns)

School Lane Co-operative Society, *c.* 1910. By 1870 School Lane, with its two cotton mills, had emerged as a quite distinct community in its own right. The figure of a woman on the extreme left of the photograph gives a good impression of the everyday dress of the period. St Aidan's School, centre left, occupied the site of the old Walton School. (*R. Burns*)

School Lane Post Office, *c.* 1910. A good example of well-built local property, erected during the boom years of the Lancashire cotton trade. The prosperity of the period is proclaimed in the high ornate door lintels and other architectural touches. (*R. Burns*)

spectacular. The population of these districts rose from 3,566 in 1871, to 5,672 in 1891. In the 1870s growth reached almost 30 per cent and remained at over 20 per cent during the 1880s. In the context of the entire district, the share rose from 43 per cent in 1871, to 49 per cent in 1881, and 93 per cent in 1891. Much of this growth was related to the construction of new mills: Stone Mill and Orr's Mill in School Lane, Mexican Mill in Aspden Street, and the construction of the railway depots at Lostock Hall. Indeed in just ten years the population of Tardy Gate–Lostock Hall rose from 712 to 1,108 (1891).

Bamber Bridge: 'Now within the pale of civilisation'

Visiting Bamber Bridge in the early 1870s Anthony Hewitson affected to be unimpressed. It was not 'a very comely village. It is long, roundabout, up and down: it is full of microscopical cottages, at desperately high rents' and 'has a queer breach made in it by an antiquated tramway'. He dwelt on the supposed dangers of the place in the early nineteenth century, 'But all that has gone by, and Bamber Bridge is now within the pale of civilis-ation ... we maintain that it may be classed as a village within the ring of civilisation, and as a place showing distinct traces of advancement'. In reality, of course, he seems to have been quite fond of the place and its erstwhile inhabitants.[2]

The village is one of the best examples of ribbon development in the region. In the 1780s such houses that existed were restricted to small clusters at the main road intersections, principally at the junction of the Wigan and Chorley road near the Hob Inn. The length of road north from here to the end of School Lane was virtually undeveloped, and a considerable area of mossland remained along Brownedge. By the publication of the first 6″ OS map in 1848 (surveyed 1844–46) the impact of the industrial revolution was very apparent, though the village remained essentially a rural one, set in expansive fields.

The principal community was clustered along the main road, to the south of the Blackburn railway line, and centred on the Club Street–Spinners Court area. Much of this development, and the tramway goods yard and coal depot beside the McKenzie Arms, originated in the earliest phase of growth around the turn of the century. A high proportion of the property was built in stone, and survives to the present day. Less than a mile to the south, a second foci had grown up around Withy Trees mill. It included the workhouse, 'Punch Row' – now Withy Grove Road, and a small row of houses suitably known as 'Judy Row'. The length of the main road north from here to the Pear Tree and School Lane was little developed, apart from the stone-built weavers' houses along the east side adjacent to Greenwood Street. A short row of brick-built weavers' step houses, 'Lilac Houses', occupied the site at Charleston Court. School Lane remained largely rural, though in 1848 building was under way here. Along the web of ancient lanes extending south from Hennel Lane (Todd Lane and Wateringpool Lane), and along Duddle Lane and Brownedge, little had changed in centuries, beyond the establishment of the Catholic chapel. As late as the middle of the nineteenth century 'Bamber Bridge' was not a village in any accepted sense of the word, rather it was an accumulation of hamlets along the Preston–Wigan road.

By the publication of the OS map of 1895 (surveyed in 1891–92), a further half-century of ribbon development and mill construction, had welded these country districts into an urban mass, though local identities were to remain strong well into the next century. Withy Trees emerged as a significant residential area, and Dean Street and Greenwood Street accommodated workers at Mexican Mill in Aspden Street. Development was well under way along Brownedge Lane and Saint Mary's Road, but Duddle Lane and the fields along the south side of Brownedge Lane remained largely untouched. The coming of the railway had resulted in further growth to the south in the vicinity of 'Bamber Bridge' railway station, whose existence did much to identify the name with this previously amorphous area, and provided the name 'Station Road' as the title of the main throughway. Extensive railway sidings had been constructed here, and at Brownedge to the west of Meanygate.

The most important change to the village was the rapid emergence of the School Lane area as a major industrial and residential centre, providing a northern counterpart to the community south of the railway. The expansion of Withy Trees, and further ribbon growth along Station Road, were able to bind these developments into an extended village. The construction of Stone mill and Orr's mill, by 1850 and 1870 respectively, provided employment for a large workforce, and accommodation was built along School Lane and its side streets, Brandiforth Street, Mill Street and School Street. The growth of this district in the second half of the century formed the basis of modern Bamber Bridge which thus emerged as the main centre in the Urban District established in 1897. Yet to the north of the 'Pear Tree' and to the south of the 'Hob Inn' the main road still ran through open fields.

The detailed census returns from 1841–91 enable these developments to be traced in detail.[3] In 1841 handloom weaving was still an important local trade. A fair number of weavers are recorded at Brownedge, in the purpose-built houses north of Withy Trees – Lilac Houses – and in the surviving houses at Holland Slack. Yet even in Club Street their number was quickly being overtaken by that of the factory workers. Here, in the premises of the former Bamber Bridge Commercial Building Society, 387 people occupied 59 houses. Of the 203 inhabitants 'in work', 179 people were employed in the textile trade, with 77 handloom weavers, 52 powerloom weavers, and 50 people in related trades. Of the powerloom hands, all were under 30 years of age, with 30 under 20 years and 11 under 15 years. Half were women. At 'Withy Trees factory' a sample of 300 people occupied 43 houses. Of 158 people in work, 141 were employed in textiles. Along the main Bamber Bridge axis the occupations of 884 people are listed, revealing 665 textile workers in a population of 1,600 people. In the largely rural area to the west of Station Road, extending across Brownedge to Todd Lane (then 'Toad Lane'), half of the workforce of 400 people was engaged in textiles (665 people, 392 at work, 205 textile workers).

A number of features thus characterise the population at this time. A very high proportion of the population worked, comprising virtually everyone apart from the very young, the great majority of them in some aspect of the cotton trade. By modern standards this was a very young population, and in the district south of the railway in Bamber Bridge, for example, only a couple of people are recorded over 80 years of age, with few people over 45 years old. The bulk of the cotton mill workforce would thus be termed 'young people' today.

After 1841 these factors begin to change markedly. By the 1851 census the railway had begun to emerge as an important employer: William Clayton (34) resided at the station with his wife Anne and their two children, describing himself as 'Railway Porter'. In the 1861 census John R. Maxwell (28) is listed as 'Railway Station Master'. Development along School Lane was now well under way, and large numbers of people described themselves as 'Cotton Factory Workers'. The census enumerator, John Greenwood, caused great consternation by altering the area of his enumeration district 'to be more convenient to him', and rather idiosyncratically recorded thatched housing at Brownedge. By 1871 the School Lane mills were well established, and G. & R. Dewhurst had taken over and begun to expand Cuerden Mill on the site of the old Clayton print works, known locally as 'Down Below' and 'Dewhursts Row'.

The progress of Bamber Bridge in the 1860s and 1870s was very marked, with large numbers of terraces erected. Handloom weavers became a rarity: Club Street had 22 in 1861, but only 7 ten years later, and none in 1881.

Brownedge Road level crossing and signal box, c. 1912. In the final decades of the nineteenth century, Lostock Hall emerged as a major railway centre, and the sounds of the railway could be heard throughout much of the district right up to the end of the steam era in the 1960s. (R. Burns)

Brownedge Lane and the end of Aspden Street, c.1920. Well into the present century Brownedge retained a certain rural charm. St Mary's Junior School can be seen in the distance, with the old farm beyond it. (R. Burns)

At No. 3 Lilac Houses, John Waring aged 70 in 1881, was among the last of the hand weavers of Bamber Bridge. Although whole rows of houses were given over to factory workers, the proportion of people in work began to fall, as a higher proportion of older people was recorded. By the census of 1891, much of the fabric of Bamber Bridge, as it was to survive up to the Second World War, was in place. The opening of the modern era was perhaps heralded by William Johnston (34), of Station Road, who gave his occupation as 'Telephone Labourer'.

Brownedge

By the 1880s Bamber Bridge had absorbed Brownedge, although the area maintained a sense of identity up to the construction of the Duddle Lane housing estates in the early 1960s. Commentators frequently alluded to its pleasant aspect, which must have been in stark contrast to the crowded rows of houses clustered around the mills of Bamber Bridge and Cuerden. Hewitson described the panorama from St Mary's Church: 'Looking from right to left: a mill, a wood, church spire, Whittle Hills, several cottages, and two or three factories; and in the immediate foreground, three hedges, twenty-two railway wagons, a pointsman's box, and one end of Bamber Bridge'. He found Brownedge 'an irregularly fashioned, quietly situated hamlet ... It stands in a flat district: and if anything special has to be seen you must either climb a tree or ask somebody for a ladder. The inhabitants are homely and kind-hearted ... Humble hard working people live in it, but they make you welcome'.[4]

The Roman Catholic church was the architectural wonder of the district.

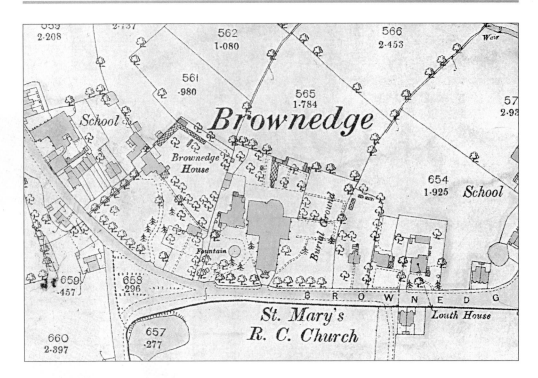

Brownedge Church and schools, a section of the 25″ OS map. The triangle formed at the junction of Brownedge Lane, Brownedge Road and Duddle Lane probably resulted from the construction of a way west along the former moss via Brownedge Road to Tardy Gate. The lower land to the south of Brownedge was not yet developed.

Mannex's *Directory* described it in 1854 as 'a beautiful Catholic chapel, in a most delightful and picturesque location'. The church took pride of place among Hewitson's *Country Churches and Chapels* – 'There is not a country church, whether Protestant or Catholic, we have yet visited which can be at all compared to this in decorative effect, in richness of tone, in elaborateness of detail, in the many hued colours and rare beauty of its sanctuary, and in the fullness and perfection of its artistic treatment throughout'.[5] The first chapel here was opened in December 1780, and was rebuilt in the 1820s. The 120′ high spire and tower had been 'recently erected' in 1873. The mission was an extremely successful one, and schools were erected close by the church in 1862. They were run by the 'Sisters of Christ', who established a convent here the following year. A new 'Boys School' was opened in 1882. In 1871 Elizabeth Drake (39), was the 'supervisoress', describing her occupation as 'Teacher in Poor School'. In all there were four nuns, rising to nine in 1881. By 1891 the flourishing establishment had 10 nuns and 15 resident 'female boarding school scholars'.

To accommodate the rapidly growing but poor parish, with few rich patrons, a series of extensions to the church was followed by a wholesale rebuilding in 1891–92. All but the tower seems to have been reconstructed to designs by Pugin & Pugin of Westminster, creating a church almost 200′ long, 70′ wide, broadening to 100′ at the transepts, and capable of holding 1,200 people. The interior was spectacular, and quite at odds with the stark and buttressed exterior. The new marble high altar was set within

Bamber Bridge level crossing, looking north along Station Road, c. 1920. The extent to which Eccles' mill, and particularly the enormous chimney, dominated the village, can clearly be appreciated from this photograph. Colin Dickinson, in his masterly study of the mills of the Preston district, suggested that round- or oval-sectioned chimneys replaced square ones about 1850. This was a circular chimney. (R. Burns)

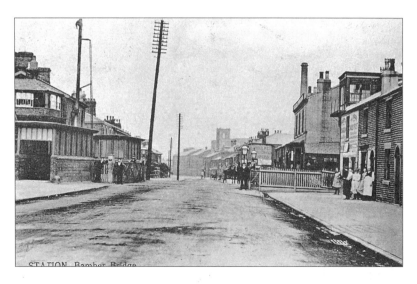

a columnade of ten polished granite pillars to stunning affect. Even the roof, with its enormous span, was a wonder.[6]

St Saviour's and St Aidan's

The rising importance of Bamber Bridge was recognised as early as 1836 by the establishment of a second Anglican parish in the district, and the construction of St Saviour's Church. The adjoining 'National School' followed

St Aidan's Church, Station Road, c. 1920. The parish was formed in 1895, and work on the church began. Built in sections, it was completed in 1914. The houses on the left fronted open fields which still extended westwards to Duddle Lane, preserving the village's rural aspect. (R. Burns)

in 1839. In 1854 Mannex's *Directory* found that 'the vicar has a good dwelling ... Here is also a very convenient and well ventilated school'. In 1886–87 the church was extended by the addition of a chancel and transept, and the nave was extended at a cost of £3,300. The Dewhurst family, the owners of nearby Cuerden mill and Higher Walton mill, were important benefactors. Anthony Hewitson was much taken with the spire, which he found also served as a chimney, and squire Parker of Cuerden Hall's pew: 'It is so arranged that the bulk of the congregation cannot see those who may be in it: the "vulgar stare" is shut off, and the fine old squire, who is fond of lofty cosy pews, may send up his orisons in it and go through either quiet meditations or fine genuflections without anybody seeing him'.[7]

The first vicar of St Saviour's, the Rev. W. Wignall (d. 16 Dec. 1867), was an important worker on the local Cotton Famine relief committee. Hewitson left a colourful picture of his successor the Rev. J. Taylor (34), 'Mr Taylor is a stalwart, strongly-built, firm muscled man, keeps his hair excellently combed: has dark cap bordered whiskers; has a brisk, clean roseate face – it always seems to have been just washed: is fiery, manly, candid; doesn't care much for dress, and knocks about in rough, strong, plain clothes ... gets into hot water sometimes with his parishioners for castigating them; has no faith in Roman Catholicism, and considers the Pope a wonderful sinner, but is not as fierce in this as he once was ... feels that he is the vicar of Bamber Bridge, and respects highly the gentleman who lives at the vicarage ... has a large head and English spirit, and a candid mind'. As at Brownedge, the congregation was mostly composed of factory people.[8] The ancient 'parish' was further subdivided by the formation of St Aidan's parish, and the present church was begun in 1895. By 1901, 'only the east end has been completed, leaving the west end for a future extension. The church, when completed, will consist of nave, side aisles, chancel and transepts ... The style adopted is late Decorated Gothic'. The church was eventually completed in 1914.

The mansions

A short distance to the south of the river Lostock, Cuerden Park enclosed a rather different world from that of the millhands and handloom weavers of Bamber Bridge. Although occupying an ancient site, Cuerden Hall has been rebuilt on a number of occasions since Dr Kuerden described the 'Ancient fabric' in the seventeenth century. The most notable rebuildings are those by 'Mr Banastre-Parker' in 1717, and Robert Townley-Parker in 1816–19. The latter was resident here in 1851, with his wife, son and daughter, and their 14 servants. No fewer than 15 visitors are listed in the census, and many of the visitors had their own servants with them. Townley-Parker was High Sheriff in 1817, and was Tory MP for Preston in 1837–41, and 1852–57. His politics, and his attempts to suppress poaching on his estate did not endear him to the locals. He died in 1879. The 1861 census describes him as a 'Landed Proprietor', and the hall had 17 servants, and a gardener, Samuel Ormerod (56), who lived at Stag Lodge. In 1906 the hall passed to Reginald Tatton. Having been used as a hospital during the First World War, and as an educational centre and the 'Anti Aircraft Headquarters' during the second, it was finally sold by the Tatton family in 1958. After use by the army and the Central Lancashire Development Corporation, the hall became a Sue Ryder Home.[9]

Bamber Bridge itself had two mansions, Withy Grove and Darwen Bank, the homes of the local millowning dynasties – the Eccles and the Rodgetts. The 1841 census lists eight members of the Eccles family living at Withy Grove, a fine house set in the fields behind Withy Trees mill. William Eccles (38) is described as a 'Master Cotton Spinner', and his wife Jane was 33. They had five children living with them, a visiting relative, and three female servants. By 1871 Eccles was 'Employer of 384 hands', and his sons William and John were also described as cotton spinners. William junior took over the firm, and he was still resident at Withy Grove in 1891, when he was described as 'Cotton Spinner and manufacturer'. Unmarried, he lived with a housekeeper, a cook, and two servants.

Darwen Bank, 'standing in its own grounds of 70 acres, occupies an eminence from which extensive and beautiful views may be obtained'. Located off School Lane, and formerly the country seat of the Pedder family, the estate had been purchased by Miles Rodgett by 1841, when the 'Master Cotton Spinner' had a household of nine, including his sons Edward, Miles, John and Richard. It was the family home for half a century, which saw the rapid progress of Higher Walton. Both Miles Rodgett (86) and his wife Tabitha (84) were still resident in 1871, with their sons Miles junior (53) 'Land owner', and John (49) 'Retired Cotton Manufacturer'. In 1881 Edward Rodgett was resident; he had 'no occupation', and lived in some style with six servants. The estate had cottages for the gardener, coachman, under gardener, and gamekeeper.

On Edward Rodgett's death in December 1892 it was reported that 'Gloom has been cast over the district of Higher Walton, where the deceased Gentleman was held in the greatest esteem'. He had left the family firm in Preston, and 'built a large establishment at Moons Mill by which the inhabitants of that village were mainly kept alive'. A 'staunch conservative', he had always exhibited the 'Deepest anxiety in the welfare of those in the midst of whom he laboured'. Ill health had forced him to retire, and on his father's death he had moved from Darwen Cottage, married, and 'became the possessor of numerous rare and valuable oil paintings'. He was also the owner of a yacht.[10]

By 1891 Darwen Bank was the palatial residence of John Humber (21), another 'Cotton Manufacturer', his wife Jane (24), and their five servants. As Mayor of Preston, Humber entertained the Duke of Edinburgh on his visit to open Preston Dock in June 1892. On the arrival of HRH in School

BAMBER BRIDGE STATION (6)

Lane, the children of St Aidan's school, 'arranged' in their school yard, sang 'Rule Britannia' and 'God Save the Queen'. The Duke passed speedily through to a banquet at the mansion, whilst a procession of floats passed enfete along the lane, cheered by the large crowds, 'but through the efforts of the police order was maintained throughout'. Bamber Bridge brass band, Higher Walton band, and the Bamber Bridge Morris men were much in evidence. Pride of place was given to a 'beautiful decorated lorry, on which were Britannia and her guards'. School Lane's great day ended with a supper at the 'Moot Hall' for members of the revived 'Mock Corporation', after which 'Fireworks were displayed'.[11]

The signal box, Bamber Bridge level crossing, c. 1915. The unique signal box at Bamber Bridge, located high on the side of a building, may indicate that property was demolished in order to carry the railway through the village. When a train was due to cross, heavy wooden gates operated by hand from the box, closed the roadway. (R. Burns)

Steam Town: Lostock Hall and Tardy Gate

Ironically it was the remote mossland edge of the old manor which best came to represent the age of steam. South of Walton Moss along the river Lostock, the early mills at Cuerden Green and Lostock Hall became the centres of small communities of mill workers. The first edition 6″ OS map of the district (published 1848, surveyed 1844–46), reveals a predominantly rural flat landscape on the edge of the great mosslands of West Lancashire, exploited and worked by a pattern of relatively isolated small farms. The district really comprised two quite distinct hamlets. 'Tardy Gate' is located on the Preston–Leyland road at the point where it was joined by the main cross-country routes linking Preston and Walton with the villages of the west. These include Brownedge Road and Wateringpool Lane from the north and east, and Croston Road and Coote Lane from the south and west. 'Lostock Hall' came to be applied to the district to the south, lying west of the actual and ancient Lostock Hall (now the site of St Catherine's Hospice). Broadly speaking, these districts came to be separated by the line of the East Lancashire railway, though in practice the length of Leyland Road–Watkin Lane became a central axis, fulfilling much the same function as Station Road in Bamber Bridge.

By the late 1840s the Blackburn line was opened, and the availability of cheap flat land, and the junction here with the North Union line (ultimately the west coast main line), and the East Lancashire–Liverpool line, led to the development of an extensive series of railway servicing facilities. These included sidings, marshalling yards and engine sheds. Lostock Hall thus emerged as something of a colony of the Lancashire and Yorkshire Railway Company. By day and night, the sights, smells and sounds of the railway pervaded the entire district.

By the OS survey of 1891–92 (published 1895) the small mill beside Lostock Hall had long closed, and Walton Moss had gone. The Cuerden Green mills had been greatly extended, and a large community had developed with the construction of Lostock View and South View. The landscape of the area was now completely dominated by the arcs of railway line which formed the important route junction. In the steam age, therefore, the ancient strategic importance of the Ribble crossing at Walton had passed to Lostock Hall. Large goods marshalling yards and sidings had been developed, with a 'goods shed' between Moss Lane Bridge and Watkin Lane, and an 'engine shed' to the west of Watkin Lane. Railway stations were positioned at Farington on the main line, and at Lostock Hall on the Liverpool and East Lancashire line. The more direct spurs from the latter to Preston, via Brownedge Crossing and Red Bridge, had a station in Todd Lane known originally as Preston Junction, and later as Todd Lane Junction. A very extensive series of reservoirs had been constructed along the Liverpool and East Lancashire line, extending three-quarters of a mile west from the intersection with the main line.

Twenty years later (1912 map, surveyed 1909) the mill of 'The Tardy Gate Manufacturing Company' had been built off Coote Lane, and further mill housing had been erected between Ward Street (formerly Bashall's Row) and the railway. Lostock Hall's growth as a railway centre had reached its greatest extent with the opening of the 'Lostock Hall connecting line', and the erection of further engine, goods and carriage sheds. A very extensive railway centre now extended along the former mosslands eastwards from Tardy Gate to Moss Lane, with more distant goods yards at Brownedge. Indeed the whole length of the East Lancashire line from Bamber Bridge to the junction with the main line ran through a series of railway facilities.

The foundation stone of St James' Mission Church was laid by Harry Dewhurst in June 1891, and the building was completed the following year. A Catholic 'school-church' dedicated to St Paulinus was also built in 1891, and a separate parish – independent of Brownedge – was formed in 1903.

A new Catholic church, dedicated to Our Lady of Lourdes and St Gerard Majella, was opened in 1913.

The census of 1841 records just six houses on Walton Moss, with ten people in work, half of them in textiles.[12] In marked contrast, the mills operated by the Bashalls and their partners at Cuerden Green and Farington employed many hundreds, accommodated in purpose-built mill cottages. At Cuerden Green 'Bashall's Row' housed 482 people in 58 houses, most of whom worked at the mill. Along Leyland Road, to the south of the river Lostock, William Bashall (40) and his partner William Boardman (40) lived in great style at Farington Lodge and Farington House respectively. By 1851 the development of the railway was well under way, and in 1861 John Holt (34) proudly gave his occupation as 'Railway Station Master: Lostock Station No. 1'. Richard Bashall (61) occupied the old mill manager's house adjacent to Cuerden Green mill (Lostock House or 'Bashall's Lodge'), whilst John Bashall (35) resided at Lostock Hall. During the 1860s the mill was taken over by Henry Ward and Sons, and in 1871 William Flitcroft was living at Lostock House and Robert Jackson at the hall. Both were cotton spinners, and Flitcroft subsequently established the Lostock Hall Spinning Company beside Cuerden Green Mill. Ten years later Harry Dewhurst (25), of the firm of G. & R. Dewhurst, the operators of the enormous Cuerden and Higher Walton mills, resided at the Hall.

The 1881 census records railway workers of all kinds – pointsmen, signal men, railway porters, clerks, platelayers, labourers and engine drivers – as Lostock Hall completed its transformation into a railway town. Since the cotton industry also continued to expand, and both of these employers reached their peaks in the final decades of the nineteenth century, the growth of the Tardy Gate–Lostock Hall area was very marked, enabling the population to increase by 65 per cent in the 1880s. The emergence of the 'new' industries at Leyland, so marked a feature of the twentieth-century history of the district, had also begun to emerge, and Henry Culshall (21) described himself as a 'Labourer at the India Rubber Works'.

By 1925 both Cuerden Green and Tardy Gate mill had become part of the firm of Thomas Moss and Sons, a member of the Consolidated Cotton Mills Trust:

> Cuerden Green mills were rebuilt by Henry Ward and Co. of Blackburn in 1861, and sold to Thomas Moss in 1888. In 1902 the whole of the preparation dept. was destroyed by fire, but it was rapidly rebuilt in the same year. Four years later a new shed was added to the establishment, containing 1,000 looms ... the output was raised in proportion to a great demand ... Tardy Gate Mill is modern in establishment, but has been modelled on principles which are the outcome of a long experience in the cotton industry. Built in 1908 by the Tardy Gate Manufacturing Company, it contained 476 looms. In 1911 the mill was acquired by Thomas Moss and Sons who carried out considerable plans.[13]

CHAPTER ELEVEN

The nineteenth century: town and country

Higher Walton

> Higher Walton stands upon an eminence, near the river Darwen, and possesses all the characteristics of a fairly civilised and growing village; it can boast a church, a chapel, a very large manufacturing establishment, sundry public houses and beershops, two finely named terraces – the Victoria and the Albert – good schools, one or two of Dunville's whiskey sign boards, and other peculiarities.[1]

Y THE MIDDLE of the nineteenth century the valley bottom around the complex junction of the Manybrooks and the river Darwen was the location of a considerable and varied industrial development. The small cotton mill site on the river had been greatly extended by the cutting off of the ox-bow and the construction of a second mill, whilst the small water mill on the Manybrooks had been transformed into a foundry and engineering workshop. Higher up the Darwen the large print works had developed at Bannister Hall. The complicated system of waterways required to service these concerns is clearly shown on the Tithe Map. With the construction of the enormous Rodgett mills from the 1850s, the term 'Higher Walton' came into respectable use, replacing the older 'Moons Mill', 'Can Bridge' and 'Kitting Burn'.

The first 6″ OS map (published 1849; surveyed 1846–47), reveals the comparatively early development of some elements of the village. The Swan Inn overlooked a very large mill pond which was subsequently drained for further mill extensions, and small terraces of mill workers' homes began to be built along Higher Walton brow. By the 1860s the model village of the Rodgetts was almost complete, and the plan apparent on the 1895 map has changed very little down to the present day. Fairly uniform housing extended along Blackburn Road, forming 'The Triangle', with further side streets opposite the church. Local millowners were important sponsors of the parish church, the Working Men's Institute, and the splendid mill school. Little expense seems to have been spared, and the enormous mills with their great chimneys, one of which at almost 300′ high still survives, dominated the scene. Industrially, socially, and architecturally this was a very compact village, a point easily appreciated today from the top of Kittlingbourne Brow.

Higher Walton, seen from Manybrooks, 1997. Beyond the stream, the mill school and All Saints Church can be seen. The whole scene, with the enormous mill as the backdrop, is still one of the great sights of industrial Lancashire. Anne Bradley has written extensively about life in the village. (*Author*)

The census returns reveal the steady and sustained growth of the village between 1841 and the Great War.[2] The 1841 census depicts a typically small mill settlement, not dissimilar to that at Roach Bridge or Hoghton Bottoms, where Edward Livesey (30) 'Cotton Spinner' sustained a community of 237 people. The foundry was well established by this date, and in 1851 Robert Whittaker is described as an 'Ironfounder and Millwright employing 87 men and boys'. He died in 1856. The Whittakers lived at Prospect House on Prospect Hill – a cluster of houses at the junction of Kittlingbourne, School Lane and Brown lane. A small community had also grown up at the Bannister Hall printworks, and 80 print workers resided there in 1841, including 'William Sharp (33) 'Print Cutter', and Adam Lamster (50) 'Designer for Printers'. The 1871 census lists ten houses here. In 1850 the Rodgetts erected a very extensive cotton mill alongside James Livesey's older factory, and the firm of Rodgett Brothers subsequently took over the whole site, whilst continuing to operate the mills separately. The years of the Cotton Famine saw the most extensive development of this community of spinners, printers and mechanics. By 1871 the redevelopment of the village was complete; a brewery was established and the census duly reveals John Hacking, 'Brewer'.

A small but significant Irish colony had emerged. Many members gave their place of birth as County Clare, and their households could be very large:

John Kanady [Kennedy?] (55) Labourer.
Catherine [Wife] (47) Housekeeper.
Mary (16) Cotton Rover.
Michael (15) Labourer.
Patrick (14) Cotton Throstle Room Hand.
Catherine (10) Scholar.

Phinter (10) Scholar.

Catherine Ragan [Boarder] (18) Cotton Rover.

Families often lived in very close proximity to each other, for their mutual benefit, but also one suspects to be able to keep an eye on each other. In 1881 this family, for example, were living by the corner of Church Street and Blackburn Road;

9 Church Street.

Elizabeth Hunt (62) Widow.

Herself and her children are all recorded as 'born in Walton-le-Dale'.

Elizabeth Anna (27) Cotton Weaver.

Mary Anna (24) Cotton Weaver.

John (22) Mechanic, unemployed.

Joseph (18) Joiner.

Blackburn & Preston Road.

Henry Hunt (26) Cotton Weaver.

Margaret [Wife] (25) Cotton Warper.

Clara Anna (3 weeks).

All Saints Church, c.1865. The spire was added to the tower in 1871. (R. Burns)

The church of 'All Saints', erected in 1862 and consecrated in 1864, marked a further subdivision of the old parish, and recognised the growing

importance of the village.[3] A spire was added to the tower in 1871, at a cost of £600, and a peal of bells was presented by Edward Rodgett in 1872. By 1877 the firm of G. & R. Dewhurst had taken over the mill, though the Rodgetts continued to take a very active part in local affairs. In 1883 the Dewhursts established the 'Higher Walton Institute' at the cost of £1,000. Anthony Hewitson was favourably impressed, both by the church and its 'large and excellent schools'. The interior was 'very pleasing ... There are few country churches equal to it in design, solidity of material, and goodness of workmanship; and we were as pleased as surprised at is capaciousness and excellence of finish'. The congregation almost 600 strong, were mostly working people. The vicar, the Rev. W. B. Shepherd, was 'white featured, red whiskered, heavily moustached, and middle sized'. A 35-year-old bachelor in possession of £150 per year, Hewitson did not think that the former curate from St Leonard's would long be in want of a wife.[4]

Gregson Lane

The country district to the south and east of Higher Walton – along Hoghton Lane and Gregson Lane – supported considerable numbers of handloom weavers well into the second half of the century. A number of distinct, but tiny hamlets, can be identified from the census returns and the 1848 6″ map. Bank Head Lane and Daub Hall Lane traverse the rolling country from Hoghton Lane to Brindle Road at 'Hospital Crossings', crossing the Fowler, Bank Head and Drum Head brooks of the Manybrooks system. Along this line a number of hamlets had developed, as at Bank Head and Livesey Green. In a number of places the streams have incised deeply, and at Drum Head the crossing was difficult and often required a detour to the west. At 'Four Lane Ends', where Bank Head Lane and Daub Hall Lane meet on Gregson Lane, a small scatter of houses had developed in the vicinity of Pickering Fold. By 1895 a small but significant community had developed at 'Gregson Lane', around the Gregson Lane mill, and Brindle Mill. In 1882 Simpson & Jackson operated 31,000 spindles and 216 looms at the former. The 1871 census records William Jackson, a 'Master Cotton Spinner employing 214 workpeople'. He occupied a gentleman's residence in Gregson Lane. Brindle Mill, built alongside the line of the railway, was run by J. & W. Bourne. This was also a combined firm, employing 276 people to operate 30,000 spindles and 330 looms. The mill's fine engine house and 'Bournes Row' survive.

The 1841 census reveals large numbers of handloom weavers in the colonies at Coupe Green, and along Hoghton Lane, Gregson Lane and Bankhead Lane. Though their numbers held up well in 1851, a decline was very apparent ten years later. Employment was maintained by transferring production to the weaving of complex, fine or costly fabrics, which could not be manufactured by power loom. In this way the trade survived, and to some extent may have prospered well in to the second half of the century. In the 1850s the weaving of worsteds and silks had become widespread. Along Hoghton Lane large numbers of worsted weavers are listed in 1871, and Jane Riley (32) had established herself as an 'Agent for the manufacture of Fancy Goods in Silk'. Further diversification clearly followed, for in 1881 Richard Riley is described as 'Oil Cloth Manufacture'. The numbers of weavers had fallen off very markedly, and in Gregson Lane John Barnes (74) 'Hand loom cloth manufacturer', was among the last survivors of the great trade.

The nearby Catholic church, St Joseph's, has an important place in the religious history of the district. A chapel of 1721 was replaced in 1786 and further enlarged in 1832. Schools for 80–90 pupils were built close by in 1831. The mission is the 'mother church' of the Catholic parishes of both Walton-le-Dale and Leyland. Hewitson disliked the stares his visits seem to have attracted at All Saints and St Saviour's ('They are great observers at Walton'), but here, 'Nobody stares vulgarly as we pass ... we feel easy amid a congregation so severe and devotional ... The people who attend this chapel are a homely, frugal, energetic class – have good appetites, and can get to sleep at the end of each day without a whiskey night cap'. The small church has thankfully changed little since the 1870s: 'They have a large regard for the chapel, and would like to carry it home if they could ... They would often carry their priest to their homes, out of pure respect, only he is heavy, and they have, as a rule, a good way to walk'.[5]

Higher Walton's prosperity during these years was marked by a degree of sporting achievement, and in the years 1884–87 Higher Walton participated in the FA Cup. The club's record is as follows:

1884–85 (R1)	Darwen Old Wanderers 1–1 (H), 1–4 (A).	
1885–86 (R1)	South Shore 3–4 (H).	
1886–87 (R1)	Third Lanark 0–5 (A).	
1887–88 (R1)	Heywood Central 8–1 (H).	
(R2)	Fleetwood Rangers 3–1 (A).	
(R3)	Bootle 1–6 (H).	

This very successful local league club was formed in 1882 and played at the 'Higher Walton Ground near the Greyhound Hotel'. South Shore, formed in the late 1870s, was a prominent amateur side before entering obscurity and oblivion on their amalgamation with Blackpool FC in 1899. Third Lanark, formed in 1872, were among seven Scottish clubs playing in the English Cup at that time, and won the Scottish Cup in 1889 and 1905. Heywood Central's 8–1 defeat was to be their solitary game in the competition. Bootle (formerly Bootle St Johns), who ended the 1887–88 cup run, were the top Liverpool club at this time. The Higher Walton club's record is made more remarkable by the disqualification and expulsion of the Preston club in 1883–84 and 1885–86, for the dangerous precedent of paying their players. The club chose not to enter the competition in

1884–85. The advent of professional football in 1888–89 heralded the end of direct entry into the 'cup' for small teams such as Higher Walton, but in 1891–92 they narrowly lost 5–4 to a team from the Fylde coast in the first qualifying round.[6]

Calvert's town: Walton village

In the first decades of the nineteenth century important changes were made to the street plan of Walton, which were to be central to the growth of the village thereafter. Frank Coupe states that Walton Cop was raised in 1822, and a parliamentary bill authorising the construction of 'New Road' (subsequently Higher Walton Road) through the townfields was obtained in 1807. These two measures greatly facilitated the spread of the village both to the east and west. By the end of the century extensive rows of terraced houses had been erected along much of the line of the Preston–Blackburn road, from the Ribble bridge to St Patrick's Church. The skyline of the village had come to be dominated by Calvert's massive Flats Mill, which provided employment for over 800 local people. The air of prosperity and security in unassailable world markets was not to be seriously challenged until the 1920s.

The quality of housing was closely related to the economic position of the inhabitants in society, and within the village quite distinct neighbourhoods emerged. These can be identified from both the OS maps of the period, and from the census returns. The housing clearance schemes of the 1930s on the corner of Chorley Road and Victoria Road (where the majority of nineteenth-century villagers had resided), and the construction of the

The village of Walton, seen from Frenchwood, c. 1900. The enormous mill, with its various extensions, entirely dominates the landscape. The chimneys of the School Lane mills can be seen on top of the Cinnamon Hill escarpment, but those of Higher Walton mill are obstructed by Walton Law. The road leading down from the Bridge Inn, to the site of the old Ribble bridge, can be seen at the extreme right of the photograph.

The White Bull Inn, at the foot of Church Brow, c.1905. Around a century earlier, the young Joseph Livesey is known to have drunk here – with predictable consequences – during a Christmas outing for St Leonard's bell ringers. (*R. Burns*)

Bamber Bridge By-pass in the 1980s, have, however, removed large tracts of the old urban landscape.

To the south of the river Darwen, Walton Green was a semi-rural enclave of small cottages owned by the Hoghton estate.[7] The 1851 census records a hundred inhabitants. Three-quarters of them claimed to have been born in Walton – the largest proportion in any part of the village. Thirty years later the population had risen to 112, but less than 40 per cent were locally born. Although Walton Green may have originated as accommodation for estate workers at Walton Hall, it seems to have supported a fair proportion of linen weavers throughout the eighteenth century. By 1851 70 per cent of people in employment here worked in textiles, a fifth of them as hand weavers. By 1871 Jane Newsham (73) was the solitary handloom weaver.

Walton Hall, rebuilt on a number of occasions and demolished around 1840, was approached along an avenue from Chorley Road: 'The hall was brick built in the square style with a quadrangular courtyard ... Stucco ceilings and other elaborate decorations adorned the interior, the whole being very tastefully conceived'.[8] A new house was erected to the west of the old hall in 1865, inhabited until 1931, and ultimately demolished in 1940–41. Richard Flowerdew, land agent, was resident here in 1871, and the hall supported a full staff of servants, gardeners and grooms. George Rollett (45) was tenant of Walton Hall Farm, describing himself as a 'farmer of 105 acres'.

The length of Chorley Road south from 'Walton Corner' to the Darwen bridge, was dominated by the corn mills. In 1841 Thomas Moore (46) was the miller, in 1881 James Briggs (47) is described as 'Miller – Employing 15 men and 3 boys', and John Ley (48) was established as 'Corn miller' in 1891. The old Unicorn Inn was one of a number of buildings which extended into the line of the highway. In 1861 Alice Pearson (26) was the landlady here. At the north end of the Darwen bridge an enclave of blacksmiths emerged. George Davis was the smith in 1861 and 1871, and Nathan Hardman's blacksmith's shop had been established by 1881. John Hilton was employed here as the wheelwright in 1891.

'Walton Corner' was the most densely populated part of the entire district. Virtually all of this area has now been cleared, and forms a car park and the car pound for Coupe's Garage. The frontage along Victoria Road from Walton corner to the old Police station, hid a maze of cramped rows of cottages which included Gray Horse Yard, Gillibrand Court, Fallowfield Brow, and Johns Row in a western group, and to the east Marginsons Row, Chapel Yard and Tongues Yard. In 1851 they were home to 213 people, 84 of them under 10 years of age, and half born in Walton.

Hardman's Smithy, between the Unicorn Inn and the river Darwen. This firm continued to operate on this site for a century. (R. Burns)

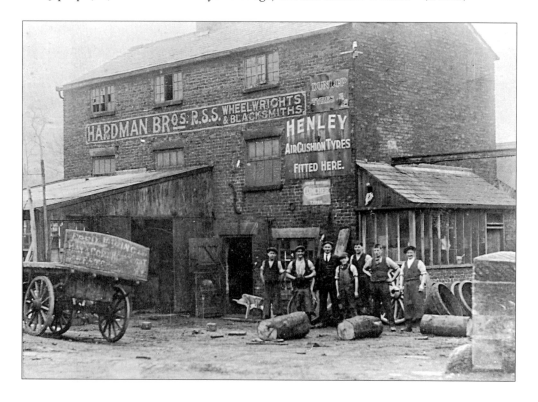

Hunt's Houses, looking north along Chorley Road to the Darwen bridge, with the chimneys of Flats Mill in the distance, c. 1910. (R. Burns)

Of those in work, 84 per cent worked in the textile trade. By 1881 the population of this locality had risen to 270, of whom 141 were mill operatives. A small Irish colony had grown up, and 51 people here gave 'Ireland' as their place of birth. To these figures from the 'side streets' must be added those people living along the frontage, so that perhaps half of the population of 'the village' may have been clustered in the vicinity. The very few houses which survive today, therefore, are a poor indication of the district's former importance.

The number of handloom weavers here declined rapidly after 1830, for plentiful work was available in the adjacent factory. Yet individual weavers continued to be recorded into the 1870s, when Margaret Ainsworth (60) and James Gorton (56) and his wife were listed. From 1851 the number of cotton workers here remained broadly unchanged. The point of saturation had been reached.

Apart from small shops, the post-office, beer houses, and the premises of tradesmen, much of Victoria Road was given over to mill workers' housing. In the length from the Yew Tree to the Ribble bridge 71 per cent of people at work in 1851 were employed in textiles, a figure which by 1881 had fallen to less than 40 per cent. In Todds Row, the line of terraced houses overlooking the river opposite to the end of Winery Lane, the figures were 86 per cent and 50 per cent respectively. In the second half of the century extensive terraced housing was erected to the north of Flats Mill, extending to the Ribble bridge. The Rope Walk, a long narrow building for the manufacture of ropes, is a major feature on the maps of the period. Five ropemakers are recorded in 1851 and John Woodhouse was 'Roper at the Ropery' in 1871.

Calvert's mills dominated Victoria Road, and the main residence of the family up to the end of the century was Walton House at the side of the mill. Unlike some of the residents of Church Brow, they seem to have lived comparatively modestly, notwithstanding their enormous wealth. In 1841 William and Mary Calvert had no 'live in' servants, and as late as 1861 (by which time William Calvert employed almost 900 people at his mill), they had only a cook and a maid. Benjamin Gartside (35) 'Manager at cotton mill' lived next door, and John Turner (46), Walton's celebrated 'Portrait artist and animal painter', lived close by. The area to the north of the mill supported a large number of gardeners, who found employment on the market gardens which developed on the Flats after 1850. The ancient resources of the area continued to provide a livelihood for Adam Pomfret, who in 1841 was a fisherman living beside Walton bridge. A gas works was established behind the Bridge Inn, and in 1871 William Masheter is described as 'Gas Stoker Foreman at the Gas Works'.

The potential size of both households, and the range of occupations which might be found within them, is illustrated by the family of John Turner (69), a 'handloom cotton weaver', and his wife Betty (54), recorded in the census of 1851. Their home contained their children – John (26) powerloom overlooker, Ann (24) powerloom weaver, James (20) and William (18) both described as 'twister for powerloom' – and Thomas Turner (31) a widower, and a platelayer on the railway. His family comprised John (11) 'working in Bank Croft', Mary (9) a scholar, and John (4). The 'County Police Station', which survives as the 'Old Police Station', was occupied by Henry Woodcock (45) the police sergeant. Chorley Road and Victoria Road thus became densely populated thoroughfares, containing an amazing assortment of people and professions, from the poor weaver to the self-made millionaire.

Among the great and good: Church Brow

Rather different social groups were to be found along the heights of Walton Law – or 'Church Brow' as it had become by the eighteenth century. Frank Coupe describes a row of three-storey buildings here, interestingly known as 'Old Baltic', which were removed early in the twentieth century, 'Approach to the upper rooms was by a flight of stone steps to a flagged terrace guarded by iron railings and running the whole length. The basement rooms were used by handloom weavers'.[9] The erosion of the riverbank in the loop of the Ribble west of Ribble Side Farm has resulted in much subsidence along the north side of Church Brow, particularly in the vicinity of the church. Some property has been lost here through erosion, which continues apace. Sadly it is not possible to prove the late E. E. Pickering's contention that the Kings Croft area was the core of the early settlement, all evidence of which has been lost to the Ribble.

The Walton-le-Dale Working Men's Institute was erected in 1881 on the site now occupied by Calvert Court, midway up Church Brow. This rather splendid structure, erected at a cost of £1,400, was the gift of Richard

The view south from the end of Walton Green, with Cinnamon Hill in the distance, *c.*1912. The cart is passing the end of the avenue leading to Walton Hall. (*R. Burns*)

Calvert. In 1891 he donated an extensive library of books, and the building was extended in 1908. The Walton-le-Dale Working Men's Association had been formed in 1858, and had a very formal constitution and strict rules. No political or religious lectures were to be entertained, and 'any member who shall be guilty of wilfully breaking any of the rules or bye-laws of the Institution, or of bringing intoxicating liquors into the Institution, or of gambling, swearing, or behaving in any way calculated to annoy and disturb the members in the rooms shall be censured by a resolution of the Committee'. This remarkable building, once an important centre of local life, retained the village's Second World War air raid warning siren up to its demolition in December 1986.[10]

On the higher ground the great and the good made their homes. Cooper Hill, now a close of modern homes, was formerly a gentleman's residence set amid extensive gardens which extended downslope to the Darwen lowlands to the south. The house is said to have been designed at least in part by General Burgoyne, victor with Henry Hoghton in the 'Great Preston election of 1768'. It has similarly been claimed that Benjamin Franklin visited his daughter here in the 1790s, and of course erected his celebrated lightning conductor here. In the 1830s the house was used as a boarding school, but by 1841 it had become the residence of Charles Swainson, cotton magnate and archery enthusiast. A sale notice of 1845 describes the house as having 12 bedrooms, gardens, meadow and six acres of townfield, in an estate of 31 acres. The house had a considerable staff of servants, with a butler, housekeeper, cook, lady's maid and the rest. By 1871 the Swainsons had left, and Cooper Hill had become the home of James Wilson (45), 'Solicitor and Deputy Clerk of the Peace of Lancashire', his wife, 8 children, a niece, a nephew, a visitor, and 6 servants.

In 1862 'Highwood' was occupied by Jane Clayton (60), 'Landed Proprietoress', and James Threlfall (58) was landlord of the 'Red Lion Inn'. By 1881 the great house was home to Henry Gran, the 'Secretary of the Preston

Gas Co. employing 210 men'. Beyond the parish church, the vicars of Walton lived in a grand style. In 1841 the 'Parsonage' was occupied by Robert Hornby (35) 'clerk', his wife Maria (30), their seven children, governess, and six servants. Thirty years later the Rev. James Kershaw (40), lived here with his wife, three children, three boarders, and just three servants. He was a tireless worker during the Cotton Famine, and established the secondary parishes of St Saviour's and St Aidan's. Hewitson reckoned the parish school to be one of the best in the district, and left a colourful description of the vicar, who was to be one of the most prominent of the nineteenth-century Walton vicars: 'Mr Kershaw will be about 40 years of age. He is small and neat in figure – has a large and what the old song would call "a dark and a roving eye" – wears stiff and methodically cut whiskers, of a warm and a gingerly hue, is precise, circumspect, and measured in his talk, considers that he is the law and the prophets in one complete edition, conceives that he is a sort of Jupiter Olympus amongst the minor Walton Gods, is cold and courteous, believes much in the authority and importance of clerical cloth ... as a rule he never rants nor roars about other people's creeds'.[11]

Knot House, at the top of Knot Lane, had strong textile connections. James Livesey lived here in 1841, and his son Thomas (44) was described as a 'Master Cotton Spinner' ten years later. By 1881 it was the home of Edmund and Charlotte Calvert. On the south side of Cuerdale Lane near to the eastern end of what is now 'The Drive', stood Calrow Hall or Walton Lodge. A sale notice of 1810 describes an estate of 115 acres, including Osbaldeston House, gardens and a 'melon ground'. Originally the home of one of the partners in the Mosney enterprise, the property was subsequently acquired by Richard Calrow, and the estate was extended to almost 350 acres. The house was demolished around 1895, and 'The Drive' was subsequently erected. The sharp distinction between the 'haves' and the 'have nots' in Victorian society was thus plain for all to see in the contrasting lifestyles of the inhabitants of 'The Barracks' and Church Brow – quite different worlds barely 200 yards apart.

Higher Walton Road and St Patrick's

The opening of Higher Walton Road, from Walton Corner to the foot of Knot Lane, enabled the village to expand westwards across the former townfields. The new road had two toll gates here, at the bottom of Knot Lane and at Kittlingbourne. Toll collectors were a notoriously dishonest lot. The collector at the former gate in 1841 was John Hunt (40) an 'Ironfounder and Toll Collector', and his wife Elizabeth. Although much of the property along Higher Walton Road dates from the early twentieth century, a number of older properties clustered around the Catholic mission here. Typical of these were the houses in Lady Place. In 1891 their 'heads of household' consisted of:

St Patrick's Church, Higher Walton Road, 1997. The foundation stone was laid in 1879, and the church was completed in 1911. The church grounds occupy a portion of the ancient Monk's Meadow. (*Author*)

No. 1   George Green (26) 'General Labourer'.
No. 2   John O'Brien (25) 'Cotton Weaver'.
No. 3   Michael Broll (30) 'Cotton Weaver'.
No. 4   John Crusidene (49) 'Gardener'.

Anthony Hewitson found the congregation of the Catholic chapel to 'consist entirely of working people, including a very considerable sprinkling of young females, rather largely enamoured of roses, feathers and captivating head gear. But all who attend, young and old, appear to be a very orderly, devout class, and, considering their means, they assist very creditably and liberally the mission to which they are attached'. The present mission dates from the mid-1850s, when land was purchased for a chapel and school. A public house – the Grove Inn – on the corner of St Patrick's Place and Higher Walton Road, was taken over as a temporary church and as a residence for the priest. The new school-cum-church was a very curious structure: 'The building has an open painted roof, 30′ from the floor to the apex; is 130′ long, 18′ broad: and will accommodate 300 persons. The walls are plain, and are pierced on the eastern side with three strong windows filled in with heavy opaque glass. In the roof there are several dormer windows of a triangular shape ... there are three and 20 ventilators in the building!'. During heavy rain part of the building flooded. Although it was estimated that the locality contained a thousand Catholics, Hewitson remarked that 'the means are not at hand for a properly constructed church'.[12] The foundation stone of the present church, dedicated to the Blessed Virgin and St Patrick, was laid in 1879, and the church was opened in October 1880. Designed by Pugin, Ashlin and Pugin, and built of Caen stone at a cost of £6,000, it was only completed in 1907. The adjacent junior school was built in 1911 at a cost of £2,700, on land given by Sir James de Hoghton.

Social trends in Mid-Victorian Walton

Detailed analysis of the 1851 and 1881 census returns for Walton village reveals the general statistical trends apparent in much of the urban area.[13] The population of the study areas was 1,791 in 1851 and 1,585 thirty years later. Since the study area in 1881 was slightly smaller, the population in fact showed little change. The number of women exceeded that of men by 71 in 1851 and 61 by 1881. This was a very young population, and the age range also changed very little; 25 per cent of the population was under 10 years of age, and 50 per cent under 20 years in both years. Conversely only 15 per cent were aged 50 years or over, with 6 per cent over 60, and 2 per cent over 70 years of age. In 1851 eight inhabitants were aged 80 or over, falling to just three individuals in 1881. A large proportion of Waltoners lived along the frontage and side streets to the south of Victoria Road between the Yew Tree and Walton corner. In 1851 552 people lived here, falling to 457 in 1881.

In 1851 and 1881 just over half of the inhabitants claimed Walton-le-Dale as their birth place, with a further 18 per cent born in the adjoining parishes. In 1851 95 per cent of the people had been born in Lancashire, falling to 87 per cent in 1881. The only significant change in the place of birth analysis was the increase in the number of people born in Ireland, the figure rose from less than 1 per cent to 4 per cent (69 people).

In 1851 the workforce comprised 978 people, 55 per cent of the population, and 80 per cent of the population of working age. The pattern of employment was dominated by the cotton industry, which provided 60 per cent of jobs, with 38 handloom weavers and 539 mill workers. The highest proportion of cotton workers was to be found in the side streets along Victoria Road (79 per cent), and in Todds Row (86 per cent). The other principal employments were: agriculture 57 people; tradesmen 133; shopkeepers 35; servants 77; and the professions 22. By 1881 the importance of the industry had increased slightly, employing 36 per cent of the entire population. The balance of employment within the trade was as follows: spinners (35 men, 9 women); weavers (109 men, 255 women); clerical (10 men, 1 woman); and 'other' (81 men, 78 women). Women employees (343) exceeded men (235) by 108.

The comparison of the two census returns thus reveals a community in which a very high proportion of the population was obliged to work, and was in paid labour. The great majority were employed in the cotton industry, at Flats Mill, and weavers predominated. Only a small proportion of the population could expect to live to 60 years of age, in what was for the time a fairly prosperous community. Great wealth and poverty were in close proximity, and the consequences of an individual losing his or her job, or failing in business, were very clear. Long hours of tiresome work in a depressing environment, with frequent pregnancies for the working women, and a short life, thus typified the golden age of the Lancashire cotton industry for the majority of people in mid-Victorian Walton.

The de Hoghton estate and the country districts

In the country district an altogether different community, more reminiscent of the old pre-industrial society, struggled to survive the flood of cheap foreign food which followed the repeal of the Corn Laws in 1846. Nineteenth-century commentators were frequently scathing of the system of farming they encountered to the south and east of Preston – the tired overworked soils, and the small, uneconomical size of many holdings. Alternatively, the proximity of the town and mill communities gave a strong stimulus to market gardening and dairying, and, in the present century, to the egg trade.

Sir Henry Philip Hoghton (1768–1835) was the last of the Lords of Walton to reside principally at Walton Hall, which is said to have been destroyed by fire in 1834. His son, Henry (1799–1862), the eighth baronet, acquired the valuable Bold estate near Wigan through marriage, and accordingly changed his name to become Sir Henry Bold-Hoghton. The sale of the Bold estate in 1858 raised well over £100,000. He is best remembered for his sportsmanship, and for his defeat in a yacht race which established the Americas Cup competition. His son the ninth baronet (1821–76) also changed his name by royal licence, to become Sir Henry de Hoghton. He invested great sums in the revival of the estates, and the restoration of Hoghton Tower. He was widely travelled, and a hint as to the source of his wealth was given in the American press at the time of his death: 'There died last week a man whose name was once rather widely known in America: Sir Henry de Hoghton, the wealthy baronet whose

A handloom weaver's house in Brown Lane, 1997. Weavers' houses such as this one were a common feature of the countryside which extends west from Higher Walton to Gregson Lane and Brindle. Here a short row of houses has been converted into two dwellings. (*Author*)

sympathies with the Southern Confederacies were strong enough to induce him to "invest" £200,000 in rebel bonds. He was understood to have held on to the last, and of course lost every penny of the sum – a million dollars in gold'. Whatever the truth of this, the Probate Register records that he left a personal fortune in the region of £200,000.[14] His obituary reveals the extent of his investment in the estate:

> The estates had been neglected and impoverished during many years before Sir Henry came into possession ... The estates were in sore need of better agriculture. The late baronet set himself energetically to work to improve the estates. Within the short period of his possession he spent more than £30,000 in land drainage alone ... The great improvements of every kind, in buildings, fences, roads, etc., upon the Walton estate, have been carried out without reference to cost and at vast outlay.

In 1873 the de Hoghton estate comprised 4,112 acres, with an annual rental of £10,144. On his death it passed to his brothers Charles (1823–93), and James (1851–1938), who completed the restoration of the Tower in 1901, and entertained King George V there in 1913.[15]

A catalogue of the Walton estate produced in 1826 describes around 1,900 acres, or almost 45 per cent of the entire land area of the district. Virtually all the existing cottage property in Walton village was owned by the estate, which continued to be the principal landowner until the estate's wholesale disposals in the 1920s. The estate was still run on old-fashioned lines, and many properties were held by lease for a given number of lives. The largest landholdings comprised Walton Hall (236 acres), Holland House (123 acres), Middleforth Hall (107 acres), Leigh House (105 acres), Leigh Brow (76 acres), Cinnamon Hill (76 acres), 'Harrisons', Toad (Todd) Lane (53 acres), and Wateringpool (51 acres). The majority of holdings were, however, extremely small.[16]

The Walton-le-Dale Tithe Map of 1839 presents an extremely detailed picture of landholding, tenancy and cultivation. Tithes were due from almost 3,500 acres, which were utilised as follows: arable 295 acres; pasture 1,928 acres; meadow 1,064 acres; gardens and nurseries 77 acres; and woodland 93 acres. The pattern of ownership was dominated by a small group of very large landowners, and very few people owned any land at all. Sir Henry Bold-Hoghton was the principal landowner with an estate of 1,293 acres, which still included a great deal of cottage property. William Calrow's Walton Lodge estate (including the Sollom House and Osbaldeston Hall farms) comprised 320 acres, and James Livesey owned an estate of over 350 acres. The largest holdings over 100 acres, in the Hoghton estate, were Walton Flats, Leigh House, Ridings Farm and Walton Hall Farm. Other large farms included Bannister Hall, Holly Bank, Sollom House and Osbaldeston Hall. Alternatively, many holdings were too small to be viable agricultural units, and farming families had a long tradition of part-time work in textiles. In 1839 220 holdings were under one acre in

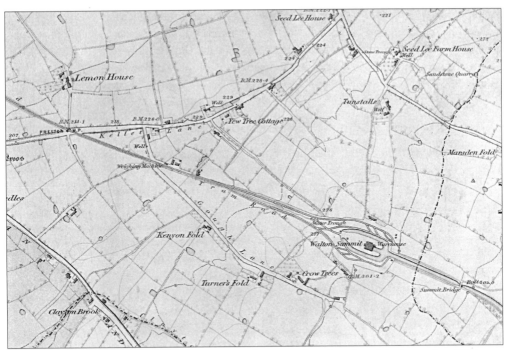

A detail of the 1848 OS map showing Walton Summit and the farms along Kellet Lane and Gough Lane. The tram lines can clearly be seen, with the warehouse and canal terminus. Many of the farms in this district were extremely productive, and Lemon House was one of the very early landholdings. Farming, and particularly dairying, remained important occupations in the district well beyond the Second World War. Much of this beautiful countryside was extensively built over by the CLDC in the 1970s as part of the Clayton Brook development.

size, and 377 were under 20 acres. Fifty-eight holdings were over 20 acres, and just 17 of them over 50 acres in extent.[17]

The personal details of the farmers, their families, and the farm labourers can be traced with great accuracy in the census returns. The small holdings often provided employment for a single family member, but provided a home to a large extended family who worked in the mills. The larger farms, by contrast, frequently employed the whole family, as the designation 'farmer's wife', 'farmer's son', and 'farmer's daughter' imply. Daughters were particularly important. Thomas Tomlinson's (45) household on Walton Flats in 1841, comprised himself and his wife Elizabeth (40), their five daughters, three sons, and two agricultural labourers, John Slinger (20), and Joseph Smith (30). William Wiggins at Mains House, and James Glover at Holland Park, also had five daughters at home.

The Shuttlingfields, which lie between Gregson Lane and Brindle Road, have been farmed since medieval times. By 1840 they comprised three farms, Lower, Middle and Upper Shuttlingfields. The latter comprised the 'Brindle Township and Walton-le-Dale Charity lands'. This was a local charity which assisted such 'aged persons' who were nominated by the clergy, with monthly payments of 2s. Funds came from the farm's rent of

£50 per year. The records for the period 1837–67 survive, and appointments were still being made in 1893. In 1867 the farm was sold, and the proceeds were invested in government stocks. Farm families could be very large, and in 1841 the three Shuttlingfield farms were home to no fewer than 32 people.[18]

Cuerdale and Clayton Brook

Cuerdale has long been a rich farming district. In 1841 the census recorded 16 households, in all just 57 people. Eight of the heads of household were farmers, with a gamekeeper and two agricultural labourers. Jonathan Richardson (40) farmed the Cuerdale Hall estate, employing an agricultural labourer and a 'farm servant'. By 1861 James Ramsey (62) 'farmer of 190 acres', employed his son William (described as a 'shepherd'), and Nancy Calderbank (45, 'dairy maid'). There was a number of large farms here, Thomas Hacking (55) farmed 94 acres at Yew Tree Farm, and Euan Hartley (55) a hundred acres at Darwen Side, in 1861. James Fisher (46) was at Webster's Farm, James Night 'farmer of 16 acres' farmed Swain's Farm, and Richard Parker (38) 'farmer of 18 acres', was at Ribble Side.

In the countryside at Clayton Brook, Margaret Harrison (80, 'widow') and her son Thomas (45) farmed 50 acres at Crow Trees in Gough Lane in 1861. His six sisters aged 35–53, all described themselves as 'farmer's daughter'. At Seed Lee Farm, Joseph Orrel (85) and his wife Ellen (74), recorded here in 1841, still managed 27 acres with their son Thomas in 1861. Quite a colony of boatmen had grown up around the canal basin. In 1841 George Scott (55) and his family of four sons and a daughter are described as 'boat hauliers', and a number of heads of household are described as 'coal heavers'. Near Gough Lane, John Darbyshire (30), 'coal heaver', supported a family of 11 children, 8 of them under 10 years of age. Many smallholders and especially their dependants were outworkers in the hand weaving trade well into the second half of the century, particularly on the farms along the length of Bank Head Lane and Kellet Lane.

By the end of the century farming had become more specialised, with dairying on the pasture lands of the Ribble valley and the higher boulder clay country of the plain, and intensive market gardening along the alluvial valleys. The latter became strongly established quite early along Winery Lane on Walton Flats, and on the Darwen lowlands south of Higher Walton Road. In 1861 Jane Mansley (70) of Walton village was described as a 'market gardener, employing 13 men', and Thomas Smith and James Thompson are also listed as market gardeners. The predominance of dairying on what were still largely self-sufficient farms, is revealed by the de Hoghton estate sale catalogue of 4–5 August 1920. The sale comprised '22 farms, 26 cottages with gardens [Walton Green], several fields suitable for market gardening. Building sites. Accommodation land and woodland'. The sale included Walton Hall Farm, which was said to comprise 125 acres of 'rich meadowland sound pasture' and arable. The importance of dairying is demonstrated by the following extract:[19]

> Wateringpool Farm. 46 acres. 'Excellent dairy farm at Lostock Hall with superior house and buildings', and shippons for 17 cattle.
>
> Holland House Farm. 82 acres. 'Excellent dairy farm ... nearly all grass', with a large barn, 3 stall stable, Harness room, 2 loose boxes, shippon for 48 cows and 10 young stirks, and 3 pig cotes.
>
> Cockshutt Farm (Duddle Lane) 62 acres 'Excellent dairy farm', with a shippon for 31 head, 6 calves, 4 pigcotes, and a Dutch barn.
>
> Limekiln Farm. (Todd Lane) 56 acres. 'A very superior dairy farm', and 'a shippon for 22 cows, 8 young things and 6 calves'.

By the end of the century these ancient farmlands, which had been worked by subsequent generations for over 800 years, were to have largely given way to suburban housing estates.

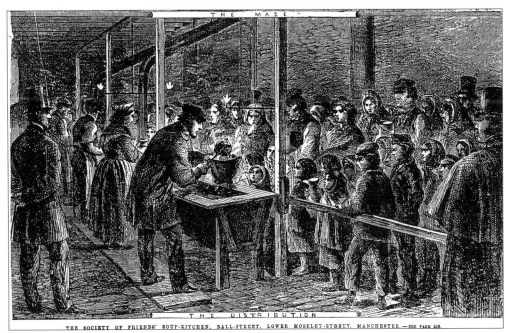

THE SOCIETY OF FRIENDS' SOUP-KITCHEN, BALL-STREET, LOWER MOSELEY-STREET, MANCHESTER.—SEE PAGE 558.

A large soup kitchen: Lancashire Cotton Famine, from the *Illustrated London News*, 1862. Such kitchens were frequently established during the cyclical crises which mark the path of the cotton trade through the nineteenth century. The papers of the Walton-le-Dale Relief Committee are preserved in the Lancashire Record Office, and include the recipe for the celebrated Walton Soup. This had a high repute. Better-off people could buy tickets at 1*d*. each; these could then be given to persons believed to be 'deserving', who would then take them to the kitchen and obtain a quart of soup.

CHAPTER TWELVE

The engine of progress

Y THE MIDDLE of the nineteenth century many of the local textile concerns were already long established. Still in family hands, they provided the district with a strong sense of continuity throughout the period of Lancashire's pre-eminence in the world's cotton industry. Failures were few, and enormous profits could be made right up to 1921. Alternatively, labour relations were often bitter, and strikes were endemic. By 1851 Richard and Edward Ashworth, 'Cotton Spinners and Manufacturers', had established Stone Mill or 'New Side' in School Lane, a mill subsequently run by Thomas Eccles and Sons. In the 1860s Orr's Mill was established to the south of School Lane. A. S. Orr's was to be in many ways the most successful of the district's mills. It remained in family hands into the 1960s and survived up to 1979. In the following decade Mexican Mill, a weaving shed, was opened by Tootal, Broadhurst and Lee, in Aspden Street, Bamber Bridge. By 1881 it was operating as Richard Aspden & Co.

An indication of what the consequences of over-specialisation in a single industry might be in the years following the First World War, was provided by the 'Great Cotton Panic' of 1861–65. Recovery from the major commercial crisis and trade slump of the autumn of 1861, was aggravated by the American Civil War. By September 1862, of the 1,750 'operatives' usually at work in the Walton and Bamber Bridge mills, 72 had full-time work, 1,092 were working part time, and 606 were entirely unemployed. Normally only about 160 people per week asked for poor relief from the Preston Poor Law Union's Board of Guardians. In November 1861 this figure doubled to 352, on 1 February 1862 it reached 847, on 4 March 1,110 people. By 7 October the number had increased to 1,576, passing 2,000 in the first week of November, to peak at 2,521 on 2 December 1862. As late as August 1863 only 136 of the 870 people employed at Flats Mill were in work, at Gregson Lane just one in 60, and at Higher Walton 56 in 510.[1]

The scale of the crisis completely overwhelmed the Guardians:

Yesterday from early morning till seven o'clock last evening, the outside, the stairs, the lobbies, rooms, and every approach to these offices [the Overseer's building in Preston] were densely crowded, not only by hundreds of Preston poor, but by large numbers from Walton-le-Dale, Moon's Mill, Bamber Bridge, Farington, Cuerden Green and all round ... The numbers that were present can hardly be estimated accurately; but they are daily on the increase. The appearance of the young women from the country, especially from Walton and Farington, is superior to that of many young women similarly situated in this town; but that may be accounted for from the better air they breath and their superior habits of cleanliness.[2]

The Walton-le-Dale Relief Committee, headed by the vicar Mr Kershaw and the principal millowners and gentry, organised a wide range of relief enterprises. Funds were raised locally, and grants were received from two bodies established to collect funds nationally, the Manchester Central Committee, and the Lord Mayor of London's fund. The millowners were expected to donate handsomely. Some did. The Rodgetts donated £340, the Swainsons £270, the Calverts £200, and Sir Henry and Lady de-Hoghton £95. In all the Walton Committee raised £5,395, comprising £1,785 raised locally, £2,025 from Manchester, and £1,565 from London. Funds were paid out on a weekly basis to boost the payments made by the Preston Guardians. 'Aged persons' were to have 3s., and everyone else 2s. 6d. each, with additional payments for children. A major row broke out, however, when it was found that the committee were paying 8s. per week for the upkeep of a horse.[3]

Supplies of coal and clothing were provided where necessary; soup kitchens were established; and adult schools were set up for the unemployed. In February 1865, for example, Elizabeth Hunt's family at Higher Walton received 15s., and were given a counterpane.[4] As late as August 1865, however, there was great consternation when it was reported that uneaten scraps of food left over by one of the school teachers had been ravenously devoured by the hungry children. An extensive programme of public works was set up to absorb the energies of the able-bodied, and the 'Forty Steps' and the stone Ribble bank revetments date from this time. Strongly influenced by Livesey's teachings, the Walton committee was a comparatively liberal institution, for 'no person who has saved money in any way is to be obliged to spend it before relief is given'.[5] Recovery came in 1864, and crowds of operatives rejoiced at the sight of the arrival of the first wagons of cotton bales on the sidings at Bamber Bridge.

Despite the Cotton Famine, the decade of the 1860s saw considerable growth in the industry, and regionally the old family firms began to lose ground. Locally, however, public companies only began to establish themselves in the last decades of the century, and many mills remained in family hands. Important changes in the ownership of the Lostock Hall and Cuerden mills took place in the 1860s. Henry Ward acquired Cuerden Green Mill from the Bashalls, and the old Clayton bleach works, operated

The Forty Steps. The Walton Committee was a liberal one, and applied Joseph Livesey's ideas as to how the poor should be treated. The able-bodied were supposed to work in exchange for their relief, and although the Board of Guardians tried to apply this strictly, the Relief Committee preferred to insist that the unemployed attended adult schools and classes. At Walton the wall along Walton Cop was constructed, and these steps were inserted into the hillside on the path between the Blue Bridge and the School Lane mills. (Author)

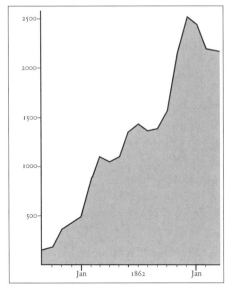

The number of people relieved by the Preston Board of Guardians during 1862, the most severe phase of the Cotton Famine. In the manufacturing district the level of unemployment was usually very low, but periods of crisis in the trade could lead to exceptionally heavy unemployment. The long-term implications of a situation in which virtually all of the population of the district depended on a single industry, which in turn was dependent on the export trade, became readily apparent, and was to bring disaster after 1924. (From Hunt, *The Silent Mills*)

in the 1850s by Robert Orrel 'cotton spinner and manufacturer', had been taken over by G. & R. Dewhurst by 1869. By 1877 the Dewhurst combine had also absorbed Rodgett's Higher Walton Mill.[6]

Within the Preston manufacturing district Calverts and Dewhursts emerged as the 'super giants' of the time, rivalling Horrockses in size. In 1882 Calvert's operated 150,000 spindles, 2,500 looms, and employed 2,200 people at Flats Mill, and India and Aqueduct Street mills in Preston. In 1904 G. & R. Dewhurst operated 63,000 spindles and 1,100 looms at Cuerden, and, 51,000 spindles and 800 looms at Higher Walton. In 1900, the Walton, Bamber Bridge and Lostock Hall mills thus contained some 450,000 spindles, 5,300 looms and employed almost 5,000 people.[7]

The formation of the Lostock Hall Spinning Company in 1874 marked a new stage in the evolution of the local cotton companies. This was essentially a co-operative enterprise, in which 6,500 £10 shares were sold in blocks of 50. The prime mover was Mr Flitcroft of Lostock House, and the initial shareholders comprised two cotton manufacturers, two waste dealers, an oil merchant, a gunmaker, and a solicitor. The four-storey mill had been rapidly built, at a cost estimated to be 28s. per spindle, and the 500hp steam engine had a drive wheel weighing 30 tons. The directors met weekly, had a series of committees, and supervised all activities in the mill directly: 'The Manager was called in and interrogated as to what was being done'. In the first decade of the twentieth century Tardy Gate Mill was built by the 'Tardy Gate Manufacturing Company'. Taken over by Thomas Moss & Sons, it was subsequently extended to operate 1,108 looms. The frenetic building boom of the 1900s is well illustrated by the Bamber Bridge Manufacturing Company's enormous Wesley Street Mill ('New Mill'). Opened in 1907, it operated 130,000 looms, and remains the largest building ever erected in the district.[8]

Self-government

The development of the institutions and expertise of local government was central to the material progress of the district after 1870. During the seventeenth and eighteenth centuries these functions had been undertaken by the manor court (with its constables, barley men, and houselookers), and the parish council or vestry. Much conflict and confusion must have occurred between these bodies, but by the early nineteenth century the vestry had come to predominate. In 1740 it was decided 'at a publick meeting at our school ... that Thomas Hawkshead our present master, have yearly allowed him, the sum of three pounds, for writing, keeping the Town's Accounts, and his troubles about the publick affairs of our

The Bamber Bridge Spinning Company's Mill ('Wesley Street Mill' or 'New Mill'), under construction, 1907. The years before the Great War saw the final great expansion of the industry, financed by joint stock companies. Similar ventures were established at Lostock Hall and Tardy Gate. An interesting feature of this mill was its tremendous engine, similar to that preserved at Trencherfield Mill, Wigan. Although the fine engine house survives, the engine was not preserved, and amazingly it was cut up for scrap in the 1960s. (R. Burns)

Township'.[9] This body, with its more open tradition, overseers of the poor, constables, and surveyors of the roads, thus formed a natural basis of functions and functionaries onto which the modern system of the local administration of public services could be developed. The cumulative impact of the New Poor Law (1834), the establishment of the Highways Board (1848), the Local Board of Health (1877), and the Urban District Council (1895), enabled the community to establish modern levels of public services. The achievement of these successor bodies in the years up to the Great War is very impressive, for local initiative was supported by national expertise, and access to central government backed funds.[10]

The old vestry

The surviving nineteenth-century vestry records date from 1826, when the body was composed of 21 men of the parish, including the principal mill

The 130,000-spindle New Mill, Bamber Bridge, c.1910. It was hoped that a second, identical mill would be added to the site. The chimney has now gone, but the engine house survives. George Woodcock, General Secretary of the TUC during the Wilson Government, worked here in the 1920s. Closure of the mill was announced in 1959. (R. Burns)

owners William Calvert, William Eccles and Charles Swainson. John Clay, the parish curate, was chairman, and meetings were held in the overseer's office in Bamber Bridge.[11] The committee was occasionally rent by internal disagreements, and a major row broke out over the election of officers in March 1860 between William Calvert and Richard Ashworth. The dispute was still rumbling on two years later. The vestry's task was to supervise the parish officers, but the Grammar School and Workhouse seem to have absorbed much of its energies. Though the vestry was responsible for 'public health', and introduced cholera regulations in 1832, provision was very rudimentary. On 22 March 1857, for example, a special meeting had to be held 'for the purpose of devising means of having the moles destroyed which are now increasing rapidly in different parts of the parish'. Great attention was given to the collection of the rates, and the rating lists are an important local history source. In 1826 it was decreed 'that a rate of 1s. in the pound be forthwith collected from the tax payers of Walton-le-dale to defray the charges against this township caused by the rioters'.

The activities of the parish's officers were watched very closely. In November 1835 it was 'Resolved that Edward Balshaw, the constable at Tardy Gate be admonished in consequence of his conduct generally, and habits of intoxication, that he be informed that the vestry is much displeased with such practices, and that he now be continued in the office upon trial'. Alternatively a too rigorous application to duty could expose the officer to danger from the populace. At the same meeting it was 'resolved that Giles Shorrock be allowed £1 15s. 0d. in consideration of damage he has sustained, in consequence of having done his duty as constable of Bamber Bridge. Further that a reward of £5 be offered to any person or persons who shall give such information as will lead to the conviction of those who have maliciously thrown vitriol upon the cotton warp in the looms of the aforesaid GS in the night of the 19th Instant.'

Much of the vestry's time was taken up with the management of the parish workhouse at Bamber Bridge. In October 1831 Thomas Tomlinson was instructed to provide the house with 'Back Draughts and briskets' at three pence per pound, and stews at three half pence a pound. John Ham was to provide 'good oatmeal' at 28s. 3d. per load, and James Ward was to deliver 'flatt red potatoes – 20 loads at 3s. 10d.: Pink Eyes – 20 loads at 3s. 8d. per load'. The 'best Chorley coal', was ordered at 8s. 8d. per ton, and George Kent agreed to supply 'good' butter and soap at tenpence halfpenny per pound and 52s. per cwt. respectively. Candles were expensive at 6s. 2d. per dozen. When supplies did not meet the required standard the dealers were swiftly called to account. The supply of coffins was a major item in the accounts. In May 1831 Matthew Brierley agreed to supply them as follows: 'For persons 1 week old to 5 years 3s. 6d. each, 5–12 years 4s. 6d., 12 years and upwards 8s. 6d.' The cost of the upkeep of the house was subsidised by income from the work undertaken by the inmates, and by the rents from the 'Poor's Land' at Brownedge. With the introduction of the New Poor law the initiative passed to the board of guardians in Preston, and in March 1852 it was agreed to let the workhouse and its lands to the Preston Union. With the opening of the new 'Union Workhouse' in Watling Street Road, Preston, in 1867 the smaller parish houses were closed.

All gas and water: The Walton-le-Dale Local Board

The first meeting of the Local Board was held in the overseer's office at School Lane End on 19 March 1877.[12] The cotton interest was ably represented by Richard Calvert, G. C. Dewhurst, and Edmund Rodgett. The other members included the vicar, Mr Kershaw, and Richard Flowerdew, steward of the de Hoghton estate. Dr Trimble was appointed medical officer on an annual salary of £30 per year, with a Clerk, Inspector of Nuisances, School Attendance Officer, and Surveyor of the Highways. The 'council' had committees for General Purposes, Gas and Water, Finance and Highways. Meetings were to be held on the first Monday of each month. In November 1879 permission was obtained from the Local Government Board to borrow £2,500 for imposing new offices (more suited to Walton's rising sense of civic dignity), to be built on the corner of Brownedge Lane. Expenditure for the first year came to £527 10s. 0d. Wages accounted for £107, lighting the streets £250, and sanitation and scavenging £25. Strict economy was long to be the great arbiter, in all things.

The offices of the Walton-le-Dale Local Board, c. 1895. A superb example of one of the Board's gas lamps can be seen on the corner of Brownedge Lane. (R. Burns)

The principal function of the new and expensive Board was to provide street lighting, and an adequate water supply.[13] Gas was easily obtained from the Preston Gas Company's plant on Walton Flats, and by October 1877 the first cast-iron gas lamp standards had been delivered. The lamps were to be lit from September to April, and lighting-up time varied with the time of the sunset. During the full moon no lights were to be lit. On 1 January 1880, for example, the lights were to begin to be lit at 3.45 p.m., and to be extinguished from 11 p.m. By the end of the month the times had moved on to 4.35 p.m. and 10 p.m. No lights were needed during the full moon, which was 25–28 January. Walton village was to have 35 lamps, School Lane 10, Brownedge 7, Bamber Bridge 25, Higher Walton 21, 'New Road' 16 (120 yds apart), Chorley Road 16, Gregson Lane 5, and Lostock Hall 10. The lamps cost £3 6s. 0d. each, and 13s. a year to run.[14]

As the stock of lamps was added to, the lamplighters were constantly in dispute over their wages. In September 1901 the rates for the rounds were increased: Bamber Bridge (86 lamps) 15s., Walton village (77) 14s., Lostock Hall (30) 9s., Gregson Lane (24) 8s. 6d., the total weekly cost being 46s. 6d. Great disputes broke out over the placing of the lamps. Most people wanted their street's single light to be placed by their house, whilst others tried to claim a rent if the lamp was placed on their property:

> 4th Oct. 1887   Lostock House
> Gentlemen,
> I find that you have a street lamp erected on our land close to the Lostock Hall Spinning Company's mill. I suppose you will not object to pay us an acknowledgement of say 1s. per annum, with an undertaking to remove when not required.
> Yours Truly
> R. H. Flitcroft.

Alternatively Henry Ward demanded 'No less than three lamps' for his row of houses at Lostock Hall. Lamp smashing was soon a problem, and the Board offered 'rewards' to any successful informant: 'The clerk reported that he had received information from PC Naylor that John Livesey (16), Robert Hilton (13), and Frank King (13), all of Walton had been seen smashing four street lamps in Church Brow, Walton'. If they were successfully convicted the informant was to receive 10s. reward.[15]

Triassic Water

Before 1877 no systematic water supply existed, and water was taken from wells, pits, mill lodges, streams and the rivers. In May of that year the new Gas and Water Committee met under the chairmanship of Richard Calvert to discuss the matter. Daily consumption was estimated at about 125,000 gallons, with 35,000 gallons used by the mills. Accordingly much of the initiative to develop a system came from the millowners who provided the backbone of the Board. Calverts required 16,000 gallons, and G. & R. Dewhursts needed 4,000 gallons at Cuerden and 8,000 gallons at Higher Walton. Preston Corporation could supply the water, but the price was regarded as high, and the water pressure from a main over Walton bridge would be too low to operate the mill fire hydrants at Bamber Bridge and Gregson Lane.[16]

After taking suitable advice, it was decided to sink a borehole near Brindle, between the canal and the junction of Pippin Street and Sandy Lane. Trial pumping began in February 1880, and the Board decided to approach the Local Government Board for permission to borrow £10,000. A well 8' in diameter and 150' deep was to be dug, fed by water rising 300' through two boreholes at the bottom. The costings were as follows: the well £1,808, engines and pumps £1,677, buildings and a reservoir £2,030, trunk and distribution pipes £3,820, pipe laying £1,284, total cost £10,625. Water was to be pumped into a reservoir from where it could feed a system of iron water mains by gravity. Pipes were to be provided by the Stanton Iron Works, and the engines were made by W. & S. Yates of Blackburn. In October 1881 the drills of the Cumberland Rock Boring Co. reached a depth of 526', and drilling stopped. It was felt that 'great waters lie beneath the belt of Kinder Scout Grit, and that this may be tapped in future'. By the end of the month the well was yielding 140,000 gallons daily.[17]

A system of mains and pipes began to spread throughout the district, at the rate of 5d. per foot, with the plumbers paid 1s. for each joint. The results were predictable: the Lancashire & Yorkshire Railway Company were among many claimants for damages, when one of their horses fell into a hole left by the pipemen in School Lane. Fire hydrants were provided at the various mills, the railway company was offered a supply for the Lostock Hall engine shed at the rate of 7d. per thousand gallons, and churches, chapels and schools were to pay a nominal 2s. 6d. per week for a supply. The water, however, proved to be very hard, and it quickly became apparent that the well could not meet the demand, as more houses began to be connected. Users were urged to be economical. The drought of the summer of 1884 brought matters to a head, when Oswald Simpson refused to pay Gregson Lane Mill's water bill. The water supply, he claimed, had been 'cut off half the time', and the thrifty inhabitants of that district 'will not pay for what they have not had'. The Brindle well was producing just 65,000 gallons a day, well short of the 400,000 gallons promised by the geologists – and production was falling further.[18]

It was decided to increase the flow by digging a series of adits or tunnels, from the well into the surrounding geological structure. In 1885, under the direction of Ebenezer Timmins, a heading was pushed almost 200 yards. The Board followed the excavations with great interest, and much excitement greeted the report: '12th September ... Very full stream tapped'. A branch heading was completed early in 1886, the flow reached 200,000 gallons, and the new works were opened in the spring. But in June 1887 the pipes again ran dry:[19]

> Pumping Station, Brindle.
> I am very sorry to say that the production of the well has fallen off, and unless the consumption is cut down we shall have an empty reservoir. I went down to the mouth of the heading on Saturday at 5 o'clock pm, and found it about one foot deep at the lower end which means it was practically empty.
> H. Barnes.

Worse was to come. In 1889 the neighbours, Leyland and Preston, had to be asked for water, and Ebenezer Timmins was suggesting that a new well be sunk at Walton bridge.

The Board had initially been wary of Manchester Corporation's Thirl-mere water scheme, but in 1891 they began negotiations to obtain a supply from the aqueduct at Hoghton. The water was soft and was supposed to be cheap. The Brindle water had a hardness of 24.8 degrees, the Thirlmere water just 1.7 degrees, and to save money the Board planned to mix the waters. Agreement was reached on 23 May 1896. An 8″ pipe, two and a quarter miles long was to deliver 140,000 gallons a day to the existing system.[20] The cost of 8*d.* per 1,000 gallons, and the ever-increasing demand, led the Urban District Council to consider the construction of a second well. A water diviner found a propitious spot, but the Local Government Board insisted that professional opinion be obtained. In 1907 Prof. Boyd-Hawkins of Manchester University reported that a well should be sunk 'through the drift sands and gravels, into the Triassic pebble bedding of the red sandstone, on the high road between Bamber Bridge and Walton'. This strata, he felt sure, could provide up to a million gallons daily. In 1909 a borehole 18″ in diameter and 500′ deep was sunk off School Lane. The well cost almost £6,500, and was a great success, gushing 82,000 gallons per day. The water was reported to be 'good and wholesome for domestic use'. A second, larger and deeper borehole was sunk in 1913–14 at a cost of £2,500, and output was increased to 200,000 gallons daily in 1917.[21]

Alongside these developments the piped water supply had been steadily extended. In 1906 a contract was placed to lay pipes along Todd Lane and Potter Lane at a cost of £234 16*s.* 9*d.* The iron pipes were to be sealed with 'the best blue soft pig lead'. In June 1907 'an application from the Trustees of the Bamber Bridge Wesleyan Chapel was read requesting a water supply with additional pressure to enable their organ to be blown by water power ...' Pumping ceased at Brindle in October 1920, and a new reservoir was opened at Gough Lane in November 1924.[22]

Public Health: the Great Sewer Competition of 1885

Only when a piped water supply was in place could the provision of sewers be considered. WCs could only work with the water to flush them! In June

1885, as a means of saving money on expensive engineer's reports, it was decided to hold a competition to decide the best system for the district. By 1889 no work on the system had begun, and the Board officially asked Preston Corporation if they would like to take over the problem. When the latter refused, a sub-committee was formed to discuss the problem further. In 1891 it was decided to develop a treatment site at Carr Wood, and the Board applied for a loan of £23,000 at three and a half per cent interest, to pay for the works, the necessary pumps, and the sewer network. Negotiations with the landowners along the lines of the sewers were protracted, and it was not until the summer of 1894 that work really got under way.[23]

The Board was soon fending off claims for damages, as carts and other vehicles came to grief in the sewer excavations. George Lawes demanded damages when his gig embarrassingly crashed into a crater outside the Board's offices in Station Road, throwing the passengers out. The superbly detailed plans of the system are preserved in the Lancashire Recrd Office, and the sewerage system became a source of great civic pride. An eastern high-level sewer drained Higher Walton and Bamber Bridge, a western high sewer drained Lostock Hall, and a low-level sewer drained Walton village. The much-improved health of the inhabitants of the district, and particularly the greater longevity they continue to enjoy thus owes much to the bringers of piped water, sanitation, and thus civilisation – the Walton-le-Dale Local Board.[24]

Each stage of development spurred on further progress. With the provision of clean water and improved sanitation, public health could advance enormously. With the greater sense of the importance of public health greater efforts could be made to educate the public, and so raise standards further. The progressive improvement of public health provision can be traced in the annual reports of the Medical Officer of Health.[25] Smallpox and typhoid were still very prevalent, and Bamber Bridge in particular had an unenviable reputation for the prevalence of infectious disease. In 1887 the isolated farm, Bradkirk House off Brindle Road, was obtained by the Board for use as a smallpox 'hospital', and in 1903 the Urban District Council's Isolation Hospital was opened in Brindle Road. The medical Officer visited the site of an outbreak of typhoid in Gregson Lane in 1898, 'I visited the house, which I found clean, well built and thoroughly drained. Up to a short time before the fever appeared, the inmates drank rain water collected from the roof where pigeons frequented; the water was stored in a cistern under the floor and had a most unpleasant smell. I cannot help thinking the cause of the illness was due to the use of this water.'

Although the reports contain great lists of the improvements undertaken in the years before 1914, sanitation remained generally rudimentary by modern standards. In 1903 the scavengers emptied 37,207 pails, and 10,315 'bogs and ashpits' were cleaned out. The work was the subject of many disagreements, and in 1913 the council decided to stop the practice of contracting the operation out, and to undertake the work itself. Steadily house owners were obliged to introduce flush toilets, but progress was slow. A survey of 1912 revealed the use of 605 privy middens, 1095 'excreta pails', 300 slop water closets, and 692 fresh water closets. Housing conditions were also often extremely bad, particularly in the side streets off Chorley Road corner, and it was here that the earliest slum clearance schemes were established. In 1911 James Leigh, Inspector of Nuisances, reported a case of overcrowding in Station Road, Bamber Bridge. In one house 12 people shared three bedrooms. The family comprised, a man and wife, their two adult daughters, and a married daughter with her husband and their four children. The last six people shared the small back bedroom.

In these environments infectious diseases could spread rapidly, infant mortality was high, and childhood illnesses such as measles frequently closed all the district's schools. The Brindle Road Isolation Hospital comprised two blocks, with an administrative building and a mortuary. Local cases of diphtheria, scarlet fever and typhoid were transported here in a special wagon, and could be incarcerated here for weeks. In 1906 Dr Trimble described it as 'well ventilated ... it is certainly as close to the ideal of a large and well planned hospital as so small a one can be'.[26] The Hospital Rule Book stipulates that visitors were only to be allowed on Tuesdays and Saturdays between 2 and 4 p.m., and 'children visitors must be refused admission without exception'. Nurses were not allowed to receive visitors, were to undertake much of the cleaning and polishing, and must be in their beds by 10.30 p.m. for 'lights out' at 11 p.m.[27]

Related signs of progress include the purchase of the first steam roller in 1890, fears as to the health hazard created by the dust storms thrown up by the early motor vehicles on the gravel road through Bamber Bridge, and the establishment of the Borough's Fire Service. Accordingly 'The Walton-le-Dale Urban District Council Fire Brigade Rules and Regulations' stipulate that

> The Brigade shall consist of a Captain, First Engineer, Second Engineer, Sergeant, and 18 Firemen, who shall be appointed by the Council ...
>
> Rule 11. Each Fireman shall have a plate provided by the Council, placed over the door of his residence, with the word 'FIREMAN' thereon in large character.
>
> Rule 19. Punctuality, zeal, activity, and civility will be expected invariably from the Brigade ...[28]

At the outbreak of the Great War enormous progress had been made in all the departments of local government. Adequate water supplies had been ensured, a sanitation system had been established, and a professional Medical Officer worked to progressively improve the standard of health and hygiene. The drive was well under way to convert privies to flush toilets, and the improvement of the notoriously filthy backstreets 'was being seriously taken in hand'. Indeed the authority now boasted that 'the health of

the district has always maintained a high standard, the death rate being especially low'. At this point of supreme optimism in the future progress of the district, and with exports of Lancashire cloth at an all-time peak, events in Eastern Europe intervened decisively.

The Walton-le-Dale Fire Brigade's crew and Leyland Motors engine, passing Withy Trees Mill, Station Road, Bamber Bridge, c.1935. Well into the 1960s the call-out siren on the Station Road fire station was a familiar sound in the village. (R. Burns)

The Great War

The outbreak of the First World War was marked by ceremonial and great enthusiasm. Preston's wartime mayor, Sir Harry Cartmell, later recalled the events of 5 August 1914. 'During the whole of that first day, and indeed for some time afterwards, great crowds of people thronged the principal streets, everyone evincing a consciousness that we were on the eve of great things'. The following day local reservists were seen off at Preston railway station, 'the crowd becoming literally wild in their display of enthusiasm'. This mood quite quickly dissipated. At the end of 1915, Cartmell visited the surviving Preston contingent at the Front: 'After a busy afternoon I took leave of our men and carried with me a picture of many smiling faces, but I could not get rid of the thought of their depleted numbers'. By the end of 1916 the people at home were also facing increasing hardships, and food rationing was introduced in early 1917.[29]

Amidst fears of an impending French invasion, a battery of artillery volunteers had been formed in Walton-le-Dale in February 1861. This became the 11th Battery Royal Field Artillery, and subsequently the 2nd West Lancashire Field Artillery (Territorial). Their annual week's training had become a well-established social event by the early years of the present century. Although local men served in all the campaigns of the war, the battery formed an important focus for volunteers at the outbreak of the

The Walton-le-Dale Isolation Hospital, Brindle Road, Bamber Bridge, c.1906. Serious infectious diseases, particularly smallpox, were a major problem faced by the Board. Childhood cases of scarlet fever, a notifiable disease, could be incarcerated here for over six weeks. These modern facilities replaced the fever house, which had been established in a former farmhouse. Only very slowly did the public health of the district improve. (R. Burns)

war. The former Drill Hall, in Pear Tree Street, off Station Road in Bamber Bridge, still exists. Reformed as part of the 55th (West Lancashire) Division, the battery served throughout Flanders, and fought at the battles of the Somme, Ypres, and Passchendaele.

Some indication of the losses suffered by the local community can be gained from the regimental lists, and the local war memorials. Many local men served in the 1st/4th Battalion of the Loyal North Lancashire Regiment. This regiment suffered 3,093 casualties during the war, comprising 873 dead, 2,093 wounded, 83 returned POWs, and 44 missing (1921).[30] Many of their names can be seen on the awesome memorial in the foyer of the Harris Art Gallery, Preston. A programme of dedicated research on the casualties listed on the local war memorials is well under way. Work on the Bamber Bridge memorials by Mr J. Rawcliffe indicates the following numbers of casualties: St Saviour's parish 54 dead, St Aidan's 27, Bamber Bridge Methodist Church 7, and Brownedge St Mary's 73. In all 167 dead, including six men whose names are on no memorial ... A figure of around 300 might therefore be the total for the district when Walton and Lostock Hall are included – and this was just one very small township in Lancashire.

The Preston newspapers could barely keep pace with the appallingly long lists of casualties. The reports still convey the intense personal cost of the catastrophe:

Preston Guardian 28 September 1918:
Official intimation has been received of the death in action (by Shrapnel) of Gunner W. Green (32) RFA of 90 Station Road, Bamber Bridge. He joined the army early in the war, and had been in France a considerable period. His battery officer writes – 'He was one of the best gunners we had, and a fine example to the battery. He was one of those grand God fearing men one does not often come across. He will be greatly missed.

Private W. T. Holland (21), for example, was a weaver at Orrs Mill, and a resident of Club Street. One of seven 'soldier brothers', he was killed on 25 July 1916. Pte Edward Monarch Jamieson (26), of Dewhursts Row, was killed on 15 October 1916 at the battle of Ancre. He had been given his distinctive second name, Monarch, after the name of the engine at G. & R. Dewhurst's nearby mill.[31]

Corporal John McNamara (30), was educated at Brownedge School, and worked as a 'Ring Jobber' at Orrs. He lived with his wife and their four young daughters in Stone Row, School Lane. Having served with the 'Loyals', he was transferred to the East Surrey Regiment. Early in September 1918, he single-handedly held off a desperate German counter-attack during the battle of the Selle. He was killed four weeks later, just three weeks before the Armistice. Although he had apparently told his brother that he was 'in for something', he died not knowing that he had won the Victoria Cross. Tragically, a significant number of local men were killed in the fierce fighting late in 1918, within weeks of the Axis collapse which finally brought about the Armistice.[32]

Events on the Home Front can be traced in most of the local sources of the period. In September 1914 the Walton-le-Dale UDC resolved to pay the wife of their employee Richard Ball, 'who has joined Kitchener's Army' 10s. per week in his absence. By April the following year Cuerden Hall was being used as a hospital for the wounded, and in May Dr Trimble the Medical Officer was given 'leave of absence ... for the purpose of enabling him to join the Royal Army Medical Corps for duty abroad'. With the shortage of manpower, and the introduction of conscription,

Local men of the 2nd West Lancashire Royal Field Artillery, at summer camp, Arthur's Seat, Edinburgh, c. 1912. The Territorials' Drill Hall was located in Pear Tree Street, Bamber Bridge. Perhaps 300 local men were killed during the Great War, including John McNamara, the Bamber Bridge VC. (J. Rawcliffe) wages rose rapidly, and the council had to increase its rates of pay in order to retain its key staff.[33]

Many areas of life became 'controlled': a local food control committee was established, and the council began to set coal prices in October 1917. Labour was also closely regulated: '1 July 1918: Resolved that the application of Mr Fred Coupe for a licence to ply for hire be postponed, for him to obtain the permission to commence a new business'. By 1918 the domestic and military position was desperate. Recreation grounds were to be ploughed up to grow food, and all the restrictions on domestic pig keeping were suspended. Old problems reappeared. In May 1917 it was decided to offer rewards in an attempt to keep down vermin and pests. One shilling was to be paid 'for a dozen rat tails, 3*d*. per dozen heads of fully fledged house sparrows, 3*d*. per dozen heads of unfledged house sparrows, and 1*d*. per dozen house sparrow's eggs'.

Anti-German feeling ran very high. Measles became specifically referred to as 'German Measles', and towards the end of the war the council passed the following resolution: '24 June 1918: Resolved. That this Council views with alarm the freedom allowed to enemy aliens at large, the continuance of naturalised Germans in Government offices, and the latitude permitted to pacifist subjects of HM in their treasonable utterances and actions whereby the enemy are directly supported and encouraged, and call upon the Government to intern all enemies and de-naturalise all Germans who have been naturalised in recent years.'

In spite of the gradually developing social crisis, the council managed to maintain the drive for domestic improvement. The introduction of water closets was driven ahead, labour and materials shortages permitting, and

Peace celebrations in Brandiforth Street, Bamber Bridge, 1919. The end of the war came at a point when the Home Front was close to total collapse. The subsequent boom in the cotton trade, which followed the enormously profitable war years, led to great hopes for the future. Yet by the early 1920s the long-term changes in the pattern of world trade, which had been accelerated by the war, were becoming apparent; the local mills began to close. (R. Burns)

plans for 400 new post-war houses were discussed as early as October 1917. The cotton trade registered record profits during the war, and the rapid growth of Leyland Motors produced a great demand for skilled men, and placed the district's infrastructure under great strain: '3 June 1916. Resolved: that the Leyland Motor Company Ltd be requested to abstain from using the Highways in this district for testing motor lurries, and if they continue to do so that payment be claimed for this extraordinary traffic'.[34]

The war had a profound effect on the health of the people, particularly that of the young and old. By its end, the general diet was extremely poor, and the great Influenza epidemic swept Europe. The impact of these events on the young can be seen, for example, in the Log Book of the Bamber Bridge Methodist School.[35] Throughout the war the school faced great staffing problems: '30th May 1915. Mr A. Longton, certified teacher of class 2 absent, owing to having enlisted in the Royal Field Artillery during Whit Week He is 2549 2/11 Battery, West Lancashire Brigade RFA'. His loss had immediate effect, '4th June 1915. No teacher for standards 3 & 4. Head master grouped standards 3–4–5–6–7 for as many lessons as possible: Timetable suspended'. Inexperienced staff were brought in, and one of the infants' teachers faced a class of 48 children, 25 of them under 5 years of age. In October 1916 the crisis led to children being sent to the adjacent schools. Throughout the war, lack of fuel and defective heating equipment resulted in very cold classrooms, particularly during the winter of 1918. As late as November 1919 fires had to be lit in the two classrooms, 'so that classes may take turns in warming themselves'.

From the summer of 1916, as a result of these difficulties, great waves of sickness swept through the staff and children. Many of the older children were 'half-timers', who spent half of their time at school, and half at the mill. In July 1918 cases of influenza and mumps were being reported, and by November a large proportion of the school had influenza. To help the war food effort, the staff and children helped out in the fields and on the wartime allotments, '16th Oct. 1918. Miss J. Hutchinson with 5 Big Boys left school at 3.20 p.m. to assist Mr Clitheroe lift his potatoes'.

Peace came on November 11th 1918; 'News arrived at 11 a.m. that the armistice had been signed by Germany. The afternoon has been given up to a holiday to celebrate the event'. The following day only half of the children turned up for school, 'And as all work people had ceased work it was decided to close the school for the day ...' Enormous numbers of children now had influenza. Victory had come at a point when the situation on the Home Front had become truly desperate.

Brownedge War Memorial, 1997. Erected at a cost of £1,184, the memorial was dedicated on 4 September 1921. In the distance the line of the ancient Brown Edge can be seen. (Author)

CHAPTER THIRTEEN

Paying for the last war and preparing for the next

HE LONG TERM IMPACT of the Great War on the cotton industry did not become immediately apparent. In 1918 Tattersall's *Annual Review* could report that 'The Lancashire cotton industry in the last year has experienced the most prosperous period in its history. More money has been made than in any previous twelve months'. 1919 was even better, and in 1920, 150 companies paid dividends of 40 per cent or over. In fact, signs of the long-term decline of the industry in Lancashire had been apparent – to those who would see them – from the 1880s, as former markets began to develop industries of their own. As Bowker concluded, 'War time and boom years had made an unexpected melodramatic climax for what had been slowly developing in the Lancashire of 1900–1914'. Manufacturers at the coarse end of the market, serving the markets of India and the Far East were particularly affected by the rise of Japan and the move of India towards economic independence.[1]

The funeral of William Parker, in 1919, was to be the last of the great public funerals which had become such a tradition in the local cotton industry. Great crowds lined the roads between his home at Withy Grove, Bamber Bridge, and Preston Cemetery: 'As a large employer of labour, he was kind and generous. Had England more masters like him there would be far less industrial unrest and jealousy ... For by distances the roads were lined with people, many in visible grief, and Bamber Bridge, Walton, and a large part of Preston were in mourning. Hundreds of men with bared heads, and thousands of men and women with bowed heads showed their sense of loss'.[2] The probate register reveals his estate to have been £156,792 9s. 2d., a sum only exceeded by the estates of Henry Calvert (1902 – £357,000), Frank Calvert (1915 – £170,000), Henry Calvert (1922 – £226,000), and Herbert Calvert (1953 – £241,000). Thus, such was the scale of the wealth created by this one firm alone, that in the twenty years 1902–22 six 'shareholders' in the enterprise left a total of £1,046,000.[3]

By the early 1920s the boom was over, and manufacturers waited for the return of pre-war conditions: 'Despised in 1900, patronised in 1913, looked at with curious indifference so late as 1922, the foreigner in 1928 has been hitting Lancashire hard for seven years. The direct export loss to Lancashire has been tremendous. The indirect loss may yet prove irreparable'.[4] The economic and industrial advantages which had brought the trade from India to Lancashire in the 1780s, had passed to other countries. Britain had become a mature industrial society, whose manufacturing advantage now lay not in primary goods, but in the production of high value-added items such as motor vehicles and electrical goods. As the old industries entered their long inter-war decline, these new industries expanded markedly. Good local examples are Leyland Motors, and Courtauld's enormous rayon plant at Red Scar.

The Consolidated Cotton Mills Trust grew out of the early period of rationalisation. A handbook published in 1925 could still look to the future with confidence: 'Tardy Gate Mill is modern in establishment, but has been modelled on principles which are the outcome of a long experience in the cotton industry ... The absorption of the energies and interests of Thomas Moss and Sons, is in itself evidence of judgement and discrimination. success which is based on a long lived reputation, either in the main body or in its components, begats further prosperity, and the record of this firm's enterprise speaks well for its future under enhanced conditions'.[5]

In 1922 Mr Harold Parker of Calvert Brothers was a member of the British Cotton Delegation which toured the United States and Australia. The visit to the cotton growing areas of Queensland, and the North Rivers District of New South Wales, was covered in great detail by the Brisbane Courier: 'Mr Parker, who is vice president of that noted football club, Preston North End, was originally one of the most prominent amateur footballers in England. Calverts, of which he is Managing Director, are the best-known cotton manufacturers in the world so far as the Eastern trade is concerned ... In one year his firm had made considerably more 36″ wide cloth than would completely encircle the globe. They employed 2,300 persons, and consumed at the mills during a year no less than 20,000 bales of cotton, each of 500lbs'. Whilst staying at Wowan, 50 miles from Rockhampton, Mr Parker visited a 'colony' of former mill folk. 'Among The Settlers – Returning in the evening Mr Harold Parker made a visit to Lancashire Lane, where he called on a Lancashire man, who had worked in Calvert's mills'. The party were much impressed by the agricultural potential of the district, and advocated immigration from England as a means of overcoming the rising tide of unemployment.[6]

By the mid-1920s, it was clear that the depression in the cotton trade was not to be transitory, and that it indicated a profound change in the fundamentals of the world trade. By 1925 five Preston mills had closed; six closed between 1926 and 1932; and nine from 1932 to 1936. Six more mills closed from there up to 1940. J. H. Spencer later described the collapse of much of the Preston trade, 'The war of 1914 gave the death blow to our vast China and India trade ... We all know how this affected Preston; all the mills serving India and China markets have closed down, and it may be said that the Lancashire cotton trade of today, and especially our local trade, is confined to the finer counts and specialised fabrics'.[7]

With the developing economic depression, hard pressed directors took

The Walton-le-Dale Grocery and Butchery branch of the Preston Industrial Co-operative Society, Walton Corner, c.1925. During the late 1930s the billboards of the village newsagents (right) gave the latest news of Preston North End's great cup runs – and Hitler's march to war. (R. Burns)

greater risks to maintain profits, leading to many commercial failures. In 1925 Richard Aspden and Co. of Mexican Mill failed, and was declared bankrupt. The premises in Aspden Street, Bamber Bridge, were sold, '28 October 1925:[8] The valuable freehold weaving shed and manufacturing premises known as Mexican Mill'. It contained 282 36″ looms, mill gearing, and a horizontal compound tandem condensing engine. Between 1926 and 1932 Thomas Eccles Stone Mill, and William Eccles Withy Trees Mill, in School Lane and Station Road, Bamber Bridge respectively, also closed. Dewhurst's enormous Cuerden Mill, which had once claimed to have the largest spinning floor in the world, closed by 1936. The firm's Higher Walton Mill was sold to the Lancashire Cotton Corporation in 1932. In 1937 it was acquired by the Preston Tyre Fabric Co., who begun to diversify production away from the orthodox cotton trade. The company's third local mill, Farington Mill, ran on well into the 1960s. Most sensational of all, however, was the collapse of William Calvert and Sons in 1931. This was the single greatest economic disaster ever to befall the village of Walton, and many thought that the village would never recover. From the available evidence it is clear that the closing of these five mills resulted in the loss of at least 2,500 jobs, and the production of 3,500 looms, and almost 200,000 spindles. Bamber Bridge was hit very hard.[9]

Life between the wars

Notwithstanding widespread unemployment, the inter-war years were not without elements of very considerable progress. The process of urbanisation gained momentum, and with the spread of semi-detached housing, an extensive suburbia began to develop. This is revealed on the 'Emergency Edition' 6″ OS map of 1938. The new housing was most apparent along the main throughways, linking the old village centres. Lostock Hall emerged as a major residential centre, with its 'commuter stations' at Lostock Hall and Todd Lane. From the latter, lines of housing spread along Brownedge Road towards Brownedge level crossing, and towards Tardy Gate. Mayfield Drive and Rosemead Avenue had begun to be developed, as had St Cuthbert's Road, Mercer Road and St Oswalds Road, off Wateringpool Lane. From Tardy Gate ribbon development had spread along Leyland Road towards Skew Bridge, and the Lostock Hall Gas Works, with its enormous gasometers, retort houses, and railway branch line had been built.[10]

In Bamber Bridge development was more restricted. Collins Road was in the course of development, and semi-detached housing had begun to spread along the north side of Brindle Road. The first houses had been built along Duddle Lane, which for most of its length was still a country lane. On Cinnamon Hill only Windsor Road and the related side streets had been laid out, and building along the lower length of Hennel Lane had reached a similar stage. The line of fine detached residences had begun to extend eastwards from Knot Lane along Cuerdale Lane, from where Preston Corporation's spectacular building schemes could be seen across the Ribble valley. New houses were also becoming a feature of Hoghton Lane and Gregson Lane, and along Higher Walton Road east of Walton corner.

The nature of the Urban District Council also began to change, as it absorbed the functions of house builder and landlord. In 1930 a dispute broke out over the appointment of the chairman. Mr Kelly of St Leonards ward, as senior member, thought he ought to be appointed 'Mr Ingham, a new member, said he did not think that while there was a Conservative

An early motor omnibus run by the Lancashire & Yorkshire Railway Company, at Bamber Bridge, c.1912. Motor transport was to re-order the local landscape drastically in the twentieth century, culminating in the construction of the motorway system through the east of the district, and in the 1980s the building of the Walton and Bamber Bridge by-pass. Easy car access also resulted in the suburbanis-ation of much of this former manufacturing district, and in the schemes for a Central Lancashire New Town.
(R. Burns)

Kay's Garage, Walton Corner, c.1935. The natural route centre at Walton Corner was an ideal site for the location of motor service stations. Cooper Hill, the large mansion overlooking the village centre, can be seen on the extreme right of the photograph.
(R. Burns)

majority of members they should have a Socialist chairman ... Mr Rigby, the oldest member of the Council declared that in all his 11 years a member, politics had never coloured meetings'.[11]

From 1928 requests for tenders to build new houses began to appear in the press; 20 houses were advertised for Collins Road, with 40 more in 1932, and a further 14 in 1938. House clearance also proceeded, and the old property in Meanygate was ordered to be demolished in October 1938. There were other harbingers of change: in 1934 the authority advertised the sale of its horse-drawn vehicles, including 'One 1906 Shand Mason, horse drawn, double cylinder vertical steam fire engine, with two lengths of 4″ suction: pumping capacity 300 gallons per minute. very little used and in excellent condition'.[12]

Until the census returns for this period become available in 2031, the Street Directories are once again an important source, providing much incidental information on everyday life.[13] The motor car was to shape the new suburbia, and in 1936 Walton had six garages, including Fred Coupe's establishment, Dodgsons Service Station, and James Rafferty and Sons ('Petrol filling etc: Telephone 4034'). Walter Lathom (164 Victoria Road) was clogger, Leonard Finch the dentist, and William Brooks and Hugh George the 'Physicians' at Charlton Beeches. The village had nine grocers, including the Preston Industrial Co-operative Society on Chorley Road, five inns, two 'fried fish dealers', and two window cleaners, Arnold Bentham and William Mayor. Mr Frederick Fletcher ran the 'Dining Rooms' at 34 Chorley Road – in the ancient Unicorn Inn. At Gregson Lane John Harkin

was the village clogger, and Jamieson Brothers ('Makers of the 'Ideal' Prize Loaf') were established in 'Gregson Lane Bakery'. The village could also boast an independent co-op, 'The Gregson Lane Co-operative Society', and quite rightly for the birthplace of the Ribble Motor Bus Company ('of Gregson Lane ... and also at Preston'), its own dance band – Matt Worsley's greatly celebrated 'Daytona Beach Boys'. In Higher Walton, John Taberner, 'Hardware Dealer' was established at 13 Cann Bridge Street, close by Jacksons Garage Company ('Wireless and Cycle Dealers').

Bamber Bridge in the 1930s was something of a metropolis. Here, in 1936, were found no less than ten 'fish fryers'. The village had three banks, six shoemakers, and four butchers, including Thomas A. Cooper and Eric Wolstenholme. The list of 28 'grocers' included the premises of 'The Bamber Bridge Industrial Co-operative Society', and 'Melias' in Station Road. There were 14 'shopkeepers'. Often using the front room of a small terraced house, the latter were important centres of the street's life. Good examples were Isabella Pilkington's small shop in Greenwood Street, and Ann Halpin's shop in Duddle Lane. The range of services available in Bamber Bridge was very large; there were 10 'hairdressers', 11 inns, three sets of surgeons (Ernest Hulme, Brownedge; Martin Ryan, Withy House; William Simpson, Station Road) and two chemists. Local garages were run by John Crook and Richard Prescott, who operated the village's bus company, the BBMS (Bamber Bridge Motor Services). The importance of coal as a domestic fuel is indicated by the 11 coal merchants. The village supported 13 confectioners, four fresh fish dealers (including Joseph Pearson at 7 Dean Street), and three tripe dealers (all in Station Road).

An early road accident, c. 1910. a steam wagon, built by the 'Lancashire Steam Motor Co.' of Leyland, in collision with the cottage at the corner of School Lane and Station Road, Bamber Bridge. (R. Burns)

Small shops also dominated Lostock Hall and Tardy Gate. Here Thomas Wadeson was clogger in Watkin Lane, but there were also five 'Boot and shoe repairers'. The 13 grocers listed in 1936 included the Watkin Lane and Ward Street branches of the BBICS. Thomas Marsden ran the local garage ('Cycle dealer, motor engineer and garage proprietor'). Prepared food outlets were numerous here, with five 'fried fish dealers', and eight confectioners.

A Bamber Bridge Motor Services 53-seat Titan double-decker undergoing final trials in the South Works of Leyland Motors, c.1938. The BBMS became an important and much-loved symbol of Bamber Bridge's pride and prestige, as well as providing a forum for the exchange of news and gossip. At Withy Trees locals would stand back to let a Ribble bus pass on the Bamber Bridge–Preston run, to catch the BBMS running behind. The nationally important Ribble Bus Company also had local roots, having been established in Gregson Lane. (*South Ribble Museum*)

Uncle Jimmy's Treat, c. 1925. The children's outings begun by James Charleston (1859–1931) became a major local event. R. A. Tatton, owner of the Cuerden Hall estate, opened the park to the children, and local shops gave refreshments. The latter, and St Saviour's Church, can be seen in the background of this photograph. The story of 'Uncle Jimmy's Treat' is told in 'Days Gone By in Bamber Bridge' by S. Gregson and E. M. Waterfield. (R. Burns)

Cuerden Sports Club, the YMCA League and Cup Winners, 1925–26. Notwithstanding divided loyalties to Preston North End and the Ewood Park club, the district has itself produced a number of successful teams and players, culminating in the recent phenomenal rise of Bamber Bridge Football Club. (R. Burns)

In the country areas, farming remained a very important industry, but was undergoing considerable transformation as the majority of farmers struggled to survive the Depression by 'make do and mend'. In the district 130 farmers are listed, including John Holroyd (Middle Shuttling Fields), Thomas Calderbank (Osbaldeston House), Hargreaves & Driver (Walton Hall Farm), and Frank Sowerbutts (Iron Gate Farm). This figure, however, includes 50 'poultry farmers', reflecting the growth of egg marketing and the chicken trade. Many smallholders along Duddle Lane and Brownedge Road kept hens, including William Dowbakin, Christopher Nagle, and James Ashworth, The Bamber Bridge area was able to support five egg dealers, and five dairies, and was the natural centre for the Milk and Egg Marketing Boards.

The return to full employment

The progressive re-armament from 1937 had an important impact on mid-Lancashire. The extension of vehicle manufacture at Leyland, the manufacture of aircraft at Strand Road, Preston, and at Warton, and the construction of the Royal Ordnance Factory at Euxton boosted local demand for labour. In the wider district the development of the aerodrome at Samlesbury, and the enormous Courtaulds' rayon plant at Red Scar, further promoted recovery. In the long term these major strategic investments were to shape the post-war history of the region. Re-armament, in short, was the catalyst for short-term investment, which in the longer term brought into being a new industrial base which was to prove strong enough to supplant even the cotton industry. Without the threat of war it is uncertain when, or how, this recovery might otherwise have been brought about.

On 14 March 1938 the *Lancashire Daily Post* carried the headline, 'Hitler Rides in Triumph from Linz towards Vienna'. In November 1938 it was announced that 3,000 building jobs would be created at Euxton, that aircraft assembly work would create work for a further 5,000, and Courtaulds factory was hoping to employ 2,000 rising to 5,000. By December 1939 the local cotton mills were reported to be running at full capacity, and cloth prices had risen 30 per cent. J. M. Keynes' arguments for government intervention in the economy as a cure for mass unemployment, scorned in

The Empire Cinema, Clayton Street, Bamber Bridge, c.1950. Originating before the Great War, this small picture house was frequently so packed by ardent filmgoers in the 1920s and '30s that the doors had to be opened to clear the smoke which obstructed the film show. Subsequently the premises were occupied by Smiths Electrical Engineers and around 1950 John Smith, with the help of an assistant on the roof, obtained the first reception of a television signal in the district, at his house in Duddle Lane. (*R. Burns*)

The new suburbia, semi-detached housing and shops along Brownedge Road, Lostock Hall, *c.* 1940. The development of Lostock Hall gathered pace greatly between the wars, with the ribbon development of Brownedge Road. An early electric street light can be seen on the left of the photograph. (*South Ribble Museum*)

New council houses along Collins Road, Bamber Bridge, *c.* 1938. The council's effort to speed up construction of new houses was put to an end by the Second World War. As in 1914, the outbreak of war came just when real progress was beginning to be achieved. (*South Ribble Museum*)

the 1920s and 1930s, had been brilliantly vindicated. Near full employment had returned in under three years.[14]

With Hitler's invasion of Slovakia in March 1939, civil defence preparations were pushed on rapidly. The Military Training Act came into force in June, and as the Danzig crisis reached its conclusion 50,000 evacuees many in their Sunday best, were said to have changed trains at Preston. Everywhere the fear was of air attack: 'There are the sandbagged buildings, now becoming almost commonplace in the familiar landscape and accepted without comment. There are the policemen, carrying their steel helmets and their gas masks: the ARP workers: soldiers much in evidence'.[15] E. H. Booths warned their customers, 'We appeal to all customers to confine their buying to their usual pre-war requirements. It is too late to stock up now. It is also unfair and unpatriotic'.[16]

The evacuees

During the crisis of September 1939 a surprisingly large number of evacuees were billeted in the area. Walton, Higher Walton, Bamber Bridge and Lostock Hall had separate reception centres and sets of records. Bamber Bridge and Walton seem to have been the primary reception areas. In the former 479 evacuees were placed in 331 homes, whilst the centre in St Patrick's Hall, Higher Walton Road, distributed 370 people among 198 homes. A further 125 adults accompanied their children, mostly mothers with babies, but returned home soon after the initial crisis. By the second phase of accounting and registration, which began on 28 October 1939, much smaller numbers of children and virtually no adults stayed on.

At Higher Walton and Lostock Hall the situation is more confused since many children were later relocated to the primary centres. From All Saints School 181 children were allocated, with a further 294 at Lostock Hall. Given the variability in the records, a figure of 1,300 is probably a good estimate of the evacuee total. The majority of children came from Manchester – Fallowfield, Didsbury, Miles Platting and Withington – with a smaller number from Bradford. Although brothers and sisters were occasionally split up, they were usually placed in adjacent houses. Alternatively the householders received 10s. 6d. per child, or 17s. for two. Sheila Burton, for example, who came from Southholme Gardens, Manchester, stayed at 45 Chorley Road, Walton-le-Dale, for 15 weeks, and the householder received £7 17s. 6d. towards her keep.[17]

Preparations for air attack

In March 1937 the clerk of the council's General Purposes Committee drew up an 'Air Raid Precautions Scheme', and in May it was announced that the Chief Constable was to be responsible for the air raid wardens.[18] The following year a special ARP Committee was formed, and by September 1938 recruitment of the wardens was well under way. The council requisitioned 40,000 sandbags, and drew up a list of suitable shelters and basements. Where these were not available trenches were to be dug. In Collins Road, Bamber Bridge, a 'model' trench shelter was dug. It was 35 yds long, 6' deep, 3' wide at the top and 2' wide at the bottom. Covered with railway sleepers, it had an 'air lock' at each end. By early December the crisis of that year had passed, and it was resolved that the trenches which had been dug at Lostock Hall should be filled in.[19]

By the outbreak of the war anti air raid provision was still rudimentary, but was extending rapidly. In November it was decided to take in parts of the various new Jubilee Playing Fields for the construction of shelters for 2,000 people. One year later 23 communal shelters had been opened, 16 of them in the previous two months. Vandalism and flooding were problems. Great efforts were now made to build further shelters, and an additional 52 communal shelters were ordered to be built. Metal 'Morrison Shelters' became available, and 120 were ordered from the manufacturers. In May 1943 the accounts of the contractors, John Moulding and John Fishwick, were settled, and almost £15,000 had been spent.[20]

By the summer of 1940 training sessions for the wardens were held on two evenings each week, and the district had been divided into six districts for the fire watchers' beats:

1   Bamber Bridge Section. HQ Prescott's Garage. Distance 9 miles.
2   HQ Section. HQ Fire Station, Bamber Bridge. 9.5 miles. Cyclist to patrol from Station Road to Meanygate via Brownedge Road, and return via Station Road.
3   Lostock Hall Section. HQ Moss's Mill, Ward St 10.7 miles.
4   Walton-le-Dale Section. HQ Kay's Garage. 7.6 miles. Cyclist to patrol along the river bank to Tram Bridge.
5   Higher Walton Section. HQ Higher Walton Mill. 6.3 miles.
6   Gregson Lane Section. HQ Ingham & Tippings corn mill. 6.3 miles.

Special rations were provided for the council's water plant employees, whose role would be vital in keeping up the water pressure during any fire fighting operations. These comprised: one tin of Irish Stew, Oxo cubes, Horlicks tablets, biscuits, and a piece of cheese. In September 1940 blankets, mattresses, rugs and petrol cans were purchased for the wardens, and great efforts were made to improve air raid warnings. Sirens were located at the Fire Station, and on the roof of the Walton Working Men's Institute. A mortuary was set up in School Lane. The Ward Street bombing gave a massive boost to local awareness of the threat, and in May 1941 the council ordered that the wardens should work 'Not less than 48 hours women, 72 hours men'.[21]

Yet events were not without their moments of farce:[22]

29 August 1940.
Mr Kay reported that Mr Will Coupe ran into his Garage in Pyjamas and dressing gown and told him he thought an unexploded bomb had fallen between his home and the vicarage as he distinctly heard the thud, and would take the necessary steps to locate it.
03.55: Police found nothing.

The Ward Street bombing

The first local air raids began in the late summer of 1940. A major attack on Leyland Motors took place on 21 October, when the works were bombed and machine-gunned, and on the 26th bombs fell in the fields off Brindle Road, Bamber Bridge. Shortly after teatime on Sunday 27 October the air raid HQ at Bamber Bridge received an eyewitness report of an enemy plane flying over Lostock Hall, followed at 18.24 hours by a report that

Ward Street, Lostock Hall, 1997. The gap in the houses along the left side of the street indicates the area of the most severe bomb damage. The Ward Street Bombing was the district's worst wartime incident. Papers in the Lancashire Record Office, Preston, detail the events at teatime on Sunday 27 October 1940, literally minute-by-minute. At 18.24 hours reports were received at the Air Raid HQ in Bamber Bridge fire station that bombs had fallen on Lostock Hall. Tragically, the 'Air Raid Messages Pad' records that the 'Air Raid Warning Red' message was only received at 18.29½ hours. Although the prompt response and desperate efforts of the recovery and medical teams was later commended, the delay had been disastrous, for the shelter at the end of Ward Street was undamaged, and twenty-five people had been killed. (Author)

bombs had fallen in the Ward Street area. At 18.27 the sirens were operated and the rescue teams were despatched. These were joined by teams from Leyland and Farington. The actual 'Air Raid Messages Pad' survives in the Lancashire Record Office.[23] It reveals that reports were constantly being received. At 18.29½ the 'Air Raid Warning – Red' was received. The delay had been fatal; there was a shelter close at hand and it was not damaged in the attack. The people had not had either a warning or the time to reach it.

The official report and the 'Bomb Damage Book' reveal the scale of the disaster.[24] The rescue arrangements worked well, and great efforts were made to get 'a considerable number of people' out of the wreckage. The last person alive was got out at 1.30 a.m. Twelve people were treated at Walton, and nine were sent to Preston Royal Infirmary. Twenty-five people had been killed in seven houses in Ward Street, including Cyril Watson (41) and his wife Helen, and six of their family, who had lived at No. 56. Two high explosive bombs had been dropped, damaging 33 houses in Ward Street (nine 'totally destroyed'), eight houses in Princess Street, and six houses in Birtwistle Street. Moss's mill was also damaged. Although the accounts are not exactly consistent, the bombs seem to have struck at 18.15 hours. The target had probably been the Farington Works of Leyland Motors.

At the council meeting of 4 November 1940 it was, 'Resolved on the motion of the chairman, the members standing in silence, that this council, express their deep and sincere sympathy with all the relatives and friends of those civilians, men, women, and children, 25 in all, who were killed in the regrettable enemy air raid on certain civilian dwellings in Ward St Lostock Hall, on Sunday, the 27th October, 1940, and also with the injured in their suffering, those rendered homeless, and those who have sustained serious loss'.[25]

In the greater Preston district over 100 incidents were reported in late 1940.[26] During the night of 29 November the largest unexploded bomb to fall in the county landed on the lawn at Darwen Bank, Bamber Bridge. A team of bomb disposal men worked to recover the 25cwt 'Herman Goering' bomb from a crater 39' deep. It is typical of many wartime incidents, that people living in the adjacent streets off School Lane knew nothing of it. On Mayday 1941 incendiaries were dropped over Lostock Hall, causing damage to a large number of properties in Wateringpool Lane, Lourdes Avenue, Brownedge Road, Laburnam Avenue, Highfield Avenue and St Gerards Road. An incendiary bomb hit St Gerard's Church. One householder in Wateringpool Lane, reported his losses as, '2 cycles badly damaged, 1 long handled brush, a child's spade, half a hundredweight of seed potatoes'. Hitler's attack on Russia brought the air raids to an end.[27]

The Bamber Bridge Incident

With America's entry into the war, the North West became an important support area for the build up to the invasion of Europe. Indeed the area around Freckleton and Warton became known as 'Little America'. In Bamber Bridge a number of Quarter Master Truck Companies composed largely of black troops were established at Adam's Hall, a camp off Mounsey Road. Ken Werrell has described this as 'a misleading name for a motley collection of army huts which housed US Army Airforce Station 569'. Problems of race were totally unknown in the district, and the black soldiers generally got on very well with the locals, attending dances and the usual events in the village's social round. By contrast racial tension and discrimination were acute in the American forces, and units were segregated. Throughout the incident which sparked off the events of the night of 24 June 1943, the locals took the black soldiers' part against the white American military policemen, and when the shooting started the former were at pains to warn them to keep out of the way.[28]

At shortly after 10 p.m., two American MPs tried to arrest one of a group of about a dozen black soldiers who were drinking in the Hob Inn. The barmaid had refused to serve him since it was 'after hours'. An argument ensued, and the MPs tried to make an arrest. A crowd gathered, and significantly, a British soldier shouted, 'Why do you want to arrest them? They are not doing anything or bothering anybody'. Events quickly got out of hand when one of the policemen drew his pistol. The policemen were forced to retreat in their jeep, a beer bottle smashing against their windscreen as they drove away to the railway crossing. Here they picked up two other MPs, and confronted the crowd on its way back to the camp. A second confrontation developed, and the vastly outnumbered policemen had recourse to their weapons. 'There were shouts, curses, insults, dares, and then in short order, a brief, confused and bloody fight.'

The police opened fire hitting one man, and further reinforcements arrived. As the soldiers reached their camp, rumours swept it that the white MPs 'were shooting blacks'. A large crowd of men gathered, perhaps 200 strong, some of them armed. A truck carrying half a dozen men crashed out of the camp, and returned to the village. The unit's commander was absent, but one of the white officers tried to calm the 'mad frenzy'. 'I know Colonel Pitcher is for you men, and I am for you. Now we cannot take these things into our own hands. Put up your rifles and go back to the barracks.' A similar appeal from the men's single black officer was effective, and the majority of the men returned to their huts. But feelings were running very high over the wounded men.

At midnight two jeeps and 'a makeshift armoured car' carrying about a dozen MPs 'roared up to the camp'. This confirmed the men's worst fears, 'Get up! They are coming in with tanks'. The officers ordered the MPs to leave, but the men had armed themselves, and two thirds of the unit's rifles had been taken. As the police withdrew they were fired on. Shooting in the village had been heard since before midnight. Richard Ashcroft, who ran a fish and chip shop in Station Road was told, 'Get inside, there's going to be a war', and a group of soldiers told the landlord of the Queens Hotel, 'You'd better get inside, boss, there's going to be plenty shooting'.

A large number of armed soldiers thus traded shots and volleys along the length of the top of Station Road and its side streets. The MPs shot from at least one upstairs window, and set up a machine gun ambush at each end of this section of Station Road. Things quietened down about 3am. About this time a US general arrived and put the black officer in charge of the camp. Under his direction nearly all of the rifles were taken back. One man, Private William Crossland, had been killed, and four wounded by gunfire.

The resulting investigation cleared most of the men. Two trials were held; at Washington Hall, Chorley the men involved in the original brawl were dishonourably discharged and given sentences ranging from one and a half to two years' hard labour. The second trial, held at 8th Army HQ Bushy Park, Teddington, concerned the charge of mutiny. Twenty-eight men received sentences ranging from three months to 15 years. The convicted men regarded these as 'Kangaroo courts', and their sentences were subsequently reduced, and the longest period actually served may only have been 13 months. The US forces thus had deeply rooted racial problems, and outbreaks such as that at Bamber Bridge were also to occur at Launceston, Cornwall, in September 1943, at Leicester in February 1944, and near Newbury, Berkshire, in October 1944.

The Freckleton Air Disaster

The region's greatest wartime disaster was the result of an accident. On 23 August 1944 the Freckleton air disaster killed 60 people, when an American Liberator aircraft was hit by lightning and fell onto the village school. Of the victims, 35 were children aged 4–6 years. Between 2,000 and 3,000 people attended the burial of 44 of the children three days later, 'The procession of relatives from the church to the graveside was a pathetic cross section of the entire village life. Young couples walked hand-in-hand and elderly men and women, supported on the arms of their children, formed up in a group as the committal service was said ... Several of the mourners fainted at the graveside'.

Many of the children's fathers were away serving in the forces, and had to be informed.[29]

The V1 Rocket attack on Gregson Lane

As the Russian army reached the Vistula, and prepared for the invasion of Poland, the German V1 rocket campaign was launched on the south east of England. In October 1944 intelligence reports suggested that a raid on the north of England was being planned. Guns and searchlights, and Morrison shelters had been sent away to the south, and the anti-aircraft system had run down. By December, Manchester had been selected as the target, and in the early hours of Sunday 24 December about 50 V1s ('Vengeance Weapon One') were launched from Heinkel bombers over the North Sea. Only one weapon hit the city, and the rest fell over a wide area. At Oldham 28 people were killed (including four members of a wedding party) , and six people were killed at Tottington.[30]

One of the rockets came down in the fields between Brindle Mill and Gregson Lane. The account given in the *Lancashire Daily Post* was very guarded, and did not say where the incident had occurred, remarking, 'There is plenty of open ground in which the Hun terror weapons can bury themselves harmlessly'. No-one was seriously hurt, but many windows in the mill were broken, and a cottage was damaged. 'Mr Joe Bolton and his family escaped unhurt from one of the cottages. Next door Mrs A. Hodgson was unhurt'.[31] The 'War Damage Report' reveals damage over a wide area of the Gregson Lane district. Over 400 windows were broken in the mill, and blast damage was reported in an area extending from Bank Head Lane to Hoghton Lane. The windows in the Black Horse Hotel were blown out.[32] The report in the Public Record Office reveals, '32' × 20' crater on farmland. 2 cottages seriously damaged; damage to farm, farm buildings; blast damage to 112 houses, 2 mills; 2 hotels, chapel and a signal cabin. 4 people homeless. 4 slightly injured ... leaflets found'. The entire operation had lasted just one hour, and clearly if all the rockets had hit Manchester a major disaster would have resulted. The weapon had fortunately come too late to affect the war's outcome, and by the end of January 1945 the campaign was over.[33]

The celebrations which greeted the end of the war in Europe, were rather muted, since a large number of local men were known to be prisoners of the Japanese. The old West Lancashire brigade of the RFA (reformed as the 88th Field Regiment Royal Artillery), for example, having been evacuated from Dunkirk, was sent to Singapore in 1941: 'In September 1942 Singapore fell, and, with the rest of the Army in Malaya, the 88th became the prisoners of the Japanese. Of the period which followed it is best not to give details. Most of the Regiment were sent to work on the notorious Bangkok–Rangoon railway. For those who were there, that is all that need be said; for those who were not, no description would be adequate. Over 300 of the 88th died from sickness and starvation'.[34]

CHAPTER FOURTEEN

The march of the times

HE BRAVE NEW WORLD found Walton-le-Dale facing an ancient and timeless problem. In December 1936 both the *Daily Express* and the *News Chronicle* had headlined 'the Great Walton Floods'. The rivers Darwen and Ribble overflowed a considerable area of Walton village and Higher Walton Road. The children at St Patrick's school watched the waters rise over the fields, and fled as the school itself was flooded. Empty barrels reached the ceiling of the cellar of the 'Robert Peel' in Victoria Road, and in Chorley Road the waters reached halfway up the windows of the Unicorn Inn.[1]

In September 1946 an enormous flood submerged a large proportion of the village to a depth of several feet. The 'Walton-le-Dale Flood Relief Fund' attracted £2,035 19s. 9d., most of which was paid out in small grants for the replacement of carpets and furniture. It was estimated that the local market gardeners had suffered losses of £46,000.[2] At a special meeting held in November 1947, 'Mr Ley painted a vivid picture of last years floods in the district ... the flood was caused, he declared, because of 100 years of accumulated neglect of the banks and the bed of the river Darwen, and because of the tipping of rubbish'.[3]

When Blackburn council did not support Walton's request for the establishment of a River Darwen Catchment Board, councillor C. W. Parker described its attitude as 'shabby', and a 'breach of responsibility and duty towards their neighbours'.[4] In December 1951 there was again extensive flooding throughout the Ribble and Darwen systems: 'Residents at Walton-le-Dale were warned by loud speaker to stand by for the danger period between 3.30 p.m. and 4.30 p.m. when a 24′ tide will back up the flooded Ribble and Darwen ... Residents in the area hastily piled up their furniture, took up carpets and carried portable belongings upstairs. Menfolk were called back from their jobs in Preston to help prepare for the emergency. F. W. Roscoe toured the district in a loudspeaker van'.[5]

Higher Walton Road was covered with 2′ of standing water, and the river at Darwen bridge rose 4′. Normally 10′ wide and 3′ deep, the Darwen was transformed into a raging torrent 50′ wide and 15′ deep, laden with trees and other debris. Floods in January 1954 submerged the shopfloor at the Atkinson lorry works, and swept away Mosney bridge, leaving Mr F. Latham to cross the river on an oil drum raft.[6] Following this third serious flood in eight years the river embankments were raised, and other flood prevention work was undertaken.

The river Ribble frozen at Walton Cop, 1947. At the height of the freeze-up it was possible to skate on the river from beyond Church Deeps to the Ribble bridge. (*R. Burns*)

The march of the times

The war, and particularly the destruction of the Japanese textile industry, gave a great boost to those mills which survived the depression of the 1920s and 1930s. The revival of foreign competition in the mid-1950s, however, revived the familiar pattern of mill closures: 'The slump in the cotton industry – blamed on imports of cheap cloth from abroad – has forced thousands of mill operatives in the Preston area to continue working on short time. The system of working a week and playing a week is now widespread at local mills'.[7] Two thousand spinners, and a similar number of weavers were said to be working short time. In 1959 the closure of the former Bamber Bridge Spinning Company's enormous 'New Mill' (a branch of Crosses & Heatons Ltd), was announced.

Both the Ritz Linen Co., which operated on a part of the old Calverts site, and Gregson Lane Mill had closed by 1951. The years 1967–68 saw a second wave of closures, and the near extinction of the industry in the Preston district. Even very modern and efficient factories, such as Tulketh Mill in Preston, were forced to close.[8] This phase saw the closure of Gatty's print works, Thomas Moss & Sons, the Lostock Hall Spinning Co., and Farington Mill. Higher Walton Mill, operated by Tyre Fabric, closed in 1977. Although Carus Vernon's Penwortham Mill is still in production 200 years after its establishment by John Watson, the closure of A. S. Orr's extremely modern and efficient School Lane Mill in 1979 with the loss of 800 jobs, really marked the end of the local textile trade. By 1980 the great spinning and weaving mills of Bamber Bridge and Walton-le-Dale had, therefore, woven out.[9]

The shifting economic and social requirements in the post-war era also had a profound effect on the railway system, centred around Lostock Hall. In the 1960s the extensive service facilities here were closed, along with the two passenger stations. A long campaign failed to save Todd Lane station from the Beeching axe, despite the fact that in the final year, 1965, 44,000 tickets were issued.[10] In the final days of the steam railway, Lostock Hall was one of only three steam depots left in the country. Train spotters came from as far afield as the United States to see the long lines of engines awaiting the breaker. A sad end for the engine sheds which had serviced hundreds of thousands of locomotives since the 1890s: 'Mr Fred Grundy, mechanical foreman at Lostock Hall, who has looked after the maintenance of steam engines since 1926, has a philosophical outlook about the change, 'It's the march of the times. Its a progress' he said'. On 5 August 1968 Britain's steam railway age ended.[11]

A very modern petrol station at the corner of Chorley Road and Duddle Lane, c. 1950. Duddle Lane remained essentially a country lane right up to the construction of the enormous housing estates there in the 1960s. Yet its various twists and turns still reflect the influence of sixteenth-century patterns of land-holding in the modern landscape. (R. Burns)

Horsley, Smith and Company

In 1871, Joseph Horsley and Alexander Smith established a timber importing business at Kingston upon Hull.[12] By the end of the century the business had recorded profits of over £250,000, and in 1901 'Horsley, Smith and Co. Ltd' was formed. With important yards at Hull and London, the firm began to import timber through Preston Dock, and had a permanent presence there from 1929. By 1938 imports into Preston had become substantial, and the acquisition of local storage and milling space became a priority. In May 1942, the local agent E. R. Kernaghan, acquired the disused Mexican Mill from R. Hothersall and Co. Here the first sawmill was established, 'There was only one machinist, but we were very pleased that we could tackle such a wide variety of work, and we did well in spite of many difficulties'.[13]

The firm expanded the site rapidly. Land on the east side of Aspden Street, intended for the completion of Greenwood and Hodson Streets, was acquired. In 1946 Horsley Smith (West & North) was incorporated as a separate company, and Poplars Farm on the east side of Station Road was purchased for £2,500. June 1948 saw the acquisition, for £2,000, of seven acres of Bashall's Farm, which extended the Mexican Mill site and provided a frontage onto the A6 opposite the Poplars Farm property. A new large saw mill, incorporating the skeleton of a former laundry, was erected on the site in 1949. With a propensity to shower the neighbourhood with burning wood shavings, this peculiar structure quickly became a

Bamber Bridge landmark. Although the location at Bamber Bridge was controversial within the company, the decision to locate here was vindicated by the development of the motorway interconnections in the 1960s.

By the mid-1960s, when the firm became a public company, Horsley Smiths had become a major importer of timber through Preston. The operation expanded enormously, as the company's products fed the house building boom of the 1950s and 1960s, enabling them to become an important local employer with a workforce of around 300, and a distinctive fleet of red timber wagons. The enormous timber storage yards became a major feature of the local landscape.

In 1968 a large site at Cuerden was acquired. Ten of the 27 acres were concreted, and the firm's enormous 'Coronation Shed' was dismantled and brought from Hull. Originally built in 1953, of wood, it is 440' long, and 163' wide. This important artefact of the industrial archaeology of Hull still dominates the skyline to the south of Brownedge Road along the river Lostock! 1968 also saw the link up with Jewsons. A fourth local site, formerly Hopwoods, was acquired on the A6 between the two main yards, increasing the firm's timber yards to 50 acres in size. In the late 1970s Jewsons took over the merchandising side of the business. With the closure of Preston Dock most of the timber yards were sold, and the Cuerden operation was moved to Widnes. The business survives, however, as Jewsons 'Timber and Builder's Merchants', on the original Horsley Smith holding in Mexican Mill, Aspden Street.[14]

Seddon Atkinson

Samuel Atkinson was a widely travelled loom engineer.[15] His sons established Atkinson & Co. (1907), a firm of millwrights and engineers, in Frenchwood Avenue, Preston. Edward Atkinson had worked for Coulthards of Preston, and with their merger with the Spurriers came to be involved in the development of Leyland Motors. By 1919 the firm employed a hundred men on a five-acre site in Kendall Street Preston. By 1929, 355 'Atkinsons' had been built. With the establishment of Atkinson Lorries (1933) Ltd, various models were produced, and the firm prospered during the war. Shortly before Christmas 1946 the company acquired a large site off Winery Lane, Walton-le-Dale, and by the end of 1947 the main factory here was completed. 'The move to Walton heralded the emergence of the company as a major power in Britain's heavy trucks business'.[16] Atkinson's famous 'Knight of the Road', badge was used well into the 1960s.

Seddons originated in 1919 as a family run transport firm in Salford. The company began to construct motor vehicles, and in 1948 Seddon Motors Ltd moved to a new site, the Woodstock factory, at Oldham. By 1959 Seddon Diesel Vehicles were employing 600 men, had thriving export sales, and in 1967–68 built over a thousand chassis. Both companies had foreign subsidiaries, and Atkinsons had branches in Australia, New Zealand

and South Africa. 1970 saw a number of attempts to take over Atkinsons. Bids by ERF and Foden failed, but Leyland Motors (owners of 20 per cent of the share capital) approved a move by Seddons. The takeover 'by the Seddon people', caused despair at Walton, from the shopfloor upwards, and the following remarkable advertisement appeared in the *Financial Times*: 'Chairman of Atkinson Lorries, following take-over, will be available in New Year to assist in any financial cum management problem where his past knowledge and other present connections of a wide nature could be of assistance. Other staff possibly available. Please write giving details of proposition which must be legal, interesting, and remunerative'.[17]

The link-up allowed the firm to rationalise the range of vehicles, and in 1972–73 a new factory was built at Walton with a planned output of 2,500 vehicles a year. By 1974 the company employed 2,000, was manufacturing 4,000 vehicles a year, had 20 per cent of the British market, and there were estimated to be 26,000 Seddon-Atkinson vehicles on the road. The company was bought by Harvester International in 1978, and successfully survived that firm's collapse, to be taken over by the Spanish producer ENASA, before its acquisition by MAN and Daimler-Benz in 1989. Amidst these changes, and the decline of the British commercial vehicle market in the slump of 1979–81, the Walton plant was closed.

Philip Baxendale and the Baxi Partnership

The new opportunities opened up by the post war consumer society are perhaps best illustrated in the remarkable growth of the firm of Richard Baxendale & Sons. Richard Baxendale is believed to have been born in Leyland in 1826. The 1851 census describes him as 'Richard Baxenden ... Iron Founder', living in Chapel Street, Blackburn, with his wife Anne, their two children, and four lodgers – all iron founders. By 1871, and living in Chorley, the family of eight included sons, Thomas (21) 'Moulder of iron and brass', and George (15) 'Turner and fitter of iron and brass'. In 1866 Baxendale formed a partnership with Joseph Heald whose family were long established in the Chorley foundry trade. In 1872 Baxendale & Heald were established at 48 and 42 respectively, Steeley Lane, 'Railway carriage and wagon builders, and machine makers. Chorley Wagon Works'.[18]

This business failed in 1879 with colossal debts of £30,000, but was substantially reformed in 1881 as 'Richard Baxendale & Sons' – Thomas and George – and took over the Atlas Foundry in Albert Street. The business was based upon general iron-foundry work and multi-purpose engineering, manufacturing castings for textile machinery, and later, domestic iron kitchen ranges. Though medium-scale, the concern proved profitable, and on his death in 1907 Richard Baxendale left a personal fortune of over £5,000 – well over half a million in late twentieth-century pounds.[19]

In 1914 the business passed to George Baxendale's sons Richard (22)

The foundry of Edwards, Russell & Company at Brownedge, c.1935. The works were established by Peter Pilkington in 1907. The Chorley iron founders, Richard Baxendale & Sons began production here in 1961. (*South Ribble Museum*)

and John (20). During the 1930s the business came to specialise in domestic heating, and John Baxendale developed the under floor draught fire, patented in 1935. In combination with a high output back-boiler, the 'Baxi Burnall' became a sustained success, and by the 1950s had 80 per cent of the market, and supported a large spare parts trade. Wartime saw the foundry go over to war work, but in 1943 the firm was incorporated as a limited company, and 'Baxi' was born.[20]

In the post-war years the firm's products dominated their market niche; production was expanded, and the firm began to move out of the general foundry business. In 1955, when John Baxendale's son Philip became General Manager, the firm employed just 55 people. By the end of the decade the company was looking for larger premises, and in 1959 it acquired the 11-acre site of a long-established foundry in Brownedge Road, Bamber Bridge. The village had begun to develop an engineering sector by the early twentieth century, for 'The Municipal Appliance Co ... Engineers, Boiler Makers, Ironfounders, Patentees and sole makers of Healey's Patent Inodorous Pitch, Tar and Asphalt Boilers: Hecla Works, Bamber Bridge' is listed in the street directory of 1901.[21]

By 1907 Peter Pilkington had established the Dowry Iron Works, 'Steam Hammer Makers', at Brownedge. This firm operated as 'Pneumatic Engineers' until the 1930s, when the foundry premises (the 'Pilkington Works') were taken over by 'Edwards Russell & Co. Ltd (Heating), Brownedge Road, Bamber Bridge. [Telephone 21]'. This firm, in turn, became a subsidiary of Thomas Blackburn & Sons Ltd, 'Machine Makers and Ironfounders'. With the development of the village as an important hub on the northern motorway system, the choice of this location was to prove a good one, though this factor does not seem to have been a consideration in the decision to move here.

The final board meeting was held at the Chorley works on 13 January 1961, and the first meeting at Brownedge took place on 27 March. Small-scale sheet metal production at the new site began in January 1961, and in June 1963 it was announced that production at Chorley would end. Typically the new premises and plant had been purchased from retained profits. Additional premises were acquired along the former railway sidings at Brownedge Road in June 1966, a floor of 'New Mill', Wesley Street, was taken in 1968 as a prelude to taking over the entire mill, and purchasing the adjacent nine acre Seddon Atkinson works in Club Street in 1982.[22]

The formal opening of the new site by Richard Wood, Minister of Power, took place in May 1963. Extremely modern plant was a feature of the works: 'Technically named the Baker-Perkins Indexed In Line Taccone Diaphragm Moulding Plant, it gives the new Baxi plant a 'science fiction feel'. This advanced system was to cause many operational problems, and the 'Taming of the Taccone' was to result in the loss of many nights of sleep for its operators. The minister stressed the long history of the business: 'Firms of this kind have managed to preserve two assets: the close friendly contact of personal managements and the stability of a continuous and connected policy'. Philip Baxendale described the company's rapid growth, 'When we moved to Bamber Bridge two years ago the new factory had seemed enormous ... Now they were thinking of installing mechanical accounting as an alternative to building new office accommodation'.[23]

The firm's long experience of household heating enabled it to produce a long series of highly innovative gas-fired products, which basically re-plicated the traditional coal fire and back boiler systems. This coincided with the return to fashion of gas as a fuel, with the coming ashore of North Sea gas, and the enormous expansion of house building. There was now a very large potential market for small and affordable, highly efficient and clean, central heating systems. One product, the Baxi Bermuda, was so successful that this former prerogative of the wealthy quite quickly became commonplace. The business expanded rapidly; the 200 employees of the mid-1960s, had expanded to over 800 by 1970, reaching 900 by 1983. The company's turnover had reached one million in 1963, but reached £4.8 million in 1972, and £37 million in 1983, despite a major setback during the 'oil crisis' of the mid-1970s. In 1965 15 per cent of houses had central heating, by 1990 this figure had risen to nearly 80 per cent, and 75 per cent of installations were gas-fired.[24]

The most remarkable of all these achievements, however, was the an-nouncement in March 1983, that the company was to transform itself into a workforce partnership: 'Shareholdings of the previous family owners have been bought out and, when the reorganisation is complete, an em-ployee trust will be created, with up to 49 per cent of shares held by members of the workforce as individual partners ... Mr Philip Baxendale, chairman of the company and great grandson of the founder, says, 'By acquiring an individual ownership stake in the business employees will be able to share in asset growth and ploughed back profits'. Although operating within a very conservative industrial sector, where man-management typically consisted of 'shouting at people', Philip Baxendale had long been interested in progressive systems of management. His vision was shared by Ian Smith, who had joined the company in 1958, becoming General Manager in 1961. In that year he introduced the Works Council, the forerunner of the Partnership Council, and a staff pension scheme. This, and a profit-sharing scheme, was extended to all employees in 1965.[25]

With the deaths of John and Richard Baxendale in the 1970s, ownership passed to Philip Baxendale and his cousin Joan Caselton. The two principal shareholders took little out of the business, and, for example, received just £7,700 of the firm's £5.84 million profit declared in 1982. Philip Baxendale was sceptical of the success of the 'hereditary principle' in business, and rejected both flotation or a take-over of the company by a larger firm, wishing to see it continue as an independent company. Accordingly in 1983 the cousins sold the firm to its employees for 'a price equal to one year's profits, or less than 15 per cent of its value'. By the end of 1993 the employee partners held 20 per cent of the equity, and the partnership principle had begun to be developed in the growing family of Baxi companies.[26]

The Trust has a commitment to assist community enterprises and ventures in its home area of Chorley, Bamber Bridge, and Preston. In September 1994, for example, the Partnership took control of a struggling, under-financed, and to all intents and purposes, bankrupt, local company called Preston North End – a former brand leader reduced to lower league status. An initial injection of capital was followed by substantial restructuring, capital investment, and a public share offer. The company's results

The headquarters of Baxi Partnership, with Brownedge Church beyond. In 1983 Philip Baxendale stunned the financial community with his plans to hand ownership of the company to the employees. The firm is now the largest employer in the area, and a world leader in the manufacture of heating systems. (Author)

improved markedly under the new management, long-term decline was arrested, and the shares became a strong 'buy' among investment brokers. In May 1996 some 15,000 of the club's supporters packed Preston market square to show their appreciation for this marked improvement in performance.[27]

An urban civilisation

The history of the district from the Second World War was dominated by the drive to provide better housing in healthy and pleasing residential environments, whilst accommodating the ever increasing number of motor vehicles. Large areas of undeveloped farmland were still available, and in contrast to the housing provided for the early cotton workers, this growth was to be carefully planned. As the new industries expanded to feed the rising consumer society of the 1950s and 1960s, the cotton industry faded. Two important pre-war concepts were central to these developments, and were enshrined in the 'Preliminary Plan for Lancashire' (1951), and 'The Central Lancashire Development Corporation Outline Plan' (1974): the construction of a new north–south road (the future M6), and the development of a new or enlarged urban area supported by Leyland's remarkable industrial base. Both of these projects were to be fundamental to the future growth of the area.

The Preliminary Plan identified a need to rehouse up to 40,000 Prestonians, by developing new centres in the adjoining townships, including Penwortham and Walton. In the years 1945–48 over 3,000 people were moving out of the town annually. Three main areas of development were proposed for Walton-le-Dale: to the west of Station Road, Bamber Bridge, including the Meanygate area; a belt further west, taking in Duddle Lane and extending to Todd Lane; and at Lostock Hall, the building-up of the district between Todd Lane and the main railway line. The Station Road district of Bamber Bridge was to be 'redeveloped', and the entire district suffered a shortage of school places. In the east the new urban area was to be bounded by a motorway (subsequently the M6), and a major motorway junction at Kittlingbourne was to connect a southern Preston by-pass with a Liverpool motorway at New Longton. The line of this new road was to run parallel to, and behind, School Lane, and to cross Chorley Road near to the end of Duddle Lane. Lostock Hall was to have its own by-pass.

The 'Preliminary Plan' highlights the rapidly changing economy of the late 1940s. In the 'Preston Employment Exchange area' the principal employers were textiles 18,000, local and national government services 17,650, the manufacture of motor vehicles and aircraft 15,800, transport and communications 11,400. Leyland was a boom town, employing 15,500 people, of whom 8,000 travelled in to work daily. Bamber Bridge was described as 'a prosperous textile area'. In the changing conditions brought about by the decline of the staple industry, and the opportunities which the war had brought about, the 'Sub-region showed a remarkable ability to adapt itself'.[28]

The nature of the Urban District also began to change, as the authority began to wrestle with these problems in the early post-war years. Gradually its role as a house provider and landlord, developing since the 1920s, began to take up much of its time. In December 1947 the 100th 'permanent house', built since the war, was handed over, and the pace of expansion was only slowed by government restrictions. Stanley Race informed the council in February 1949, for example, that of the 80 houses the authority was to be allowed to build in that year, work on 34 houses was already underway. By the early 1970s the council was the owner of some 800 houses and flats.

In the late 1950s and 1960s the local housing boom really got underway, and extensive private housing estates also proliferated. Good examples are the Duddle Lane estate (where 700 new houses were completed by 1962) and the Cinnamon Hill estate. In 1963 it was reported that 674 corporation houses and 2007 private house had been completed since the war, and between 1966 and 1972 a further 1826 homes were completed.[29]

In 1947 the first woman was elected to the Urban District Council, and in May 1954 Mrs M. P. M. Parker duly became the first chairman. The development of social facilities gained momentum, with the start of a campaign for a secondary school (subsequently Walton-le-Dale Secondary Modern) in 1948, and in September 1951 a day nursery was opened in School Lane, Bamber Bridge. Health scares showed little sign of ever being consigned to the past, however. At the end of May 1959 it was thought that the local polio scare was over, the last case having been reported in Fulwood in April. In the Preston district 24,013 children, and 2,134 adults had completed their first course of injections, and a further 7,111 had received 'boosters'. The year 1967 saw the great epidemic of 'Foot and Mouth' disease, and the quarantine of local farms. In July 1970, George Corbishley, the public health inspector, warned of the dangers of alien plants which had appeared, as if from outer space, along the banks of the rivers Darwen and Ribble. For 1970 was the summer of the 'Giant Hog-weed'.[30]

The district's colourful history had long been a source of great pride. Expression was given to this important strand of local identity with the publication of Frank Coupe's *History of the Village* in 1954, the acquisition of a coat of arms for the UDC in 1951, and the continuing excavations through the 1950s on the Roman fort at Walton by Ernie Pickering, Dick Livesey, and the Walton-le-Dale Archaeological Society. Homage was paid to Kathleen Ferrier in February 1956, when a commemorative plaque was placed on her birthplace in Higher Walton. Her father, Sidney Ferrier, had been appointed headmaster of the village school in July 1903, Kathleen Ferrier was born in April 1912, and the family moved to Blackburn in August 1914. A greatly loved figure, and the finest singer this country has produced, genuinely national mourning followed her premature death.

The Unicorn Refreshment Rooms, Chorley Road, c. 1970. During the floods of 1936 the waters entered the building through the windows! George Fletcher, who followed his father as owner of the Unicorn, was one of the village's great characters. In November 1972 the writer was working on a school project on the history of the village, and George Fletcher suggested that he contact E. E. Pickering to discuss the scheme with him. Over a quarter of a century, this work has been essentially the working-out of many of his ideas. (*South Ribble Museum*)

One of Pickering's trenches, c. 1956. His report of the work is one of the great achievements of amateur archaeology. There was a strong feeling that the 'finds' should be displayed locally, and the possibility of a local museum was mooted as early as 1947. (*South Ribble Museum*)

Excavations off Winery Lane, c. 1956. The series of 'digs' organised by Ernest Pickering and Richard Livesey under the auspices of the Preston Scientific Society and later the Walton-le-Dale Archaeological Society, did much to revive the always considerable interest in the district's local history. (*South Ribble Museum*)

Nearly half a century later, a memorial garden was dedicated to her memory beside the river Darwen in the village of her birth.[31]

During the 1960s George Woodcock rose to great prominence in the Labour movement, holding the office of secretary of the Trades Union Congress during the Labour government of 1964–70. Born in Bamber Bridge, and a former mill hand at the 'New Mill', he recalled his early life during a visit in 1969 to re-open School Lane working men's club – which he had joined in 1926. In the popular media, Bernard Popley, landlord of the Victoria Hotel, Higher Walton Road, 1960–62, found fame as an actor in a popular television series of the period, *Coronation Street*. He played the part of Stanley, the ne'erdowell husband of gossip Hilda Ogden.[32]

By the early 1970s, amidst the rising controversy over the New Town plans, a wholesale reorganisation of local government was announced. The prosperous but small authorities south of the Ribble, Walton-le-Dale, Leyland, and Preston Rural District (Penwortham, Longton, Hoole), were to be amalgamated to form a single large authority. All had felt threatened from time to time by their acquisitive neighbours, or by plans for extremely large local government units. The new district was to be known as South Ribble Borough Council, and local loyalties were outraged when it was announced that the municipal vehicles were to be sprayed orange. Accordingly, during the night of 31 March 1974, Walton-le-Dale Urban District Council passed away, bringing to an end over a thousand years of local independence.

Funerals & resurrections

The sporting traditions of the district continued to find expression, and hopes for a genuinely successful local football team, were realised in the 1990s through the amazing rise of Bamber Bridge FC. The present club was founded in 1952, and the development of their Irongate ground on Brownedge Road began in 1986. 'In a very short period of time they have progressed from the Preston District League, through the Bass North West Counties division two as champions (1991/2), and the Bass Counties division 1 as runners up (1992/3). In this period they reached the semi final of the FA Vase'. The season 1994–95, saw these new Invincibles win promotion from the first division of the Unibond League, and win the A.T.S. Lancashire Cup (2–1 v. Morecambe FC at Deepdale) and the Unibond Challenge Cup (2–1 v. Bishop Auckland at Burnden Park). Club secretary, John Hargreaves said, 'The transformation in the club is like a dream that just seems to keep going on'.[33]

Attracting crowds of well over 1,000, the team which had been playing in the Preston District League just six years earlier, swept to the championship of the Unibond Premier League the following season. The success of 1996 was marked by the historic game played against the Czech national side during the build up to the Euro '96 competition. The Czechs progressed to the final at Wembley to lose narrowly to Germany.

Of the two local football league clubs during much of the post-1960s era, perhaps the less said the better. In 1961 many thousands of mourners gathered along Station Road, Bamber Bridge, to pay their last respects at the funeral of Preston North End, and the solemn interment of the mortal remains in the cellar of a local hostelry. Many local Blackburn Rovers supporters were seen to be greatly moved. The origins of this local tradition of interring the clubs on their relegation are obscure, though the friendly rivalry between the respective groups of supporters dates from the 1880s. Joint action against a common threat was, however, possible, and was manifested in the Great Bamber Bridge Beer Strike of the late nineteenth century. Locals successfully picketed the local alehouses until an increase in the price of beer was withdrawn.

May 1967 saw the relegation and funeral of Blackburn Rovers. Great crowds lined the streets to pay their last respects, and the coffin was followed by a long procession of the bereaved dressed in black: 'The coffin was laid to rest in a most moving scene . . . The 'Parson' Harry Waddington conducted the service. In a short but poignant speech he welcomed Rovers to division two. Loud applause followed his announcement that the only good point about their relegation was that Preston was assured of four points towards their promotion next season. Then with much lament the body of Rovers was laid at rest'.[34] The deeper burial of Preston North End into the Third Division in June 1970 was attended by over 2,000 people. The last lament was played by a piper thoughtfully supplied by the Blackburn Rovers contingent at the Trades Hall, and the remains were sunk even lower into the cellar of the Old Original Withy Trees Inn.[35] One year later the joy of resurrection for the Preston faithful was tempered by feelings of the deepest sympathy for the Blackburn brethren whose club had changed places with PNE. The revival of both of these clubs in the 1990s came as a great shock to all.

The Preston By-pass

The motor traffic problem called forth a variety of responses. In 1951 'speeding' was reported to be a major problem on Cinnamon Hill, and it was suggested that a carefully placed mirror might cure the problem on the very tight junction of Brownedge Road and Leyland Road at Tardy Gate.[36] All west-coast traffic – commercial as well as private – had to pass along the A6, through Bamber Bridge, and cross the Ribble by the bridge at Walton. On 9 December 1953, the Ministry of Transport announced the go-ahead for the construction of the Preston by-pass. The work was to be undertaken in 1956–57, and the road was to cost £2 million, almost half of the actual cost. This impressive road would take two million vehicles a year from Preston and Walton: 'Over most of its 8 miles length the Preston bye-pass will radically change the face of the countryside some of which has remained unchanged for centuries. It will need more than 30 bridges, including one of 250′ span over the Ribble, and huge cuttings'.[37] Work began in June 1956, and the *Manchester Guardian* explained the radical new motorway concept to its readers, as 'a road exclusively for the use of motor vehicles'.[38]

In March 1958 the giant girders of the Samlesbury bridge, weighing 1,100 tons, were lifted into place, and the new road was opened by premier Harold Macmillan on 5 December. The road's statistics were reminiscent of those published a century earlier by the new railway companies: 3,400,000 tons of excavated earth, 668,000 tons of filling material, 176,000 tons of ashes, 288,000 tons of red shale under-bed, 120,000 tons of macadam, 55,000 yards of drains, 35,000 cubic yards of concrete, 2,900 tons of structured steel, and 220 miles of pre-stressed wire. After driving along the new road in suitable style, Mr Macmillan addressed the nation, and the motorway age was born in a field at Cuerdale: 'In the years to come the county and the country alike may look at the Preston by-pass – a fine thing in itself, but a finer thing as a symbol, as a token of what was to follow. The government believes in planning for a Motorway Age ... Sometime in the future we shall doubtless be widening and improving this new by-pass'.[39]

In January 1959 it was reported that the locals were shunning the new road, claiming that 'it was not needed'. At the end of the month, amidst much government secrecy, the road had to be closed due to poor drainage, and 34 miles of drains were to be laid in six days. The Preston and Lancaster by-passes were linked in December 1964 to complete that section of the new M6 motorway.[40]

The Central Lancashire New Town

The direct investment of post-war Central Government funds in the district reached a peak in the plans for the Central Lancashire New Town, announced in the House of Commons in 1965. Enormously expensive, the whole 'New Town' concept was fast losing ground, Central Lancashire was to be the last area so designated, and only narrowly avoided cancellation. As the implications and impact of the new residential and industrial developments became clear, the scheme quickly lost such popular local support that it had ever possessed. As Edward Gardner told Peter Shore, Environment Secretary, in the House of Commons, the new town was 'One of the most unpopular developments ever to be imposed on an unwilling community'.[41] Amidst rising costs, and a failing national economy, the scheme was cut by 80 per cent. Further cuts were ordered by Michael Heseltine in February 1980, and two years later it was announced that the Central Lancashire Development Corporation was to close at the end of 1985. It was formally dissolved on 31 March 1986, when its assets were transferred to the Commission For New Towns.[42]

The New Town plans for the Walton district were spectacular: 'We propose an addition of about 32,000 people in the township and to distribute this growth as an expansion of three groups of existing settlements at Penwortham, Lostock Hall/Tardy Gate, and Walton-le-Dale/Bamber Bridge. This will bring the population of each of these three districts to over 20,000 people'. By 2001 it was proposed to increase the population of Lostock Hall/Tardy Gate from 8,050 (1971) to 22,050, and Walton/Bamber Bridge from 15,830 to 21,830; an increase overall of 20,000.[43] In fact, the population of the broader district has risen fairly gradually from the 1971 figure, to just over 30,000 in 1991. The greatest period of growth fell in the decades before the new town era, in the 1950s and 1960s, as the census figures show; 1951, 14,709; 1961, 18,964; 1971, 26,854.

Yet the Development Corporation did represent the largest inward investment that the area has ever received. The infrastructure and particularly the road system were greatly improved, and the establishment of new industrial estates laid the basis for future growth. In the Walton district the major industrial investment was at Walton Summit. Plans to develop the rather beautiful open country adjacent to Kellet Lane and the former canal basin were strongly opposed by the 200-strong Walton Summit Protest Committee: 'Chaos hit a Bamber Bridge public enquiry into new town plans for Walton Summit today as protesters, including housewives with banners, turned up in force at Walton-le-Dale council chamber'.[44]

Planning permission was granted in March 1974, and the development went ahead: 'The site was planned for both advance factories of small starter units known as Nursery Factories, and also for standard factories. There were also a number of fully serviced sites for purpose-built factories, as well as a hotel development. Once planning was under way, plans were made for residential development nearby. The first was to the south-east of the employment area and was initially called the Walton Summit residential development. The name was later changed to Clayton Brook'.[45]

The geography of the district, particularly in the Bamber Bridge area, was considerably modified by the construction of new roads, and the development of the series of motorway intersections in the late 1980s and 1990s. Prominent among these projects was the link with the East Lancashire motorway through Cuerden, the second widening of the M6, and the construction and later widening of the Bamber Bridge by-pass. This new system of communications in turn began to spawn a further level of service developments, serving a wide area. Notable examples of this tendency were the large Sainsbury's store and Tennis Centre at Bamber Bridge, and the growth of the 'Capitol Centre' in Walton village. Significantly these had been the sites of G. & R. Dewhurst's Cuerden Mill and Calvert's Flats Mill respectively. The Walton Park estate was constructed to the west of

Changing times: the remnant of William Calvert's main spinning block awaits the demolition men, and the coming of the Capitol Centre, c.1985. Graphic evidence of the shift of investment from manufacturing into service industries in the 1980s. (*South Ribble Borough Council*)

Hennel Lane, and the Holland House Farm estate was built to the east of Chorley Road.[46]

1991: the final twentieth-century census

The immense changes in lifestyles experienced during the twentieth century can be seen from a comparison of the 1891, 1951, and 1991 censuses. In 1891 the population of the district was 10,556, rising to 14,709 at the mid-century, and 28,316 in 1991. Through the three censuses the proportion of children and young people in the overall population fell steadily, from 55 per cent in 1891, to 44 per cent in 1951, and 34 per cent in 1991. Alternatively, the proportion of 'pensioners' (women over 60, men over 65) has risen, from 5 per cent, to 13 per cent, and 17 per cent. Put most graphically, in 1891 over half of the population was under 25 years of age, by 1991 almost three quarters was over 25. Two major influences can be recognised in the ageing of the population during the twentieth century, the enormous improvement to public health provision in the 75 years up to 1950, and the improved care of the elderly apparent in the subsequent decades.[47]

If the most significant trends in the age-structure of the population had become apparent by 1950, the benefits of the 'new society' predominated thereafter. In 1951 43 per cent of households were without a fixed bath, and 9 per cent were without a WC. Just 56 per cent of households possessed the combination of piped water, a cooking stove, a kitchen sink, a WC, and a fixed bath; 44 per cent did not. By 1991 over 99 per cent of households had a bath and a WC, and less than 1 per cent did not have an inside toilet. Most households possessed a car (ranging from 72 per cent in Bamber Bridge Central ward to 85 per cent in All Saints), and around 30 per cent had two. Three-quarters of houses had central heating. Since 1951 social conditions have changed very markedly. In that year just 19 men and 23 women, 42 people in all, had been divorced. By 1991 5 per cent of households contained a single-parent family with dependent children. Educational provision had expanded enormously; in 1951 of the 4,573 men 'in work', 3,847 or 84 per cent had left school before their 15th birthday. Just 63 men had begun work beyond their 20th birthday, so that less than a half of one per cent can have completed a course of further education or have attended a university.

The increasing wealth of the population can most clearly be seen in the extension of home ownership. The 1885 Walton-le-Dale Valuation list shows very few people to have owned their home.[48] The textile companies were very large landlords; Thomas Eccles & Sons owned 92 houses in School Lane and Brandiforth Street, A. S. Orrs owned 47 houses, G. & R. Dewhurst had over 70 properties in Bamber Bridge, and almost 200 in Higher Walton. At Lostock Hall the Spinning Company owned 20 houses, and Henry Ward owned 40. In Walton village the de Hoghton Estate was

Council Offices and Station Road, Bamber Bridge.

Vanished Empires: the Council Offices, the Withy Trees Hotel ('Top House') and northern Station Road, c.1950. A delivery is being made at Tot Sergeant's hardware shop. The freedom of the people of the ancient manor to manage their own affairs directly came to an end as the Walton-le-Dale Urban District Council slipped into history at the stroke of midnight on 31 March 1974. (R. Burns)

the principal landlord, though individual streets often had smaller scale landlords. Thomas Marginson, for example, owned the 20 cottages which comprised 'Marginsons Row'. In 1991 the vast majority of people owned their home, as the figures reveal, All Saints ward 92 per cent, Bamber Bridge Central 85 per cent, Bamber Bridge South 85 per cent, Lostock Hall 91 per cent, and Walton 94 per cent.[49]

The 1993 Census of Employment reveals further enormous changes. Cotton had long ago ceased to be a significant employer. Though manufacturing was still an important employer, with almost 850 employed at Baxi Partnership, and over 600 employed at Bosal (UK), the sector as a whole accounted for less than a quarter of all jobs. The largest sector was 'distribution' which comprised 3,840 of the total of 12,901 jobs (30 per cent). Bamber Bridge was the main employment area with 9,795 jobs. The Walton Summit employment area had over 130 businesses, 25 employing over 50 people, and 12 over 100. This pattern of many, diversified, small companies is clearly very different from that of the few enormous employers dependant upon a single sector (cotton), of a century earlier.[50]

And yet it moves ...

By the end of the century urban development extended eastwards to the line of the M6, much as the 1951 plan had foreseen. The only extensive areas of countryside to remain lay along the valley floors and at Cuerdale, and within the area lying to the east of the motorway and to the north of the East Lancashire railway line. Employment in new service industries and advanced manufacturing plants, serving a standard of living and opportunities undreamed of a generation before, had replaced a life of toil in the spinning mills and weaving sheds. Virtually the entire district had been transformed into a suburbia, in the seventy years since the end of the Great

War. The future history of the district must henceforth be essentially an urban history.

The history of the Bamber Bridge and Walton-le-Dale district clearly supports the general contention that although economic change is generally gradual and cumulative, it does manifest periods of intense acceleration when the attendant problems of social disruption become apparent. The final decades of the twentieth century was such a period, and similar signs and potents of prosperity and disaster (in fairly equal amounts) have seen before, not least in the 1860s:[51]

STARTING OF THE FARINGTON, CUERDEN AND WITHNELL MILLS.
A SOCIAL CONCLAVE AND THEIR DISCUSSION

'Ids better news nur we'n hed for o lung time' said old Clayton, as he reared himself the other forenoon against a table in Club-Street, 'un o' th three stertin ad wonst, Bashaw's, Dewoses, un Perks ad Winnell'.

'Aye, Aye', said Craven a neighbour, 'un nod afor id wor time. Id's bin welly like clammin un starvin for two ear, un trades bed enuf still. Praties un point wen wa cud ged om, un skilly un whack, un scouse un soop, until o fello's ribs stick aet like t'pegs in a pop shop'.

'Still,' chimed in Hodge, a loomer, as he knocked the ashes out of his short pipe, 'Aer place izn't nam'd yed. Am shudn't wunder iv Mester Rutchot Ashoth 'll bi th next, un then we'll send 't Braenidge Band fro one end of Bomer Bridge to 't tother, daen't Skooloan ta Kittlingburn, un on't Moon's Mill. We'll hev o supper ut th'Original, un yo'll see we'll donce o hornpipe to th tune o *Bad Times Come Again No Moor*'.

References and notes

Walton-le-Dale: a brief note on the sources

The materials on which any 'history' of Walton-le-Dale must be based are extremely mixed, both in range and quality. The manorial records have suffered greatly through mishap and successive rounds of land sales. The records of the early cotton industry, which came to be such a formative influence on the district, are extremely frustrating, and are largely restricted to those of a single firm, that of Wm Bashall & Co. (LRO, DDX 819). The local government records after 1877, by contrast, are very full, reflecting the considerable local pride that the Urban District Council took in its heritage. Here, therefore, the local historian must spend much time gathering up the fragments.

The full publication of the report of the excavations at Winery Lane will shed much new light on the origins and early history of the settlement, and future workers can do much to expand on the model of early settlement put forward here. The *Victoria County History* is still an important starting place. Much of the material relating to the de Hoghton estate was described by George Miller in 1949, and Lumsby catalogued many of the known estate papers, publishing his findings in 1936. Long before this date, many of the originals had been lost, surviving only through the transcripts made in the 1690s.

The original manor papers preserved in the Lancashire Record Office (LRO) are very sparse. Critically, the Manor Court and Parish Vestry records are restricted to only single volumes (respectively: LRO, DDHo 542, 'The Book of Verdicts' 1672–90; and LRO, PR 2948/2, 'The Walton Book' 1703–96). The de Hoghton land deed manuscripts are similarly limited to a series of uncatalogued and mostly late eighteenth-century bundles (LRO, DDHo 503–23). This contrasts markedly with the Farington Estate archive which is available for Leyland (LRO, DDF). Central to the latter is the superb bound set of estate plans and inventory drawn up in 1725 (LRO, DDF 81). A similar plan was begun for the Walton estate in 1802, but never completed (LRO, DDH 497).

The de Hoghton collection must be consulted in tandem with the superb Preston solicitor's accumulation deposited by A. T. R. Hoghton (LRO, DDH 600–756), which contains much relevant and interesting material, including a large collection of land deeds, and legal records relating to transactions during the rise of the local cloth printing trade. The archive of smaller collections (LRO, DDX) is well worth trawling, and contains many important items. The local sequence of events following the Reformation, and the subsequent series of troubles and tribulations, has been much dipped into by writers, and the main original materials are readily to hand in the publications of the Catholic Record Society, and the Chetham Society. The de Hoghton records contain important papers relating to the 1715 and the 1745, many of them catalogued and published by George Miller.

From the late eighteenth century whole series of county and local maps become available, culminating in the tithe maps and the first edition of the 6″ OS map. Pride of place must go to William Yates' fine map, and the Lancashire County Library Service are to be much credited for ensuring its re-publication. Though published in 1786, it must be stressed that Yates completed much of the local surveying work by 1780 – too early to record the majority of the first cotton mills emerging in the 1780s. These maps reveal not only the changing pattern of settlement during the industrial revolution, but are an important source for the reconstruction and interpretation of the early landscape. The documentary sources for the 'industrial revolution', in marked contrast to the surviving industrial archaeology, are generally very restricted. Here materials from a wide range of sources must be drawn together, ranging from newspaper advertisements, parish rating lists, rentals, trade directories and strike papers. Relatively few complete sets of cotton mill records have survived, in stark contrast (at least until comparatively recently) to their industrial archaeology. Many important local details simply cannot be adequately determined, and must await future research, and many items remain lost to the researcher in private hands.

The nineteenth- and twentieth-century local government records, by contrast, are very complete, though access to the papers of the Central Lancashire Development Corporation is denied well into the new century. The council papers throw light on all aspects of everyday life, are little used by students, but doubtlessly with the development of 'Life in the Twentieth Century' university modules, they will have their day. The 'Overcrowding Survey' of 1935, for example, contained in 25 large binders, is a most remarkable description of living conditions, containing all the district's inhabitants (LRO, UDWd 56). The records from the Second World War are particularly interesting (LRO, UDWd: Air Raid Precautions 68/11–21, 6/1; Evacuees 68/6–10; Civil Defence 68/13–20).

In addition to these essentially local varieties, the familiar range of 'local history' sources are available, and the quarter sessions papers contain a great mass of relevant data. The large number of surviving wills and inventories, only partially sampled here, are an important source of information on everyday life and customs, and the Walton coroner's records are a particularly interesting source. Although a great effort has been put into exploring the sources held in the LRO at Preston, a great deal of material of local interest is known to be contained in the Public Record Office in London, and would handsomely repay the attention of future students.

The right to ask more questions than the available sources seem to be able to answer is certainly the prerogative of the local historian. That such materials are available at all at the end of the twentieth century owes much to the work of R. Sharpe-France and his fellow workers at the Lancashire Record Office, and to that small handful of interesting people who, throughout the ages, have recognised the importance of such apparently obscure records to a distant posterity.

Notes to the text

Chapter One

1. B. Barnes, *Man and the Changing Landscape: A Study of Occupation and Palaeo-Environment in the Central Pennines* (1982). Bronze Age finds; Harris Museum, Preston. For the evidence of Pre-Roman activity at Walton, see *Cumbria and Lancashire Archaeological Unit* (1988) (hereafter *CLAU*), 'The Roman depot at Walton-le Dale, Lancashire: an Archaeological assessment of the area south of Winery Lane', p. 5. Interested students should consult *The Archaeology of Lancashire: Present State and Future Priorities* (1997) (forthcoming at the time of writing).
2. C. Hardwick, *A History of Preston* (1857) (hereafter, Hardwick). E. E. Pickering, 'Roman Walton-le-Dale, 1947–1957', *Transactions of the Historic Society of Lancashire and Cheshire* cix (1957), pp. 1–46. See fig. 1 for the presumed course of the Darwen. The current excavations have only been published provisionally, *Lancashire Archaeological Bulletin*, viii (1982) pp. 4–5. *CLAU* (1988), *CLAU* (1990) 'The Roman depot at Walton-le-Dale, Lancashire: an archaeological assessment of the area north of Winery Lane', *CLAU* (1997) 'Excavation Press Release'. The former course of the Darwen is clearly shown on Robert Porter's map of 1738. See Lancashire Record Office, Bow Lane, Preston (hereafter LRO), DP256.

3. D. Kenyon, *The Origins of Lancashire* (1991) (hereafter Kenyon), See also, M. C. Higham 'A Geographical Interpretation of the Pre-Conquest Origins of the Early Teritorial Organisation of Blackburnshire, Examined in the Light of its Subsequent Evolution', *unpublished M.Ed. Thesis*, University of Lancaster (1969). For an account of early Leyland see M. A. Atkin, 'Early Territorial Organisation in the Hundred of Leyland in Lancashire', *unpublished M.Phil thesis*, University of Leeds (1985), copy in LRO.
4. M. Gelling, *Signposts to the Past* (1988), pp. 93–5. E. Ekwall, *Placenames of Lancashire* (1922; reprinted 1972). H. H. Wyld and T. O. Hurst, 'Addenda and Corrigenda to

Ekwall's Place Names of Lancashire'. *English Place-Names Society Journal*, xvii (1985).

5. F. A. Philpott, *A Silver Saga:
Viking Treasure From The North-
West* (1990). M. M. Archibald,
'Dating Cuerdale: The Evidence of the Coins', in J. Graham-Campbell (ed.), *Viking
Treasure From the North West:
The Cuerdale Hoard in its Context* (1992), pp. 15–20. Archibald suggests a date of A.D.
905. For a contemporary survey of the findspot prepared for
the Duchy of Lancaster, see
Graham-Campbell's fig. 1.7; for
maps of the settlement context
of the find see figs 3.2 and 3.1.
For the contemporary account
of the discovery, see *Preston
Chronicle*, 22 Aug. 1840.

6. Kenyon, *op. cit.*, pp. 114–15.
See her fig. 5.1.

7. For the Domesday account, see
C. P. Lewis, *The Lancashire
Domesday* (1991). W. Farrer
and J. Brownbill, 'Domesday
Survey', in *The Victoria County
History of Lancashire* (hereafter
V.C.H.), i (1906), p. 283.
P. Morgan, *Domesday Book:
Cheshire including Lancashire,
Cumbria and North Wales*
(1978). For a detailed local
regional analysis see M. C. Hig-
ham 'The effects of the Nor-
man Conquest on the North of
England, with particular refer-
ence to the Honors of Hornby
and Burton in Lonsdale'. *Ph.D.
Thesis*, University of Lancaster
(1992), copy in LRO.

Chapter Two

1 J. H. Lumby, 'A Calendar of
the Deeds and Papers in the
Possession of Sir James de-
Hoghton. bart.' (hereafter
DHDP). *The Record Society of
Lancashire and Cheshire* (here-
after *RSLC*) 88 (1936).

2. *V.C.H.*n vi (1911) p. 291.
DHDP 929. For a description

of the seventeenth-century
boundaries of the manor, see
LRO, DDHo 209 and 210.

3. DHDP 929.
4. DHDP 940.
5. DHDP 959.
6. In sequence, DHDP nos 932/3,
933, 933, 933, 936, 938, 939,
941, 945, 947, 952, 955, 964, 965.
7. *V.C.H.*, vi. (1911), p. 291 footnote 25.
8. R. B. Smith, *Blackburnshire: A
study of Early Lancashire History* (1961) (hereafter Smith), p.
68. For a general account see
V.C.H., ii (1908), pp. 1–167.
9. *V.C.H.*, vi. (1911), p. 291. F.
28. The identification of holdings is based on the documents
in DHDP, pp. 169–94.
10. DHDP 1008.
11. Smith, *op. cit.*, Appendix.
12. *V.C.H.*, vi. p. 289. D. A. Hunt
A History of Preston (1992)
(hereafter Hunt 1992), p. 30.
13. W. A. Abram. *History of Blackburn, Town and Parish* (1877)
(hereafter Abram), p. 706.
14. Abram, *op. cit.*, p. 701.
15. G. J. Piccope, 'Wills and inventories from the Ecclesiastical
Court, Cheshire', *Chetham Society* 33 (1857), pp. 246–55.
16. Abram, *op. cit.*, p. 710. For a
general account of the feudal
baronage see *V.C.H.*, i (1906),
pp. 255ff.
17. A. Hewitson (1872), *Our
Country Churches and Chapels*
(hereafter Hewitson 1877) p.
22. For accounts of the architec-
ture see *V.C.H.*, vi. (1911), pp.
297–300, N. Pevsner, *Lancashire (2) The Rural North*
(1969), p. 255. For the ecclesiastical history of the district see
Coupe (1954), pp. 36–76, F.
Gastrell 'Notitia Cestriensis, or
Historical Notices of the
Diocese of Chester' (hereafter
Notitia Cestriensis), *Chetham
Society*, 21 (1849), pp. 289–92.
18. F. Coupe, *Walton-le-Dale: A
History of the Village* (1954)
(hereafter Coupe), p. 55. I am

most grateful to Jack Humble
for drawing my attention to the
original document in the LRO.

19. Hewitson (1872), *op. cit.*, p. 26.
20. Coupe, *op. cit.*, p. 48. See also
LRO PR 2948, 2/13.
21. E. Baines, *History of the County
Palatine and Duchy of Lancashire* (1836) (hereafter Baines),
iv, p. 59. Hewitson (1872), *op.
cit.*, p. 24.
22. Hewitson (1872), *op. cit.*, p. 25.
23. *Ibid.* For the early parish and
church records see LRO PR
2948/2/1. For the problem of
subsidence to the north of the
site, see LRO DDHo 533.
24. A detailed ecclesiastical history
of this period is given in J. E.
W. Wallis. *A History of the
Church in Blackburnshire* (1936);
see pp. 84–7. Wallis also puts
forward an argument for the
existence of a series of pre-
Conquest administrative units,
based on federations of townships. Robert Banastre's estate,
he suggested, may have been
the descendant of such a group-
ing, which he interestingly
entitled 'Walton-*shire*', p. 48.
25. *V.C.H.*, vi (1911), p. 296.

Chapter Three

1. LRO, DDX 1272. For an account of the early Preston and
Leyland Townlands, see respectively; D. A Hunt (1992), *op.
cit.*, ch. 3, map p. 36, 38, 40, 42,
and D. A. Hunt, *A History of
Leyland and District* (1990),
ch. 2, map on p. 19.
2. DHDP 1107. See also DDF
808 – DDF 820.
3. LRO, DDHo 11, p. 51.
4. W. A. Hulton. 'The Coucher
Book or Chartulary of Whalley
Abbey' (hereafter Coucher
Book), *Chetham Society* 20,
(1847), pp. 345–6. Discussed in
R. Cunliffe-Shaw, *The Royal
Forest of Lancaster* (1956) (hereafter Cunliffe-Shaw 1956), pp.
345–6. For an account of the

lists of local monastic chartul-
aries etc. see Hunt (1992), *op.
cit.*, p. 272, f. 11.

5. LRO, DDHo 1121.
6. LRO, DDH 774.
7. Coupe, *op. cit.*, p. 182.
8. *V.C.H.*, vi (1911), p. 293.
9. Cunliffe-Shaw, *op. cit.*, p. 346.
    Coucher Book, p. 1141.
10. *V.C.H.*, vi (1911), p. 302, f. 11.
11. W. Farrer, 'The Chartulary of
    Cockersand Abbey' (hereafter
    Farrer 1898), *Chetham Society*
    38 (1898), p. 490. For the Cuer-
    den manuscripts, see pp. 488–94.
12. Cunliffe-Shaw, *op. cit.*, p. 346.
    Coucher Book, p. 1141.
13. DHDP, pp. 169–89.
14. *V.C.H.*, vi (1911), p. 295.
15. Abram, *op. cit.*, p. 730. DHDP
    1034.
16. *V.C.H.*, vi (1911), p. 296. Los-
    tock Hall, p. 295.
17. *Ibid.*, p. 296.
18. DHDP 1082, 1113.
19. LRO, DRB 193, The Walton-
    le-Dale Tithe Map and Award
    (1839) (hereafter Tithe Map).
    See also DHDP 952, 992–3.
20. Anon., *Lancashire and Cheshire
    Antiquarian Notes* ii (1886), p. 4.
    The extent and nomenclature of
    the early mosses, can be seen
    on the first edition 6″ OS maps.
21. DHDP 970, 972.
22. *V.C.H.*, vi (1911), p. 290, f. 6.
    For Kuerden's Map see LRO,
    DDX 194/23.
23. LRO, DDH 601.
24. LRO, DDHo 301.
25. LRO, DDHo 542, p. 103.
26. LRO, DDHo 542, p. 111;
    DDHo 304.
27. LRO, DDHo 556, box 6.
28. LRO, QSP 806/25/1.
29. LRO, UDWd 34/31.
30. Hewitson (1872), *op. cit.*, p. 139.
31. *V.C.H.*, p. 289.
32. DHDP, p. 1048.
33. *V.C.H.*, vi (1911), p. 284, f. 4.
34. *Ibid.*, p. 240.
35. *V.C.H.*, vi (1911), p. 240.
36. Respectively: LRO, QSB
    225/39–40, QSB 271/7, QSB
    202/29, QSB 463/5.

37. LRO, QAR 7/2/51.
38. LRO, DDHo 267.
39. LRO, DDHo 269.
40. LRO, QSP 213/24.
41. LRO, DDHo 272.
42. LRO, DDHo 274, 276. QSP
    483/7.
43. LRO, DDHo 534: 6 Feb. 1741;
    5 July 1782; 30 June 1760. The
    considerable debate which fol-
    lowed the presentation of the
    writer's researches on the Wal-
    ton mill race, at the local his-
    tory conference at the
    University of Central Lanca-
    shire in November 1996, took a
    majority view counter to his,
    that the flow was from the Dar-
    wen. The Environment Agency
    were duly consulted, and sup-
    ported this interpretation. The
    Agency has measurement sta-
    tions within a short distance of
    both of the former race termi-
    nals (Environment Agency:
    Dec. 1996. pers. com.). For the
    detailed plan of the road pro-
    posed in 1807, which shows
    both the mill races and the
    townfields, see LRO, PDS 17. I
    am most grateful to John Baker
    who found this vital document.
44. Farrer (1898), *op. cit.*, p. 527.
45.
    DHDP 950, 963; 979.
46. DHDP 1043.
47. DHDP 1119.
48. LRO, WCW, *Wills at Chester*
    (hereafter WCW), Peter Bur-
    scough 1624.
49. DHDP 1106.
50. LRO, QSB 189/48; QSP
    258/207; QSP 883/6.
51. LRO, QAR 6/2.
52. LRO, UDWd 63/4.
53. LRO, DDHo 277.
54. LRO, QSB 620/8.
55. LRO, DDHo 277; QSP 701/17.
56. LRO, DDHo 534; 15 Dec. 1737.
57. LRO, DDHo 284; 287.
58. LRO, DDHo11, p. 81.
59. LRO, DDHo 8, Sept. 1807,
    May 1809.
60. LRO, DDHo 526, Uncatalo-
    gued papers, plans, estimates etc.

Chapter Four

1. DHDP 1094; C. Haigh, *Reformation and Resistance in Tudor
   Lancashire* (1975) (hereafter
   Haigh). p. 157.
2. *V.C.H.*, vi, p. 298.
3. DHDP 1098.
4. *V.C.H.*, vi, p. 298, f. 110.
   Haigh, *op. cit.*, p. 259.
5. J. Gillow, 'Lord Burghley's
   Map of Lancashire in 1590'
   (hereafter Gillow), *Catholic Record Society* (hereafter CRS), iv
   (1904), p. 19. J. S. Leather-
   barrow, 'The Lancashire Catholic Recusants', *Chetham Society*
   110 (1947), p. 105.
6. M. Hodgetts, 'Elizabethan
   Priest Holes. v – The North',
   Recusant History 7, pp. 254–79.
7. G. Miller, *Hoghton Tower*
   (1948) (hereafter Miller), pp.
   68–78. For papers concerning
   Thomas Hoghton's death at
   Liege in 1580, see LRO,
   DDHo 543.
8. *Ibid.*, p. 166.
9. Gillow, *op. cit.*, p. 1.
10. *V.C.H.*, vi (1911), p. 312.
11. *Ibid.*, p. 298.
12. H. Bowler, 'Recusant Rolls 3
    and 4, 1595–96', CRS 61
    (1970), p. 167.
13. LRO, MF 1/25.1642 Protesta-
    tion Return (hereafter Protesta-
    tion Return).
14. J. S. Hansom, 'A list of Con-
    victed Recusants in the reign of
    King Charles II', CRS 5 (1909),
    pp. 153–9.
15. *V.C.H.*, vi (1911), p. 312.
16. *Ibid.*, p. 300, f. 149.
17. M. Mullett and L. Warren, *Mar-
    tyrs of the Diocese of Lancaster*
    (1987); Anon., *Blessed Edmund
    Arrowsmith: A Contemporary Ac-
    count* (1960). For the contem-
    porary positions, and the local
    difficulties in Preston and Ley-
    land, see respectively, Hunt
    (1992), *op. cit.*, pp. 48–58, and
    Hunt (1990), *op. cit.*, pp. 35–40.
    For the early surviving Cath-

olic parish records see 'Lancashire Registers; Brindle 1721–1834, Samlesbury 1752–1837', *CRS* 23 (1922). These contain much related material, and the Brindle register, in particular, records many Walton people. For Brownedge (1764–1822), see LRO DDX 241/32.

18. Miller, *op. cit.*, p. 147
19. *Ibid.*, p. 151.
20. *Ibid.*, pp. 160–1.
21. *Ibid.*, p. 161.
22. *Ibid.*, p. 162.
23. DHDP 1102. This new material in the Public Record Office, London, has kindly been made available to me by Nigel Morgan. PRO, C2 Eliz./L. 2.2/45; 'Thomas Langton vs. John Lacy of London, Charge of Usury, 1601'.
24. Miller, *op. cit.*, pp. 87–90. DHDP respectively; 1102 (1596), 1103 (1612), 1105 (1618), 1107 (1623), 1108 (1623), 1109 (1624), 1119 (1674), 1120 (1676).
25. LRO, DDHo 365.
26. This account is largely based on E. Broxap, *The Great Civil War in Lancashire 1642–51* (1910; republished 1973), and the two Chetham Society volumes. W. Beaumont (ed.), 'A Discourse of the Warr in Lancashire', *CS* lxii (1864) (hereafter 'Discourse of the Warr'). This is believed to be the account of the parliamentarian, Edward Robinson, of Buckshaw Hall near Leyland. G. Ormerod (ed.), 'Tracts relating to the Military Proceedings in Lancashire During the Great Civil War', *CS* ii (1844) (hereafter Civil War Tracts). For detailed accounts of the battle of 1648, see R. Holmes, *Preston 1648* (1985), and S. Bull, *Bloody Preston* (1998, forthcoming). For a fuller contemporary account see Civil War Tracts, 'Diurnall of Occurences' pp. 22–4, Hunt (1992), pp. 95–110.
27. Miller, *op. cit.*, p55.

28. *Ibid.*, p. 55, Broxap, *op. cit.*, p. 59.
29. 'Discourse of the Warr', pp. 21–2.
30. *Ibid.*, p. 128.
31. Broxap, *op cit.*, p. 137.
32. 'Discourse of the Warr', p. 55.
33. *Ibid.*, p. 65.
34. Civil War Tracts, p. 262. Cromwell's letter to Speaker Lenthall.
35. *Ibid.* pp. 264–5.
36. 'Discourse of the Warr', p. 68.
37. Miller, *op. cit.*, p. 107.
38. Civil War Tracts, pp. 277–8. 'Pestilence in Lancashire'.
39. For a fuller local account of this period, see Hunt (1992), pp. 111–20. The Lancashire Composition Papers are arranged alphabetically, and have been published by the *RSLC*. Volume numbers are in brackets:
　1. SURNAMES A–B (24) 1891;
　2. C–F (26) 1892; 3. G–H (29) 1894; 4. I–O (36) 1898; 5. P–R (36) 1898; 6. S–We (95) 1941;
　7. WE–Y (96) 1942.
40. LRO, QSB 668/27.
41. For accounts of the 'Mock Corporation', see Hardwick, *op. cit.*, pp. 250–3, Coupe, *op. cit.*, pp. 141–9.
42. Quoted by Hardwick, *op. cit.*, pp. 250–1.
43 H. W. Clemesha, *A History of Preston in Amounderness* (1912) (hereafter Clemesha), p. 195.
44. Mock Corporation Book, Harris Museum, Preston. I am grateful to the curator for access to this document.
45. LRO, DDHo 475. DHDP, p. 275. Quoted by Miller, *op. cit.*, pp. 111–22.
46. For an account of the battle at Preston see S. Hibbert Ware (ed.), Lancashire Memorials of the rebellion of 1715 (hereafter Hibbert Ware) *CS* v (1844); Particularly 'A Journal of Severall Occurences from 2d November 1715 ... By Peter Clarke', and 'The Merse Officer's Account'.

47. Hibbert Ware, *op. cit.*, p. 190.
48. LRO, QSB 1114, QSB 1191/13, QSB 1186/12.
49. Miller, *op. cit.*, p. 116. See also DHDP, pp. 276–87; Miller Transcripts, see LRO DDHo 475. Miller *op. cit.*, Appendix 4 'The Lancashire Militia in 1745'.
50. Miller, *op. cit.*, p. 119.
51. *Ibid.*, p. 119.
52. DHDP 130. Quoted by Hardwick, *op. cit.*, pp. 253–5.

Chapter Five

1. The Walton parish registers and papers are preserved in the LRO, PR 2948/1. An important section of the records has been published in G. E. C. Clayton, 'Walton-le-Dale 1609–1812' (1910) (hereafter Clayton), *Lancashire Parish Record Society*, 37. For the published records of the adjoining parishes, see Hunt (1990), *op. cit.*, p. 152.
2. LRO, DDX 241/32.
3. Clayton, *op. cit.*, p. 343.
4. LRO, MF 1/25. These, and subsequent statistics, can clearly be only highly speculative.
5. LRO, MF 1/27. I am most grateful for access to W. E. Waring's analyses of the region's Protestation and Hearth Tax returns.
6. LRO, WCW. Each will quoted can be located in LRO by giving the details presented in the text: name, year, and place (Walton-le-Dale). For an interesting study of the activities of those not finding the deceased's wishes to their liking, and their efforts to undo them, see J. Addy, *Death, Money and the Vultures: Inheritance and Avarice 1660–1750* (1992).
7. See LRO, DDHo 534, The Coroners' Records. These papers have no internal catalogue, but the extracts quoted here can be located using the name and year of death of the deceased.

For a historical note on the cor-
oneship, see Miller, *op. cit.*, pp.
7–8, and DHDP, pp. 193–4.

Chapter Six

1. LRO, DDHo 1.
2. LRO, DDHo 3.
3. The main financial elements,
   rentals and leases in the known
   surviving papers comprise: *Rentals*, DDHo /1 (1648), /2
   (1720). *Lease Books*, /5 (1759),
   /6 (1801), /8 (1807–30). *Accounts*, /11 (1783–1800). *Accounts
   and cash Books*, /477 (accounts
   1742–4, 1746, 1754, 1769–73,
   1778–1807, 1816–24; ledgers
   1826–56; cash books 1845–53).
   Deeds /503–523 (1771–1853).
4. LRO, DDHo 497, 498. See Miller, *op. cit.*, p. 46.
5. LRO, DDHo 503–523.
6. Tithe Map, *op. cit.*, The census
   returns are available at the
   LRO 1841–51, Leyland Library
   1841–91.
7. LRO, DDHo 542, 'The Book
   of Verdicts: Hoghton, Walton,
   Alston, Lea, Ashton Courts'
   (1672–90). Of the long list of
   court rolls given in DHDP, p.
   270, only a single volume, from
   which these extracts have been
   taken, has been traced in the
   LRO, Only single volumes of
   these two central sets of administrative records thus appear to
   have survived; LRO, DDHo
   542 (Manor Court), and LRO,
   PR 2948 2/1 (Parish Vestry records). This is thus one of the
   greatest weaknesses in the histo-
   riography of the district.
8. LRO, DDHo 301.
9. LRO, DDHo 542.
10. LRO, PR 2948 2/1, 'The Wal-
    ton Book'.
11. Handbill (copy) 'Abstract of
    the Overseers Accounts 1821'.
    Leyland Museum.
12. LRO, PR 2948 2/1.
13. *Notitia Cestriensis*, p. 201.
    Coupe, *op. cit.*, pp. 73–4, see
    also the references in LRO, PR

2948 2/1. For Peter Bur-
scough's will (1624), see LRO,
WCW.
14. LRO, DDHo 177–182.
15. *Preston Journal*, 7 July 1810.
16. LRO, PR 2948 2/1: 10 July, 16
    and 24 Oct., 13 Nov. 1834.
17. *Preston Pilot*, 29 Nov. 1834.
18. *Preston Pilot*, 17 Dec. 1835.
19. LRO, UDWd 1/1.17 April
    1857.
20. Inscription on the school build-
    ing.
20. Coupe, *op. cit.*, p. 74. The
    ancient foundation was dis-
    solved in 1862, when the
    premises were transferred to
    the subsequent St Aidan's pri-
    mary school. The old building
    was demolished in 1870, when
    the present buildings were
    erected on the site, with further
    additions in 1879 and 1901. See
    Anon., *A Short History of St
    Aidan's Church and Parish*
    (1902). I am most grateful to
    Jenny Scott for the loan of this
    rare book.

Chapter Seven

1. Abram, *op. cit.*, p. 201. For a
   modern analysis of the development of the cotton industry see
   M. B. Rose (ed.), *The Lancashire Cotton Industry – A History
   since 1700* (1996) (hereafter
   Rose). See especially, the biblio-
   graphy, pp. 361–93.
2. Clemesha, *op. cit.*, p. 100.
3. R. Eaton, *A History of Samlesbury* (1936) (hereafter Eaton),
   p. 179.
4. Abram, *op. cit.*, pp. 201–2.
5. The Blackburn Trade Directory, 1818.
6. Eaton, *op. cit.*, p. 179.
7. LRO, WCW.
8. Clayton, *op. cit.*,
9. *V.C.H.*, vi, p. 298.
10. For general accounts of Mos-
    ney, see Abram, *op. cit.*, pp.
    224–7; Coupe, *op. cit.*, pp. 150–
    3, P. A. Whittle, *Blackburn As
    It Is* (1852), p. 218.

11. LRO, WCW; will and inven-
    tory of John Charnley, 1754.
12. LRO, DDHo 509. Uncatalo-
    gued box.
13. LRO, DDHo 507.
14. Abram, *op. cit.*, p. 226.
15. *Ibid.*, p. 224.
16. J. Graham, 'The Chemistry of
    Calico Printing, 1790–1835, and
    History of Printworks in the
    Manchester District from 1760
    to 1846', quoted in J. G. Turn-
    bull (ed.), *A History of the
    Calico Printing Industry of Great
    Britain* (1951) (hereafter Turn-
    bull), p. 72. Graham's manu-
    script is preserved in the
    Manchester Central Reference
    Library.
17. O'Brien, 'Treatise on Calico
    Printing', quoted in Turnbull,
    op. cit., p. 72.
18. S. D. Chapman and S. Chas-
    sagne, *European Textile Printers
    in the Eighteenth Century* (1981),
    p. 20.
19. Graham Ms. quoted in Turn-
    bull, *op. cit.*, p. 184.
20. LRO, DDPSl 13/7.
21. LRO, DDX 343.
22. Turnbull *op. cit.*, pp. 184–5.
23. Graham Ms. quoted in Turn-
    bull, *op. cit.*, p. 72.
24. 'A Country Banker', 'Remarks
    on Five Guinea and other
    Promissary Notes', quoted in
    L. S. Pressnell, *Country Banking
    in the Industrial Revolution*
    (1956), p. 174.
25. H. F. Healy, *A Historical Nar-
    rative of a Swainson Family from
    the Counties of W. Yorkshire and
    Lancashire 1513–1880*, pp. 100–6
    (Harris Reference Library).
26. LRO, DDH 751, 752.
27. LRO, DDH 754, 755.
28. *Preston Journal*, 7 Jan. 1808; 6
    Feb. 1808.
29. For the Bannister Hall works,
    see M. Scheser '"Shewey and
    Full of Work" Design"', in
    Rose, *op. cit.*, pp. 187–209, for
    pictures of the fabrics pro-
    duced, see plate 7.
30. LRO, UDWd 3/11.

31. LRO, UDWd 3/4.

32. 'S. Potter', quoted by Abram, *op. cit.*, p. 201.

33. LRO, DDX 510.

34. Insurance records in the Guildhall library, London; Sun, No. 599126, 13 April 1792. I am most grateful to Chris Aspin for access to these and the other insurance records cited, and for access to his studies of the contemporary Blackburn and Manchester newspapers.

35. *Manchester Mercury*, 14 July 1802; *Preston Journal*, 30 May 1811.

36. *Preston Pilot*, 24 Dec. 1836.

37. Coupe, *op. cit.*, pp. 178–89.

38. LRO, TTe 1.14, June 1755. Minute book (1755–92), TTe 1, account books, TTE 2–3.

39. LRO, TTE 1. 9 April 1767. 21 Dec. 1774. 1 Jan. 1783. 19 Nov. 1792. See also LRO, QSP /PDS 17. The Harris reference library contains a valuable collection of Turnpike Trust record books, including the 'Blackburn & Walton Cop Turnpike Trust; Estimates of Expenses'.

40. LRO, TTE 1.18 Oct. 1764. 14 Aug. 1771. 27 April 1756. 21 July 1778.

41. Coupe, *op. cit.*, p. 185.

42. C. Hadfield and G. Biddle, *The Canals of NW England*, vol. 1 (1970) (hereafter Hadfield and Biddle), pp. 190–211. G. Biddle 'The Lancaster Canal Tramroad', *Journal of the Railway and Canal History Society* ix (1968), no. 5, p. 88. Hewitson (1883), *op. cit.*, pp. 198–9. C. E. Stretton, *The History of the Preston and Walton Summit Plateway: A Paper read at Walton Summit on the Occasion of the 80th Anniversary of the Line 1 June 1883 (and 1903)* (hereafter Stretton. I. P. Moss, *Farewell to the Summit* (1968). For a slide and photograph collection of the line (1965), see LRO DDX 973.

43. *Manchester Mercury*, 14 June 1803.

44. Hadfield and Biddle, *op. cit.*, p. 190.

45. LRO, DDHs 1/1. p. 135.

46. LRO, UDWd 3/1.

Chapter Eight

1. British Parliamentary Papers; 1816 (391) III p. 392.

2. Fire Insurance Policy records; C. Aspin pers. com. *Manchester Mercury*, 18 Nov. 1801.

3. LRO, DDH 595.

4. *Blackburn Mail*, 4 Dec. 1805.

5. Hunt (1992), *op. cit.*, pp. 145–8.

6. *Blackburn Mail*, 2 Aug. 1808.

7. British Parliamentary Papers 1833 (450), XX, pp. 268–9.

8. Eaton, *op. cit.*, p. 190.

9. E. Shorrock, 'Penwortham Workhouse 1796–1868', *Lailand Chronicle* (The journal of the Leyland Historical Society) 33, pp. 8–15.

10. J. Livesey, *Autobiography* (1881) (hereafter Livesey), pp. 9–10.

11. British Parliamentary Papers 1816 (397) III, p. 424.

12. Preston Journal 25 May 1811.

13. LRO, DDHo 507.

14. LRO, UDWd 3/2.

15. For Vestry, see LRO, UDWd 1/1, Employment statistics *Preston Chronicle*, 29 August 1863, and the 1885 rates list LRO, UDWd 47/5. For the dates of the Coupe Foundry, see A. Bradley *et al.*, *A Nostalgic and Historical walk Round Moons Mill* (1992), p. 16.

16. Sun Fire Insurance Office; 22 March 1792, Company policy no. 597977.

17. *Blackburn Mail*, 10 June 1799. Mr W. J. Bleasdale kindly brought this important notice to my attention.

18. For 'history', see *Preston Chronicle*, 6 June 1862; the fire *Preston Journal*, 23 February 1811; and the sale LRO, DDL 918.

19. LRO, QSP 2479/1. I am most

grateful to Geoff Timmins for pointing out this reference.

20. For the valuation, see LRO, UDWd 3/2., for the 1834 letting see *Blackburn Alfred*, 12 Feb. 1834. *Preston Pilot*, 1 March 1834.

21. Preston Trade Directory, 1851.

22. Preston Chronicle 6 June 1862.

23. For theft, see LRO, QSB 1/85/63; for sale notice see *Blackburn Mail*, 1 April 1795.

24. The 'estates' of mills along the river Lostock overlap the Walton and Cuerden (DRB 1/59) tithe maps.

25. C. Aspin, pers. com.

26. LRO, UDWd3/1.

27. For the history of Farington mill, see Hunt (1990), *op. cit.*, pp. 89–108.

28. LRO, DDX 819.

29. LRO, UDWd 1/1.

30. LRO, DDH 758.

31. *Blackburn Mail*, 9 June 1799.

32. LRO, DDH 751.

33. LRO, DDH 11.

34. LRO, DDH 594.

35. LRO, DDH 747.

36. George Fletcher, pers. com. May 1990.

37. *Preston Guardian*, 24 Sept. 1904.

38. Parker Family Papers. I am most grateful to Jeremy Parker for giving me access to this collection (hereafter Parker Papers).

39. *Preston Chronicle*, 'Special Railway Edition', 3 Nov. 1838.

40. *Preston Chronicle*, 3 Feb. 1838. 10 March 1838.

41. *Preston Chronicle*, 'Dreadful and Revolting Outrages with Loss of Life', 26 May 1838. For an account of the 'Battle of Farington', see Hunt (1990), *op. cit.*, pp. 97–100.

42. *Preston Chronicle*, 9 June 1838.

43. *Preston Chronicle*, 3 Nov. 1838.

44. *Preston Chronicle*, 6 June 1846.

45. *Preston Guardian*, 6 June 1846.

46. For an account of the development of the local railway system, see G. Biddle *The Railways Around Preston* (1989);

J. Marshall, *'The Lancashire and Yorkshire Railway* (1969).

Chapter Nine

1. L. Rawstorne, *Some Remarks on Lancashire Farming and on Various Subjects* (1843), p. 22.
2. Livesey, *op. cit.*, p. 4.
3. R. W. Dickson, *A General View of the Agriculture of Lancashire* (1815).
4. LRO, DDHo 11.
5. Hewitson (1883), *op. cit.*, p. 170.
6. For Livesey's early life in Walton, see D. A. Hunt 'The Moral Reformer', in I. Levitt (ed.), *Joseph Livesey of Preston: Business, Temperance and Moral Reform* (1996), *Harris Papers 1* (hereafter Levitt), pp. 57–74. For the sources of Livesey's life, see also pp. 75–7.
7. Livesey, *op. cit.*, p. 5.
8. *Ibid.*, p. 14.
9. For Livesey's business interests, see M. Clark, 'The Business and family Man', in Levitt ,*op. cit.*, pp. 11–31.
10. Livesey, *op. cit.*, pp. 8–9.
11. F. J. Singleton, 'The Flax Merchants of Kirkham', *TLCHS* 126 (1977), pp. 73–100. M. M. Singleton, 'The Slave Trade from Lancashire and Cheshire Ports Outside of Liverpool, 1750–90'. *TLCHS* 126 (1977), pp. 30–72.
12. LRO, DDHs 1A.
13. G. Timmins, 'Handloom Weavers Cottages in Central Lancashire', *Centre for North West Regional Studies* (hereafter CNWRS) 3 (1977).
14. *Preston Journal*, 24 Aug. 1811.
15. LRO, DDX 120/1. Michael Houghton, pers. com.
16. Coupe, *op. cit.*, pp. 115–26.
17. LRO, PR2948 2/8 Walton Ecclesiastical Census, 1864.
18. R. Allen, *History of Methodism in Preston and Vicinity* (1866), p. 43, p. 61.
19. W. Pilkington, *The Makers of Wesleyan Methodism in Preston,*

and the Relationship of Methodism to the Temperance and Tee-Total Movements (1890), p. 111.
20. *Ibid.*, p. 115.
21. *Ibid.*, pp. 116–18.
22. W. F. Richardson, *Preston Methodism's 200 Fascinating Years* (1976), pp. 162–4.
23. Pilkington, *op. cit.*, p. 135.
24. T. Kelly, 'An early Lancashire Adult School', *TLCHS* 110 (1958), pp. 128–47, p. 131 and p. 133. I am grateful to John Baker for drawing this article to my attention.
25. *Moral Reformer*, ii, no. 7 (1832). For a discussion of the main elements of his public life see J. Baker 'The Public Figure', in Levitt, *op. cit.*, pp. 33–56.
26. For the long list of Livesey's publications, see D. A. Hunt 'The Writings of Joseph Livesey: A Provisional Checklist', in Levitt, *op. cit.*, pp. 78–82.
27. J. E. King, 'Richard Marsden and the Preston Chartists 1837–48', *CNWRS* 10 (1981) (hereafter King).
28. Quoted by King, *op. cit.*, p. 2; See also *Northern Star*, 2 March 1839.
29. King, *op. cit.*, p. 7, f. 17.
30. *General Evening Post*, 28 Oct. 1779. C. Aspin, pers. com.
31. *Preston Journal*, 16 May 1810.
32. *Preston Chronicle*, 16 April 1831.
33. LRO, DDPr 138/87B. See H. I. Dutton and J. E. King, *Ten Per Cent And No Surrender* (1981).
34. *Northern Star*, 10 Nov. 1838.
35. *Preston Chronicle*, 13 Aug. 1842.
36. *Preston Chronicle*, 20 Aug. 1842.
37. LRO, QJD 1/188, 1/189. A large number of local people gave evidence, LRO, QJD 1/163–189.
38. *Preston Chronicle*, 20 Aug. 1842.
39. LRO, QJD 1/218–9, 6 Sept. 1848.
40. Pilkington, *op. cit.*, p. 116.

Chapter Ten

1. The descriptions of the district during the nineteenth century, in chapters 10 and 11 are largely based on analysis of the detailed census returns 1841–91, and the 6″ OS map series. The boundaries of the census sub-districts were often changed, and for each census the districts had to be drawn onto a separate 1″ map. By using clear overlays it was possible to provide a key for the changing districts. The full set of census returns for the South Ribble district are available in Leyland library, which also possesses a good map collection.
2. Hewitson (1872), *op. cit.*, pp. 144–50.
3. Bamber Bridge, including 'School Lane' and 'Brownedge', are covered by the following census enumeration districts: 1841 census (districts 3–4–5–6–7), 1851 (2–3–4–5), 1861 (4–5–6–7–8), 1871 (4–5–6–7–8–9), 1881 (4–5–6–8–9–10), 1891 (4–5–6–8–9–10–11).
4. Hewitson (1872) *op. cit.*, pp. 137–44.
5. *Ibid.*
6. Details of specific buildings, churches, etc., in chapters 10 and 11 are based on the descriptive notes given in the *Preston and District Street and Trade Directories* in the collection of the Harris Reference Library, for the years, *1851, 1854, 1869, 1873, 1874, 1877, 1881, 1882, 1883, 1885, 1889, 1895, 1901, 1907, 1913.*
7. Hewitson (1872), *op. cit.*, pp. 144–50; P. Milner, *The History of the Parish of St Saviour's Bamber Bridge* (1987).
8. *Ibid.*
9. 'A History of Cuerden Hall'. Central Lancashire Development Corporation leaflet. *V.C.H.*m vi (1911)m pp. 23–6;

for Dr Kuerden's account, see p. 26, f. 10. The great doctor seems to have found gardening a pleasing relaxation from the rigours of writing local history; for here he describes his own home at Cuerden, as 'another *fair* square fabric, a brick building *adorned about* with tall pine and fir trees, *situated pleasantly* upon the edge of Cuerden Green, not long since built in a *fair* court, and *a spacious orchard and garden* on the south side thereof *planted by Richard Kuerden, Doctor of Physic*, being an ancient inheritance descended upon him'.

10. *Preston Chronicle*, 19 Dec. 1892.

11. *Preston Chronicle*, 26 Dec. 1892.

12. Lostock Hall and Tardy Gate are included in the following census enumeration districts: 1841 (2–3), 1851 (5), 1861 (6), 1871 (7), 1881 (7), 1891 (7).

13. The Consolidated Cotton Mills Trust, *Concerning Cotton* (1925): 'Thomas Moss & Sons'.

Chapter Eleven

1. Hewitson (1872), *op. cit.*, pp. 132–6.

2. Higher Walton and Gregson Lane are included in the following census enumeration districts: 1841 (4–7–8), 1851 (3), 1861 (2–3–5), 1871 (2–3–4), 1881 (2–3–4), 1891 (2–3–4).

3. For references to buildings etc., see chapter 10, footnote 6.

4. Hewitson (1872), *op. cit.*, pp. 132–6.

5. *Ibid.*, pp. 150–6.

6. M. Collett, *The Guinness Record of the FA Cup* (1993).

7. Walton village is included in the following census enumeration districts: 1841 (1–4–8), 1851 (1–2), 1861 (1–2–4), 1871 (1–2–6), 1881 (1–2–6), 1891 (1–2–6).

8. Coupe, *op. cit.*, pp. 164–5. See also LRO, DDH 757, '1826 sale Catalogue – Walton Hall'.

9. Coupe, *op. cit.*, p. 174. For the long standing problems of erosion along the Ribble, see LRO DDHo 533.

10. D. A. Hunt, 'The Walton-le-Dale Working Men's Institution', *Lailand Chronicle* (1987), p. 29.

11 Hewitson (1872), *op. cit.*, pp. 20–9.

12. *Ibid.*, pp. 128–32.

13. Detailed analyses of the census returns for Walton, Hutton, New Longton, and Leyland (1841 and 1881) were undertaken by the writer's evening classes during the years 1984–91. See D. A. Hunt (ed.), *Materials for a Demographic History of South Ribble*, unpublished manuscript (1991), Leyland Library Local History Collection. The study also contains a population analysis based on many of the published parish registers from the region.

14. *Preston Chronicle*, 9 Dec. 1876; LRO Probate Registers.

15. For pen portraits of the family members, see Miller, *op. cit.*,

16. LRO, DDH 757.

17. LRO, Tithe Map.

18. LRO, DDHo 483. *V.C.H.*, vi, p. 300.

19. LRO, DDX 1261.

Chapter Twelve

1. D. A. Hunt, *The Silent Mills: Preston and the Lancashire Cotton Famine*, Leyland Historical Society Occasional Papers Series, 1 (1991) (hereafter Hunt 1990). For the workings of the Preston Union, see pp. 1–6; the origins of the 'panic', pp. 7–11; for the crisis in Walton and district, pp. 46–58. The papers of the Walton Relief Committee contain the detailed statistical returns and tables: see LRO, PR 2948/2/8. See Hunt (1991), *op. cit.*, p. 51.

2. *Preston Chronicle*, 15 Oct. 1862.

3. LRO, PR 2948/2/8 list of contributors.

4. *Ibid.*, Parish clothing book.

5. *Ibid.*, List of the scale of payments of the Walton-le-Dale Relief Committee.

6. Trade and Street Directories 1850–1900, Harris Reference Library.

7. 1882 figures from Hewitson (1883) *op. cit.*, pp. 185–6. For 1904 figures see *Cotton Spinners and Manufacturers Directory: Lancashire* (1904).

8. LRO, 938, Lostock Hall Spinning Company.

9. LRO, PR 2948/2/1.

10. The local government archive for Walton-le-Dale in the LRO is UDWd. For a brief 'history', see *Preston Guardian*, 15 Feb. 1913. *V.C.H.*, vi (1911), p. 289.

11. LRO, UDWd 1/1. Vestry records 1826–66.

12. LRO, UDWd 5/1 Minutes.

13. LRO, UDWd 11/1–2–4. Minutes, Gas and Water subcommittee.

14. LRO, UDWd 11/1. Minutes of the Local Board 1877–85.

15. LRO, UDWd 60/1. Uncatalogued Gas supply papers.

16. LRO, UDWd 11/1. Minutes of the Local Board 1877–85.

17. LRO, UDWd 11/1. See also UDWd 59/1, the uncatalogued Walton waterworks papers. These contain a detailed geological section of the Brindle well. Detailed 'history notes', prepared in the 1930s?, can be seen in LRO, 59/20 (Uncatalogued).

18. LRO, UDWd 11/1. Minutes of the Local Board 1877–85.

19. LRO, UDWd 11/2. Brindle waterworks papers.

20. LRO, UDWd 59/20. 'Report of the Select Committee appointed to Investigate the Present Condition of the Water Supply, 1895.

21. LRO, UDWd 59/1. Waterworks papers. UDWd 59/20 'history notes'.

22. LRO, UDWd 11/4; 59/1; 59/20.

23. LRO, UDWd 12/2. 'General Purposes Committee 1885–90'. UDWd 18/1.

24. LRO, UDWd 59/4. UDWd 50/2. 'Sewer Plans'.

25. LRO, UDWd 50/1. Annual Reports of the Medical Officer of Health 1898–1914.

26. LRO, 50/1. The 1906 report.

27. LRO, UDWd 51/3. 'Hospital Rule Book 1914'.

28. LRO, UDWd 38/6. 'Fire Brigade Regulations 1909'.

29. H. Carmell, *For Remembrance: An Account of Some Fateful Years* (1919). p. 23, p. 25.

30. W. E. Waring, pers. com.

31. Private Holland: *Preston Guardian*, 25 July 1916. Private Jamieson: *Preston Guardian*, 15 Oct. 1916.

32. J. Rawcliffe; file; Bamber Bridge servicemen killed in the Great War.

33. LRO, UDWd 12/6.

34. *Ibid.*

35. LRO, SMWa 6/1. I am most grateful to Leslie Ross for informing me of the existence of this interesting document.

Chapter Thirteen

1. W. Bowker, *Lancashire Under the Hammer* (1928) (hereafter Bowker), pp. 31, 41.

2. Newspaper cutting, Parker Papers, *Preston Guardian*, 1919.

3. LRO, Probate Registers.

4. Bowker, *op. cit.*, p. 55.

5. The Consolidated Cotton Mills Trust, *Concerning Cotton* (1925) 'Thomas Moss & Sons'.

6. Parker Papers; Souvenir scrapbook 1922. The tour was covered in great detail by the Australian press, see *The Brisbane Courier*, 16 Oct. 1922; *The Queenslander*, 4 Nov. 1922. Enroute the party had crossed the Atlantic by luxury liner in the former state rooms of the Kaiser, and toured extensively in the United States. I am most grateful to the staff of the University of Queensland Library, and the large number of people in the Rockhampton district of Queensland, Australia, who answered Aidan Turner-Bishop's appeal for information about the Walton colony at Wowan.

7. *Preston Herald*, 18 April 1941. Details of mill closures are based on the analysis of the Barrett's *Preston Street & Trade Directories* for 1922, 1929, 1932, 1936 1948, 1952. Much related information is contained in the LRO collection of cotton industry year books.

8. LRO, UDWd 37/2. p. 15.

9. *Preston Street & Trade Directories 1920–40.*

10. Important collections of the OS series are held by the LRO, Leyland Library, and the Harris Reference Library, Preston.

11. LRO, UDWd 5/12, 6 Feb. 1930.

12. *Lancashire Daily Post*, 5 March 1934

13. This section is based on the information contained in *Barretts Directory of Preston and District 1936* – a year chosen at random. A superbly detailed account of housing provision in the district is contained in LRO, UDWd 56. In 25 large binders, the *Overcrowding Survey* lists the inhabitants of every house in the district, with details of the owner, rent, number of occupants, room sizes etc.

14. *Lancashire Daily Post*, 2–9–21 Nov. 1937. For an account of the effect of the two world wars on Leyland Motors Ltd, see Hunt (1990), *op. cit.*, pp. 129–139, 142.

15. *Ibid.*, 6 Sept. 1939.

16. *Ibid.*, 15 Sept. 1939.

17. LRO, UDWd 68/6. Register of accommodation for evacuees.

18. LRO, UDWd 12/10. General Purposes Committee, 31 March 1937, 3 May 1937.

19. LRO, UDWd 12/10, 19 Sept 1939.

20. LRO, UDWd 68/12, Air Raid Shelters papers.

21. LRO, UDWd 68/2, ARP papers.

22. LRO, UDWd 68/1, 29 Aug. 1940.

23. LRO, UDWd 68/11. Air raid messages notepad.

24. LRO, UDWd 68/4. UDWd 68/5. The official report on the Ward Street bombing.

25. LRO, UDWd 5/13, Wartime council minutes.

26. For a wartime account of this 'blitz', see *Lancashire Daily Post*, 7 Oct. 1944.

27. LRO, UDWd 68/4. Register of War Damaged property.

28. This account is based on K. Werrell, 'The Mutiny at Bamber Bridge', *After The Battle; World War Two Then and Now*. 22 (1978), pp. 1–10.

29. *Lancashire Daily Post*, 24–26 Aug., 7–8 Sept. 1944. See also N. Garfield, 'Lancashire's Aberfan', *Lancashire Life*, Sept. 1976. pp. 50–4.

30. D. Upton, 'Flying Bombs Over Lancashire', *Lancashire Magazine* Nov-Dec 1987. (hereafter Upton) pp. 15–17.

31. *Lancashire Daily Post*, 26 Dec. 1945.

32. LRO, UDWd 68/4.

33. Upton, *op. cit.*, p. 16.

34. A. W. Simpson, *288 (2nd West Lancashire) Light Anti Aircraft Regiment, Royal Artillery, Territorial Army: A History* (1960), p. 27.

Chapter Fourteen

1. *Daily Express*, 15 Dec. 1936; *News Chronicle*, 15 Dec. 1936.

2. *Lancashire Daily Post*, 30 Sept. 1946. LRO, UDWd 37/3 Flood relief Fund.

3. *Preston Guardian*, 8 Nov. 1947.

4. *Lancashire Daily Post*, 8 April 1948.

5. *Lancashire Evening Post*, 5 Dec. 1951.

6. *Lancashire Evening Post*, 21 Jan. 1954.

7. *Lancashire Evening Post*, 6 May 1958.

8. *Lancashire Evening Post*, 1 Jan. 1968, 11 Jan. 1968. The LRO collection includes the following important sources for the end of the local textile industry on which this account is based; *The Lancashire Textile Trade Directory* (1944, 1951, 1958, 1961, 1962), *Skinner's Cotton Trade Directory of the World* (1941, 1944, 1951, 1954, 1957, 1959, 1961, 1963, 1967). See also, Hunt (1992), *op. cit.*, pp. 230–3, 248–50.

9. *Lancashire Evening Post*, 29 Nov. 1979.

10. *Lancashire Evening Post*, 15 May 1963, 14 Aug. 1965.

11. *Lancashire Evening Post*, undated cutting June 1968, courtesy of Peter Houghton, Leyland Historical Society.

12. This account is based on A. D. C. Smith, *Horsley Smith and Company 1871–1971* (1971) (hereafter Smith). I am most grateful to former employees Harry Ashurst and Harry Hunt for advising me on this section.

13. Smith, *op. cit.*, p. 80.

14. Neil Harrison, pers. com.

15. This account is based on N. Baldwin, *The Illustrated History of Seddon Atkinson Trucks and Buses* (1990); P. Kennett *Seddon Atkinson* (1978) (hereafter Kennett).

16. Kennett, *op. cit.*, p. 44.

17. *Ibid.*, p. 76.

18. I am most grateful to Howard Hammersley, of Baxi Partnership, for access to his researches into the development of the firm, and especially the early census returns.

19. LRO, Probate Register 1907.

20. 'What Makes Baxi Burn', *Management Today*, Feb. 1977. pp. 43–9, 106 (hereafter Management Today). H. Hammersley, 'Profile: Philip Baxendale', *The Partner* (The staff magazine of the Baxi Partnership) 25, pp. 8–15 (hereafter Hammersley).

21. *Preston and District Directories*, 1901, 1907, 1927, 1933, 1940,1955.

22. Richard Baxendale & Sons: Minutes of Directors Meetings. (Baxi Partnership).

23. *Chorley Guardian*, 31 May 1963.

24. *Management Today, From Partnership to Participation*. Baxi Heating (1983) pp. 6–7 (hereafter Partnership to Participation).

25. *Financial Times*, 31 March 1983. See also Hammersley, *op. cit.*,; Partnership To Participation, *op. cit.*,

26. *The Partner*, 17 (1994) pp. 7–9, 15 (1993) pp. 8–9. Hammersley, *op. cit.*, p. 17.

27. *Preston North End Share Offer Prospectus* (1995).

28. *A Preliminary Plan For Lancashire* (1951) pp. 70–1.

29. *Lancashire Daily Post*, 6 Dec. 1947. *Ibid.*, 8 Feb. 1949.

30. (Polio) *Lancashire Daily Post*, 28 May 1959; (Foot and Mouth Disease) *Ibid.* 30 Nov 1967; (Giant Hogweed) *Ibid.*, 9 July 1970.

31. (Roman Finds) *Lancashire Daily Post*, 7 May 1953; (Kathleen Ferrier) *Ibid.* 6 Feb. 1956. Both Mr Pickering's finds and the Kathleen Ferrier illuminated address can be seen in Leyland Museum.

32. *Lancashire Evening Post*, 9 Oct. 1969, 24 Aug. 1967.

33. *The Partner* 21 (1995), pp. 16–18.

34. *Lancashire Evening Post*, 19 May 1966.

35. *Ibid.*, 1 June 1970.

36. *Ibid.*, 21 Aug. 1951, 23 Jan. 1951.

37. *Ibid.*, 8 Dec. 1953.

38. *Manchester Guardian*, 13 June 1956.

39. *Lancashire Evening Post*, 5 Dec. 1958.

40 *Ibid.*, 14 Jan. 1959, 29 Jan. 1959, 7 Dec. 1964.

41. *Ibid.*, 4 April 1977.

42. For a very perceptive analysis of the New Town, see G. L. Woodcock, *Planning, Politics, and Communication* (1986). For a review, see *Lancashire Evening Post*, 4 March 1986.

43. *Central Lancashire Development Corporation: Outline Plan* (1974) pp. 140–1 (hereafter *Outline Plan*).

44. *Lancashire Evening Post*, 7 Aug. 1973.

45. LRO, CLDC catalogue; Walton Summit 'Prologue'.

46. Existing facilities are described in *A Social Atlas of Central Lancashire*, CLDC (1976). For a description of the planned improvemnts to the transport system, see *Outline Plan*.

47. The 1891 Census of England and Wales 3 (1893), p. 338. Census 1951: *County Report: Lancashire* (1954), Tables 3, 10, 22, 25, 27. *1991 Census of Population: Report for South Ribble* (1994) (hereafter 1991 Census).

48. LRO, UDWd 47/5.

49. 1991 Census, *op. cit.*

50. 1993 Census of Employment: South Ribble.

51. *Preston Chronicle*, 1864, quoted in Hunt (1991), *op. cit.*, p. 59.